The New Public Health Law

The New Public Health Law

A TRANSDISCIPLINARY APPROACH
TO PRACTICE AND ADVOCACY

SCOTT BURRIS

MICAH L. BERMAN

MATTHEW PENN

AND

TARA RAMANATHAN HOLIDAY

OXFORD
UNIVERSITY PRESS

APHA PRESS
AN IMPRINT OF AMERICAN PUBLIC HEALTH ASSOCIATION

Oxford University Press is a department of the University of Oxford. It furthers
the University's objective of excellence in research, scholarship, and education
by publishing worldwide. Oxford is a registered trade mark of Oxford University
Press in the UK and certain other countries.

Published in the United States of America by Oxford University Press
198 Madison Avenue, New York, NY 10016, United States of America.

Library of Congress Cataloging-in-Publication Data
Names: Burris, Scott, author. | Berman, Micah L., author. |
Penn, Matthew, 1967– author. | Holiday, Tara Ramanathan, author.
Title: The new public health law : a transdisciplinary approach to practice
and advocacy / Scott Burris, Micah L. Berman, Matthew Penn, Tara Ramanathan Holiday.
Description: Oxford ; New York : Oxford University Press, [2018] |
Includes bibliographical references and index.
Identifiers: LCCN 2018002743 | ISBN 9780190681050 (hardcover : alk. paper)
Subjects: | MESH: Public Health—legislation & jurisprudence |
Legislation as Topic—ethics | United States
Classification: LCC R725.5 | NLM WA 33 AA1 | DDC 174.2—dc23
LC record available at https://lccn.loc.gov/2018002743

9 8 7 6 5 4 3 2 1

Printed by Sheridan Books, Inc., United States of America

Micah Berman's work on this project was supported in part by the National Cancer Institute of the National Institutes of Health under Award Number K07CA197221. The content is solely the responsibility of the authors and does not necessarily represent the official views of the National Institutes of Health.

This book is dedicated to everyone who works for the public's health.

CONTENTS

ABOUT THE AUTHORS

Scott Burris, JD, is Professor of Law and Public Health at Temple University, where he directs the Center for Public Health Law Research. Over a three-decade career as a public health law researcher and advocate, his work has focused on HIV/AIDS, drug policy, health governance and the empirical evaluation of the effects of law on health.

Micah L. Berman, JD, is Associate Professor of Public Health and Law at The Ohio State University. He works with state and local health departments on issues relating to tobacco control and chronic disease prevention, and he served as a senior advisor to the FDA Center for Tobacco Products.

Matthew Penn, JD, MLIS, is public health attorney with over 15 years of experience in public heath litigation, environmental health, and emergency preparedness. He was formerly a staff attorney with South Carolina's Department of Health and Environmental Control and is currently Director of CDC's Public Health Law Program.

Tara Ramanathan Holiday, JD, MPH, is an attorney specializing in state and local law related to healthcare quality and financing and health system transformation with 15 years of public health experience. She currently serves as the team lead for research and translation in CDC's Public Health Law Program.

INTRODUCTION

This book offers a new approach to teaching and learning public health law. At its heart is a "transdisciplinary" model of public health law, one that recognizes that many different kinds of professionals in public health are using law and need to have the training and skills to apply it effectively in their work: non-lawyers in public health design legal initiatives, advocate for legal reform, implement the law, and monitor and evaluate its effects. For their part, lawyers in public health law practice also do many things beyond their core job description and training in law. They work with epidemiological and behavioral data that define problems and inform legal solutions. They collaborate with others to study the law's implementation and impact. They make the case for public health in the political process. This book supports a public health law and policy course that teaches students in law schools, schools of public health, social work, and other non-JD programs to do these things—and do them collaboratively, using shared frameworks and language.

The book is designed to be used in law courses and in public health programs, and follows the core competencies for each. It offers an accessible account of basic concepts, allowing the instructor to add specialized reading, case studies, exercises, or more advanced content in lectures. For instructors who flip the classroom, as we do in our classes, the book prepares students for in-class activities that flesh out the themes and information in the text. We have prepared exercises and activities for all the chapters, which are available to instructors on request to the authors.

The book begins with four chapters giving students the necessary background to public health law. Chapter 1 sets out the scope of public health law and defines its key terms. It explains that law must be understood not just in terms of what it says but also what it does. Chapter 2 describes the public health system, putting all students on a common footing in their knowledge of how and by whom public health services are delivered in the United States. Chapter 3 introduces students to the book's underlying model, including the relationship between traditional public health practice and the emerging discipline of legal epidemiology. The final chapter of Section I describes the several ethical frameworks and concerns underlying public health law work.

Section II of the book introduces tools, concepts, and skills needed for the effective development of policies and public health laws. Chapter 5 is a primer in descriptive and analytic epidemiology, a refresher for public health students, and essential new knowledge for law students who need to understand public health evidence. The next chapter, on choosing a legal approach, presents law's basic toolkit, the many ways that law can be used for health, from mandating a behavior to spreading new social norms. The section concludes with a chapter on "Using Evidence and Knowledge Critically in Policy Development," which describes sources of information and a process for "evidence-informed" legal innovation for health.

Section III takes the course into the core legal doctrine of public health law. Chapters 8 through 10 describe the legal authority for public health action at the federal, state, and local level, covering as well the intricacies of federalism, delegation, and preemption. Chapters 11 to 13 canvas the principal constitutional limitations on the exercise of that authority. Chapter 14 explains how administrative law figures in public health law practice.

Section IV turns to the process of getting a public health idea "onto the books" as law or policy. Both lawyers and non-lawyers need to understand how law actually gets made and how political acumen and strong advocacy networks are crucial to success. Chapter 15 describes the strategic considerations that go into developing a public health law that can be both effective and politically feasible. This feeds directly into Chapter 16, which introduces evidence-informed legal drafting. Chapter 17 is an introduction to advocacy strategy and to the laws that limit the advocacy activities of federally supported organizations and government entities involved in public health practice.

Section V is about putting rules into effective practice: implementation, enforcement, and legal and political defense against challenges. Chapter 18 provides a practical framework for understanding what regulation is, how it is done, and the opportunities for innovation in regulatory practice.

Chapter 19 follows with a closer legal look at the enforcement process, covering key issues of authority and the main legal challenges regulators face. Chapter 20 discusses the "defense" of public health laws—the important work of government and private lawyers and leaders in fending off legal challenges to laws or their enforcement.

The book and course of study conclude in Section VI with "Scientific Evaluation in Transdisciplinary Public Health Research and Practice." Chapter 21 explains how legal monitoring and evaluation are integral to the cause of using law in public health, and help spread laws that work from city to city and state to state.

This book would not have made it to print without the contributions of many great people. Our editor at Oxford University Press, Chad Zimmerman, was a model of patience, forbearance, and critical enthusiasm. Ohio State law and health administration student Audry Klossner was an intelligent reader, cite checker, copy editor, research assistant, and advisor rolled into one efficient package. Bethany Saxon, director of communications at the Center for Public Health Law Research, took command of the final stages to bring order, consistency, and clarity to the manuscript and to shepherd it through the technicalities of publication. We would also like to thank several readers who helped with specific chapters: James Buehler, Julie Harris, Joseph Blocher, Darrell Miller, Rachel Bloomekatz, and several members of the faculty of Ohio State's Moritz College of Law. Thanks as well to those who provided early feedback on the book's direction, including Lainie Rutkow, Ross Silverman, Robert Gatter, Amy Campbell, Mathew Swinburne, and anonymous peer reviewers. Finally, we are incredibly grateful to our families for their love, support, and tolerance as weekends and holidays became work days.

Scott Burris
Micah L. Berman
Matthew Penn
Tara Ramanathan Holiday
January 2018

I | Foundations of Public Health Law and Ethics

1 | Public Health and Law

Learning Objectives

- Identify the core features of the field of public health and explain public heath's population-based perspective.
- Define the terms *public health, law, public health law, health disparities*, and *social determinants of health* and provide examples of how they interrelate.
- Provide examples of different types of public health laws.

Introduction

Public health is "what we as a society, do collectively to assure the conditions to be healthy" (Institute of Medicine, 1988). Accordingly, the study of public health examines what makes populations sick or injured and what can be done to prevent it. As one of the key mechanisms through which we structure society, *law* can be both a cause of illness and a powerful tool to improve the population's health.

In the 20th century, average life expectancy in the United States rose by nearly 30 years. The vast majority of that increase is credited to advances in public health, rather than advances in medical care, and legal interventions played a critical role in these advances. For example, requirements that children be vaccinated before they attend school played a central role in reducing occurrence of vaccine-preventable diseases. Smallpox and polio, which were once feared and deadly diseases, were eradicated from the Western Hemisphere (with smallpox eradicated worldwide), while the number of new measles cases dropped from more than 300,000 in 1950 to fewer than 100 in 2000. Likewise, following the introduction of extensive vehicle and roadway safety laws starting in the mid-1960s, the number of highway deaths decreased from roughly 51,000 in 1966 to 42,000 in 2000, even as the number of miles driven per year increased nearly 300%.

Though lawyers are trained to write laws, they are not necessarily skilled at identifying health problems, assessing the evidence supporting competing policy options, or evaluating the impact of legal changes. Similarly, though public health professionals are trained to understand, analyze, and quantify community health concerns, they are not always comfortable translating those findings into policy recommendations or advocating for change through legislative or administrative processes. Lawyers and public health experts need one another to affect change. At the intersection of public health and law—the place where lawyers and public health experts come together—is *public health law*. The academic field of public health law can be defined as "the study of the legal powers and duties of the state to identify, prevent, and ameliorate risks to the health of populations, as well as the study of legal structures that have a significant impact on the health of populations" (Berman, 2013). In more practical terms, public health law is what lawyers, public health researchers, policy advocates, community mobilizers, and others do *together* to research, develop, advocate for, and implement evidence-based legal interventions to prevent disease and reduce injuries. This, in short, is the *transdisciplinary* approach to public health law referenced in this book's title.

Before exploring what public health law is in more detail, however, we begin by delving further into what is meant by the terms *public health* and *law*.

What Is Public Health?

As the definition at the outset of this chapter suggests, public health is something that "we, as a society, do collectively." It is a collective ("public") responsibility, geared toward improving the health and well-being of an entire community—or state, or country—as opposed to diagnosing or treating particular individuals. In addition, public health addresses the "conditions to be healthy," meaning that it is focused on "the prevention of disease and the promotion of health" (Institute of Medicine, 1988), as opposed to medical care for those who are already ill. These key features of public health—as well as some additional key concepts—are explained further next.

Populations

Public health studies the causes and distribution of disease and injury in *populations*. This is one of the defining differences between public health and healthcare. What does it mean to focus on populations? First, it means that public health starts with population-level conditions and threats, as captured in statistics (which are the product of, and require the development of, extensive data-collection efforts). It is only with statistics that we can identify public health challenges and determine whether interventions are having their intended effect. Based on one's personal experience, for example, it is impossible to accurately assess whether the number of traffic fatalities in one's city is going up or down, whether the rate of traffic-related deaths is higher or lower than in other cities, or whether a law prohibiting texting while driving is having any effect. These are questions that can only be answered by collecting data and examining statistics. We may have intuitions based on our own experiences about whether certain intersections are particularly dangerous or whether a texting-while-driving ban is having an impact—but these intuitions are, at best, informed guesses that can only be confirmed or rejected by looking at statistical data.

Looking at populations—and population-level data—provides us with insights that we cannot see at the individual level. Consider, for example, the issue of adolescent obesity in the United States. Obesity is often thought of as the result of "bad" decisions by individual actors—the children, their parents, or both—but according to the Centers for Disease Control and Prevention (CDC), the percentage of 12- to 19-year-olds defined as obese more than tripled (from 5% to 18.1%) between 1980 and 2007 (Ogden & Carroll, 2010). It is highly implausible that this pronounced trend—now being replicated in countries around the world—is simply the result of millions of independent, unconnected decisions. Instead, it appears clear that powerful population-wide environmental, economic, and social patterns (in which law plays a significant role) are influencing obesity rates. Individual-level factors may, of course, still play an important role in obesity in any given case, but shifting the lens from the individual to the population, as public health does, clarifies that the "obesity epidemic" has resulted in large part from collective, societal choices and as a result can be addressed only through communal policymaking. This broader lens suggests that policy solutions focused on individual-level behavior—such as encouraging teens to exercise more and eat better—are unlikely to adequately address (or even make a significant dent in) the problem. Instead, communities and countries must identify and reconsider the "government policies, marketing practices, and social norms [that] have coalesced to create what some have called an obesogenic environment" (Parmet, 2016).

Taking too wide a population-based perspective, however, can be problematic, because public health also seeks to address *health disparities*—differences in health outcomes correlated with socioeconomic status, race, geography, or other characteristics. Overall statistics showing that a community is generally healthy may hide the fact that those disproportionately suffering from poor health are in particular neighborhoods, belong to particular racial/ethnic groups, or share another common feature. For example, Kansas has an infant mortality rate (5.5 deaths per 1,000 live births from 2011–2013) that is not very different from the national average (5.1 deaths per 1,000 live births). However, its infant mortality rate for African Americans is the highest in the nation (14.2 deaths per 1,000 live births) and is nearly three times higher than that of white babies (Thoma, Mathews, & MacDorman, 2015). The causes of this clear and massive disparity are undoubtedly complex, but only by carefully examining population-level data can such disparities be identified—the first step toward considering why they exist and how they can be addressed. Ultimately, minimizing health disparities is necessary to achieve public health's goals of producing not just a *high level* but also a *fair distribution* of health.

Prevention

Public health focuses on *preventing* disease and injury, as opposed to treating it. The emphasis on prevention is another key feature that distinguishes public health from other health-related fields like medicine and nursing. While these other health-related disciplines also care about preventive health, public health is unique in placing prevention at its core.

Health scholars have identified different levels of prevention: primary, secondary, and tertiary. *Primary prevention* refers to efforts to prevent disease or injury from occurring at all, by eliminating risk factors. For example, primary prevention efforts relating to heart disease tend to focus on things like healthy eating, physical activity, avoiding tobacco use (and exposure to secondhand smoke), and managing stress. Primary prevention tends to be the focus of public health efforts.

Secondary prevention, by contrast, seeks to detect a disease at an early stage, often before it has become symptomatic, and prevent it from progressing to a more dangerous state. For example, physicians typically test their patients' blood pressure and provide medication for patients with hypertension (high blood pressure). Such medication, though it does not prevent the onset of hypertension in the first place, can help to prevent heart attacks from occurring. Thus, secondary prevention is at the intersection between healthcare and public health; it is a form of prevention, but it comes at a later stage and is typically much more individualized (and, as a result, more expensive per person) than primary prevention efforts.

Finally, *tertiary prevention* seeks to prevent the worsening of symptoms in an individual already suffering from disease and to improve his or her quality of life. For example, stroke rehabilitation programs work with people who have already suffered strokes to restore their strength and to compensate for any physical or mental limitations caused by previous strokes. Tertiary prevention is not the main focus of public health, but some tertiary prevention functions (e.g., support groups for those suffering from addiction) are sometimes housed in public health agencies.

Public health focuses on primary prevention in part because of its potential to powerfully impact health by reducing disease or injury levels across an entire population. In this way, primary prevention saves "statistical lives," rather than identifiable individuals. That is, primary prevention reduces the number of people who become sick or get injured, but it is typically impossible to identify *which* people have been aided by a primary prevention initiative. For example, modestly reducing the amount of sodium in processed foods would likely prevent far more stroke deaths than providing medication to every person with hypertension (and at a much lower cost). This is because reducing sodium levels across a wide swath of the population would significantly reduce the number of people who develop hypertension. However, it would likely be impossible to identify the particular individuals who were prevented from developing hypertension as a result of such a policy.

The fact that public health saves "statistical lives," rather than the lives of identifiable people with names and faces, poses a political challenge for public health. The effects of medical treatment are more easily recognizable than those of primary prevention efforts, even if the population-level impact of the latter is greater. As David Hemenway (2006) explains:

> A woman with appendicitis knows she is sick and is grateful to the medical providers who treat her. . . . But the consumer who does not get poisoned because unsafe products are kept off the market does not even know that her life has been saved, partly as a result of the efforts of the public health community.

Social Determinants of Health

Because of their focus on uncovering and addressing the underlying causes of disease, public health experts have, in recent decades, recognized that the *social determinants of health* must be a core focus of public health efforts. The social determinants of health are the resources and conditions in our social and physical environments that influence exposure, vulnerability, and immunity to causes of disease and injury. These include factors such as economic opportunity, educational attainment, residential segregation, and concentrated poverty—all of which are strongly associated with health outcomes.

Indeed, one of the most consistent and robust findings of social science has been that the greater the family income, the longer one's life expectancy. This is sometimes referred to as "the income gradient of health," or, more simply, "the gradient," and is depicted in Figure 1.1. A similar

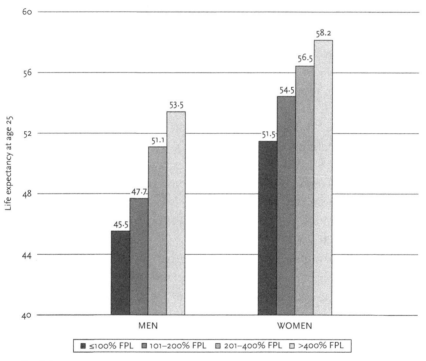

Family Income
(Percent of Federal Poverty Level)

FIGURE 1.1. The income gradient of health.

Center on Social Disparities in Health at the University of California San Francisco. (2008). Higher Income, Longer Life: Robert Wood Johnson Foundation. Prepared for the Robert Wood Johnson Foundation by the Center on Social Disparities in Health at the University of California, San Francisco; and Norman Johnson, U.S. Bureau of the Census. SOURCE: National Longitudinal Mortality Study, 1988–1998. Copyright 2008 Robert Wood Johnson Foundation/Overcoming Obstacles to Health gradient also appears in population-level analyses of the relationship between social inequality and a wide range of health and social outcomes. The exact causal relationships between income, social inequality, and health are complex and disputed, but Bruce Link and Jo Phelan (1995) suggest that those with more income tend to have "access to resources that can be used to avoid risks or to minimize the consequences of disease once it occurs," while others do not. In their view, the lack of these resources, including "money, power, prestige, and/or social connectedness," contributes powerfully to the higher disease burden in certain populations. Importantly, access to these resources is often strongly correlated with social factors such as race, ethnicity, and gender, in addition to income and educational attainment.

Building on this insight, former CDC Director Thomas Frieden has developed a five-tier "health impact pyramid" that puts social determinants of health at its base (see Figure 1.2). As Frieden (2010) writes:

> The health impact pyramid . . . postulates that addressing socioeconomic factors (tier 1, or the base of the pyramid) has the greatest potential to improve health. . . . Although the effectiveness of interventions tends to decrease at higher levels of the pyramid, those at the top often require the least political commitment. Achieving social and economic change might require fundamental societal transformation.

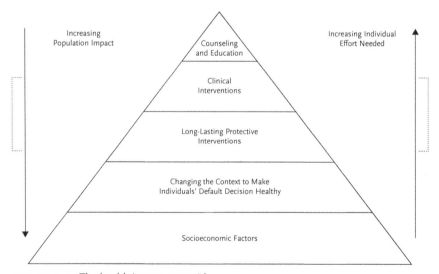

FIGURE 1.2. The health impact pyramid.

Frieden, T. R. (2010). "A framework for public health action: the health impact pyramid." American Journal of Public Health 100(4): 590-595.

Frieden's pyramid suggests that in order to meaningfully improve health, public health professionals must work in partnership with a wide range of other stakeholders—including community organizations, attorneys, and policymakers—to grapple with difficult and politically charged questions of inequality and social policy.

For example, think about how the health impact pyramid could be applied to the issue of obesity. At the top of the pyramid, public health education efforts about eating healthy food and exercising more are politically noncontroversial, but they are unlikely to be effective on their own. Clinical interventions—whether short term (e.g., appetite-suppressant medication) or longer term (e.g., bariatric surgery)—occupy the next two levels on the pyramid. These interventions are focused on individual patients and tend to be much more expensive. The next level of the pyramid, "changing the context to make individuals' decisions healthy," includes what is often thought of as traditional public health regulation. This might include things like improving the nutritional content of foods sold in schools or increasing taxes on sugary beverages. Finally, we come to the base of the pyramid—the social determinants of health. This level of the pyramid recognizes that decisions about food and physical activity are deeply influenced by one's social and physical environment. Even if one wishes to eat healthier food and exercise more, it may be extremely difficult to do so if (a) one cannot afford to purchase healthier food or join a gym; (b) there are no gyms or healthy food retailers nearby; (c) one is working multiple low-wage jobs, spending hours each day travelling to and from work, with no time to exercise or cook healthier food; (d) there are no safe spaces nearby to play or exercise outdoors; or (e) the pervasive stresses of living in poverty are contributing to one's obesity, as well as other health effects such as depression and hypertension. These are challenges brought on by socioeconomic conditions: poverty, economic inequality, limited transportation options, neighborhood violence, and more. Needless to say, these are difficult problems to take on, but they cannot be left out of the conversation about obesity. Indeed, their placement at the bottom of the health impact pyramid suggests that they are fundamental building blocks for any comprehensive approach to improving the public's health.

Government

Governmental action is the primary means by which the public acts collectively to address threats to health (and makes decisions about how best to do so). Although nongovernmental organizations and other private-sector partners are also engaged in efforts to improve population health, government action is at public health's core. Indeed, the term *public* can refer to either the general population or to the government.

Accordingly, the study of the public health system tends to explore what government can do to improve the health of populations. As discussed further in Chapter 2, there are different governmental public health entities at the local, state, and national level engaged in public health practice. Local public health departments, though a lesser-known (and often underfunded) component of local government, are in many ways the backbone of our nation's public health system. These entities monitor threats to health locally and engage in a variety of programmatic and enforcement activities related to environmental health (e.g., food safety and housing inspections), communicable disease control, chronic disease prevention, maternal and child health, and more. Beyond health departments, many other federal, state, and local government entities—including law enforcement, housing authorities, and sanitation departments—play essential roles in protecting and improving public health.

Science/Empirical Evidence

Finally, public health is a scientific discipline that seeks to promote health through the rigorous examination and use of empirical evidence. The core science of public health is *epidemiology*, which quantitatively examines the causes, patterns, and prevalence of diseases or other health hazards in populations. Epidemiologists are sometimes referred to as "disease detectives," a nod to the field's origins in the effort to identify the major causes of disease. An early pioneer of epidemiology, John Snow, tracked the distribution of cases during the 1854 London cholera outbreak. By carefully documenting both the location of new cases and the behavior patterns of those who did (and did not) develop the disease, he was able to correctly deduce that cholera was a waterborne disease, and he was able to trace the outbreak back to its source, the Broad Street Pump. In the mid-20th century, American and British epidemiologists used both longitudinal studies (following the same group of people over time) and cross-sectional studies (comparing different groups of people at the same point in time) to definitively identify smoking as the major cause of lung cancer.

Today, governmental entities and academic researchers engage in a significant amount of epidemiological surveillance, conducting large-scale surveys and tracking various types of health data. This data is used to help identify the causes and patterns of disease, disparities in public health outcomes, and the effectiveness of interventions intended to improve public health.

What Is Law?

Laws are rules issued and enforced by government entities with the authority to do so. Law is the means through which populations organize their governments, regulate social and economic interactions, and guide behavior. The influence of law is so pervasive in our society, it is rarely noticed or remarked upon. But interaction with law is an unavoidable feature of daily life. The water you drink, the food you eat, the pharmaceuticals you consume, the roads on which you drive, the computers you use, the websites you visit, and much, much more—all of these things are governed by an overlapping web of local, state, and federal (and sometimes international) laws. As will be discussed throughout this book, laws come in myriad forms. Laws may be federal, state, tribal, local, or territorial; civil or criminal; procedural or substantive; constitutional, statutory, administrative, or judge-made.

And those are just the "laws on the books." How the law is understood and applied by the public and by those tasked with enforcing it—sometimes referred to as the "law on the streets"—can be as important as what the law says. For instance, a local law may require bicyclists to wear helmets while riding, but if the law is widely ignored by the public and is not enforced, then looking only at the law's text will provide a misleading impression of what occurs in practice. Similarly, laws may be enforced differently against different populations. For example, between 2004 and 2011, 84% of those stopped by the New York Police Department's "stop and frisk" program were black or Latino, even though those groups accounted for only 52% of the New York City's population (and were *less* likely than white residents to be found carrying a weapon or contraband when stopped; *Floyd v. City of New York*, 2013). Nothing in any criminal law dictated that the stop and frisk program be carried out in this manner, and indeed, a federal judge later ruled that the police department's implementation of the stop and frisk program was unconstitutional. As this example suggests, law cannot be understood without examining how it is implemented in the real world and considering the sociopolitical context in which it operates.

Two important features of law deserve further mention. First, law is far less definitive than most people assume it to be. Non-lawyers often think of the law as a set of clear, black-and-white rules, but this is far from the case. Take the Fourth Amendment to the Constitution, which states in part that "[t]he right of the people to be secure in their persons, houses, papers, and effects, against unreasonable searches and seizures, shall not be violated." This basic constitutional protection leaves the key term "unreasonable" undefined. What does it mean for a search or seizure to be "unreasonable"? The Constitution simply does not say, leaving it to subsequent Supreme Court and lower court cases to iron out what is and is not "reasonable" in particular situations. Likewise, the text of the Fourth Amendment does not tell us what a house is (is a backyard part of a house?), what should happen when an unreasonable search occurs (can the evidence be used in court?), or whether "papers" includes electronic files stored on a Google server. That is not to say that there are no answers to these questions. But those answers are typically nuanced and subject to numerous exceptions and qualifications. A close examination of legal texts, therefore, often raises more questions than it answers. Legal reasoning is the process of identifying, thinking through, and arguing about those questions.

Second, in addition to being nuanced and indeterminate in particular circumstances, law is always subject to change. Court decisions, such as the Supreme Court's 2015 decision recognizing a constitutional right to same-sex marriage, can upend settled legal practice and expand our understanding of what constitutional protections like "Equal Protection Under the Law" mean (*Obergefell v. Hodges*, 2015). In addition, legislatures at the federal, state, tribal, local, and territorial levels can pass new laws to amend existing laws, overturn court decisions (in some cases), or initiate new programs. Any critical analysis of law must recognize that "the law" is not fixed and that it is important to thoughtfully—and, where appropriate, empirically—examine whether existing laws are working, for whom they are effective, and how they could be redesigned.

Law as a Tool to Promote Health

Recognizing that the development of law is a dynamic and ongoing process is the starting place for this book. Most of this book examines how lawyers, public health experts, and others can come together to use law as tool to improve population health. Thus it is important to think about the various ways that law shapes society—and how laws can be changed in ways that improve population health.

At the most basic level, laws can *encourage healthy and safe behaviors* and discourage unhealthy and dangerous ones by shaping incentives (rewards) and deterrents (punishments). There are myriad legal levers that can be used to influence individual or corporate behavior, and each legal option can and should be studied for its effectiveness, both in absolute terms and relative to potential alternatives. Among the legal tools commonly used to promote healthy behaviors are taxation and subsidies, changes in the information environment (e.g., warning labels), changes in the built environment (e.g., sidewalks and bicycle lanes), and punishing misconduct through private lawsuits (tort litigation). As suggested earlier, however, it is important to remember that having a new "law on the books" is only the first step; careful attention must be paid to how these legal tools are implemented and enforced.

Beyond the level of individual or corporate behavior, laws can also influence health by *changing the physical environments* in which people live, work, and play. For example, zoning rules, clean indoor air laws, and laws regulating the condition of rental properties can directly shape residents' exposures to noise, environmental toxins, and stress. Occupational health and safety laws affect workers' exposure to hazardous conditions on the job. And product regulations protect consumers from a range of hazards arising from the use of consumer goods, from pharmaceuticals to power tools.

In addition to changing the physical environment, law can also be used *to shape the social environment*. Law may shape people's health knowledge and attitudes, the way they perceive the risks and benefits of different choices, and the social norms against which their health decisions are set. For example, research on the effects of indoor smoking prohibitions suggests that such laws, in addition to protecting people from secondhand smoke, change social expectations about smoking behavior and influence social norms about smoking more generally (Burris et al., 2010).

At the same time it plays all of these other roles, law can also *influence the social determinants of health*. Through legal levers including tax laws, welfare regulations, housing codes, healthcare policy, and more, law influences the distribution of wealth, employment opportunities, and living conditions. For example, though limited research has been done on the subject to date, increasing the minimum wage could potentially help citizens improve their (and their children's) health by facilitating better nutrition, promoting housing stability, and reducing psychological distress, among other possible effects.

Finally, law *structures the public health system* by creating public health entities and endowing them with certain powers and responsibilities. These laws are sometimes referred to as "infrastructural" public health laws. In 1988, an influential report by the Institute of Medicine suggested that the nation's public health infrastructure was in "disarray," in part because infrastructural public health laws were "in many cases seriously outdated" and "inadequate to deal with contemporary problems" (Institute of Medicine, 1988). Since that time, there have been some efforts to both evaluate and update the laws organizing the public health system, but ensuring sufficient legal authority—and capacity—to respond appropriately to both ongoing and emergency threats to public health remains a challenge.

Conclusion

In this chapter, we have introduced and defined basic concepts we will use throughout the book. Public health is what we as a society do collectively to promote health and prevent disease, taking into account health disparities and the social determinants of health. Laws are rules issued and enforced by government entities with the authority to do so. And public health law stands at the intersection of these two dynamic fields and provides a range of powerful tools for improving health. In the next chapter, we go into greater depth on the nation's public health system and law's place within it.

Further Reading

Centers for Disease Control and Prevention. (1999). Ten Great Public Health Achievements—United States, 1900–1999. *MMWR: Morbidity and Mortality Weekly Report*, *48*(12), 241–243.

Parmet, W. E. (2009). *Populations, Public Health, and the Law*. Washington, DC: Georgetown University Press.

Parmet, W. E., Smith, L. A., & Benedict, M. A. (2011). Social Determinants, Health Disparities, and the Role of Law. In E. Tobin Tyler, E. Lawton, K. Conroy, M. Sandel, & B. Zuckerman (Eds.), *Poverty, Health and Law: Readings and Cases for Medical-Legal Partnerships* (pp. 3–36). Durham, NC: Carolina Academic Press.

2 | The Public Health System

Learning Objectives

- Define the public health system and understand its structure and the basic services it provides.
- Describe the differing roles of federal, state, and local public health agencies in the public health system.
- Explain how funding influences the public health and healthcare systems.
- Name three drivers of public health system performance improvement.

Introduction

Chapter 1 laid the groundwork for the study of public health law by defining *public health, law*, and the *social determinants of health*. This chapter will explore the public health system as a whole, including the organizations, activities, and people who promote public health in the United States. We describe the agencies at the federal, state, local, tribal, and territorial levels that have been granted legal authority to act on behalf of public health. We close with a short discussion of the evolving effort to improve the public health system through accreditation.

The Public Health System and Its Functions

Although much of their work happens out of public view, people in every community around the country are actively protecting and promoting the public's health. The *public health system* is the interconnected set of public, private, and voluntary entities that contribute to the protection of public health in communities, states, and the nation. Among other duties, the public health system is responsible for

- ensuring that we have drinkable water and safe food;
- reducing exposure to environmental toxins such as lead;
- protecting against infectious diseases;
- preparing for and responding to public health emergencies;
- preventing injuries;
- encouraging healthy behaviors and discouraging unhealthy behaviors;
- collecting public health data; and
- conducting research.

Federal, state, tribal, local, and territorial public health agencies are at the core of the public health system, but environmental protection agencies, healthcare providers, philanthropies, schools, and organizations working in public safety, housing, human services, recreation, and transportation can all be considered a part of the broader public health system. For example, a community where it is as convenient and safe to walk, bike, or take the bus as it is to drive will help to reduce obesity among its members by encouraging physical activity, but developing these features—like sidewalks with accessible ramps, public transit lines, and bike lanes—requires the active cooperation of transportation, zoning, and urban planning agencies.

Over time, the role and the scope of the public health system has changed as the threats we face and the tools we use have changed. Historically, public health agencies focused on preventing and controlling communicable diseases and maintaining health-related records (e.g., birth and death certificates). In part because of the success of public health measures like vaccination and sanitation, communicable diseases stopped being the leading causes of preventable death; they were replaced by heart disease, stroke, cancers, other noncommunicable diseases, chronic conditions, and injuries. In response, public health entities shifted their focus. While still concerned about preventing infectious diseases, they began to place more of an emphasis on discouraging unhealthy behaviors (like smoking and drunk driving) and promoting healthy ones (like physical activity and healthy eating). In recent decades there has been increasing recognition that educating people about health-related behaviors is not enough to change deeply engrained behavioral patterns. Health-related decision-making is deeply influenced by the social, cultural, environmental, and economic contexts in which it occurs. Accordingly, the public health system has, to varying degrees depending on the issue, turned its focus toward addressing the social determinants of health, inequality, and the broader policy environment in which health-related behaviors occur. This new orientation, of course, requires links with a wide range of entities and organizations that may not see public health as central to their missions. Of course, it also requires the use of law to help create the conditions in which people can be healthy and interagency collaboration can occur.

In 1994, the U.S. Department of Health and Human Services, with guidance from a wide variety of stakeholders, defined *Ten Essential Public Health Services,* the set of community-wide prevention and protection programs that are needed to assure the conditions people need to live healthy lives (Turnock & Handler, 1997). These 10 services are shown in Figure 2.1. These services do not focus on preventing any specific disease or addressing particular public health challenges; instead, they reflect a larger mission to maintain a dynamic public health system that can respond to a community's needs.

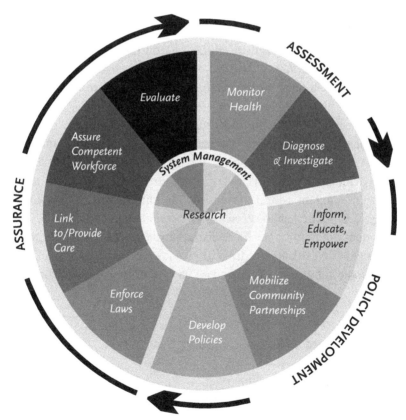

FIGURE 2.1. The Ten Essential Public Health Services.
CDC, https://www.cdc.gov/nphpsp/images/phs-figure2.gif

The Ten Essential Public Health Services can be grouped into three categories:

- *Assessment.* Public health agencies must monitor the health status of the community and promptly diagnose and investigate health problems and hazards.
- *Policy Development.* Public health agencies must inform and empower people about health issues, build community partnerships, and develop policies and plans that address public health issues.
- *Assurance:* Public health agencies must assure a competent public health workforce, evaluate the effectiveness of their services, enforce public health laws and regulations, and, when needed, link people to needed healthcare services.

The circular design of Figure 2.1 is meant to illustrate that the provision of public health services is iterative and ongoing. New public health concerns require new policies and programs, which must then be implemented and evaluated. Those evaluation activities in turn lead to reassessment and improvement of existing practices. Reflecting on this process should show you that *public health law*—the laws and policies that contribute to and result from this iterative policymaking cycle—plays a central role in the provision of public health services.

Public health services differ from the clinical preventive services offered by healthcare providers, such as cancer screenings, immunizations, and prenatal care. While some public health agencies, particularly at the local level, provide preventive services, most governmental public health work focuses on population-level prevention, not clinical care. To be sure, the line between public health services and preventive services can be fuzzy, but this does not imply a lack of cooperation and coordination: even public health agencies that do not directly provide vaccinations, for example, may promote the use of vaccines and carefully track their uptake in the population.

Organization of the Public Health System

The core of the public health system's infrastructure is governmental. Legislatures set priorities for public health action by passing laws and allocating funds, and administrative agencies are responsible for the day-to-day promotion of public health. Federal, state, and local health agencies, as well as tribal and territorial governments, implement public health programs within their purview and coordinate with each other to share information on best practices. This section outlines the functions of these agencies in promoting public health in the United States.

Federal Public Health Agencies

The U.S. Department of Health and Human Services (HHS) is the primary federal agency responsible for health promotion. Led by the Secretary of Health and Human Services, it employs nearly 80,000 people around the country and administers federal laws that incentivize and assure national and regional public health programs. The Public Health Service Act (PHSA), initially passed in 1944 to fund programs to contain the spread of infectious disease, currently authorizes HHS to support research, conduct surveillance, collect and protect patient data, ensure safe food and drinking water, prepare for and respond to emergencies, and provide a host of other services (PHSA, 1944). HHS oversees numerous subagencies to undertake these responsibilities.

Some subagencies, like the U.S. Food and Drug Administration (FDA), are primarily regulatory in nature. The FDA regulates pharmaceuticals, medical devices, (some) food, veterinary products, tobacco products, and more. Indeed, "FDA-regulated products account for about 25 cents of every dollar spent by American consumers each year." (FDA, 2016). Other parts of HHS focus on clinical and laboratory research (e.g., the National Institutes of Health), fund issue-specific research and services (e.g., the Substance Abuse and Mental Health Services Administration), and reimburse for medical care (e.g., the Centers of Medicare and Medicaid Services).

The Centers for Disease Control and Prevention (CDC) is not primarily a regulatory agency, although it does have limited regulatory authority over interstate and foreign quarantine, health hazards and biological toxins, and clinical laboratory standards. Its main duties include (a) conducting disease and injury-related surveillance and research; (b) preparing for and responding to public health emergencies; and (c) providing funding, training, and other assistance to state, local, and tribal public health entities. Laws at other levels of government occasionally incorporate CDC guidelines by reference, elevating their weight to that of law.

HHS guidelines can also carry the weight of scientific evidence, particularly recommendations issued by the U.S. Preventive Services Task Force. Convened by the Agency for Healthcare Quality Research, the Task Force is an independent panel of nationally recognized experts in prevention and evidence-based medicine that convenes to recommend clinical preventive services such as screenings, counseling, and preventive medications to the public and reports critical gaps in evidence and research to Congress annually. Similarly, the Federal Interagency Workgroup leads the Healthy People initiative to provide science-based, national objectives for health improvement. Healthy People 2020 establishes benchmarks and monitors progress across 42 health objectives, many using law and policy, based on public comment and input across agencies and from a federal advisory committee convened by HHS.

The HHS unit with the longest history is the U.S. Public Health Service Commissioned Corps, which traces its roots back to a 1798 law signed by President John Adams. The 6,000 members of the Corps serve in positions throughout HHS and other federal agencies and respond to public health emergencies. The Corps is organized along military lines, with uniforms and strict requirements for service, and is headed by the U.S. Surgeon General, who provides leadership on public health issues and is sometimes referred to as the "Nation's Doctor."

The federal public health system extends well beyond HHS. For example, the Stafford Act authorizes the president to declare a major disaster or emergency and direct the Federal Emergency Management Agency (FEMA) to coordinate disaster relief to states (Robert T. Stafford Disaster Relief and Emergency Assistance Act, 1988). However public health administration is organized, Congress ultimately sets the jurisdiction and authority for federal health initiatives, and those authorities change over time. For example, the 2009 Family Smoking Prevention and Tobacco Control Act authorized the FDA to restrict underage sales and certain advertising and marketing of tobacco products to the public but not to ban or eliminate nicotine in tobacco products entirely. Table 2.1 describes other key federal agencies that play important roles in promoting and protecting public health.

State Public Health Departments

Health departments are the primary entities responsible for public health at the state level, administering public health programs and engaging in regulatory activities. State public health departments primarily support a host of public health programs. They collect information through reporting requirements, routine surveys, and testing for various conditions or environmental substances. Using that data, they then conduct disease

TABLE 2.1. Key Agencies in the Federal Health System

NAME OF FEDERAL AGENCY	AREAS OF PUBLIC HEALTH-RELATED AUTHORITY	EXAMPLES OF PUBLIC HEALTH ACTIVITY OR REGULATION
Environmental Protection Agency (EPA)	The EPA supports environmental health and safety and administers regulations related to air and water quality, pesticides in foods, hazardous materials, and the safety of drinking water. It also supports programs that research climate change, environmentally sound infrastructure and transportation, and land use and clean-up.	Safe Water Drinking Act; Endangered Species Act; Clean Air Act
U.S. Department of Agriculture (USDA)	The USDA sets dietary standards through the Center for Nutrition Policy and Promotion; regulates the safety and labeling of meats, poultry, and eggs through the Food Safety and Inspection Service; regulates veterinary vaccines and biologics through the Animal and Plant Inspection Service; and funds school breakfast and lunch programs nationally.	Animal Welfare Act; Federal Regulations Regarding Nutrition Labeling; Federal Insecticide, Fungicide, and Rodenticide Act
Department of Veterans Affairs (VA)	The VA runs the Veterans Health Administration, the single largest healthcare administration in the United States, serving 8.76 million veterans in over 1,700 facilities.	Veterans Benefits Act of 2010; The National Defense Authorization Act of Fiscal Year 2013
U.S. Department of Housing and Urban Development (HUD)	HUD administers healthy and affordable housing programs, provides financing and insurance to homeowners through the Federal Housing Administration, and supports homelessness prevention and the redevelopment of abandoned and neglected property.	The HUD Act; Housing and Community Development Act; Civil Rights Act of 1964; Lead-Based Paint Poisoning Prevention Act and Residential Lead-Based Paint Hazard Reduction Act; Americans with Disabilities Act
Federal Trade Commission (FTC)	The FTC regulates unfair, deceptive, or fraudulent practices in advertising, which can affect public information about foods, drugs, devices, and tobacco and alcohol products.	Comprehensive Smokeless Tobacco Health Education Act of 1986; Children's Online Privacy Protection Act; Do-Not-Call Registry Legislation

(*continued*)

TABLE 2.1. Continued

NAME OF FEDERAL AGENCY	AREAS OF PUBLIC HEALTH-RELATED AUTHORITY	EXAMPLES OF PUBLIC HEALTH ACTIVITY OR REGULATION
Consumer Product Safety Commission (CPSC)	The CPSC is an independent regulatory agency that oversees the safety of hazardous substances, injury prevention through products such as child safety seats and lead-based paint, and information dissemination through labeling and packaging.	Flammable Fabrics Act; Federal Hazardous Substances Act; Child Safety Protection Act
National Highway Traffic Safety Administration (NHTSA)	NHTSA is an agency of the U.S. Department of Transportation, with the mission to save lives, prevent injuries, and reduce traffic-related healthcare and economic costs.	Federal Motor Vehicle Safety Standards
Federal Aviation Administration (FAA)	The FAA is an operating mode of the U.S. Department of Transportation that runs aerospace safety and procedures.	Federal Aviation Regulations

investigations, respond to public health emergencies, inform the public about emerging issues, develop public health interventions, and train healthcare and public health workers. Nearly all states also engage in some activities focused on addressing minority health and health equity concerns. In some states, the state health department may also be designated as a service provider under federal law, requiring it to provide certain health or mental health services at the local level and "pass through" funding from federal programs to local or even private entities that support these services.

On the regulatory side, state public health departments may license, set rules for, and inspect laboratories, restaurants, healthcare facilities, nursing homes, childcare facilities, tattoo parlors, and more (although some of this licensing and inspection may instead be conducted at the local level). They may also be responsible for licensing and regulating healthcare professionals such as physicians, pharmacists, and emergency medical technicians. Where health departments are authorized to enforce regulatory provisions, they may assess fines, revoke licensure, or take noncompliant parties to court.

State public health agencies can differ widely in structure, functions, staffing, expenditures, political engagement, and regional relationships. State public health departments can be led by a single appointed official (often a member of the Governor's cabinet), overseen by a state board of health, or incorporated into a larger agency that also oversees Medicaid, social services, and mental and behavioral health programs. For example, Montana, like many lower-population states, has an umbrella agency, the Montana Department of Health and Human Services, that, in addition to addressing public health, includes divisions responsible for child protective services/foster care, senior and long-term care, and disability services. As of 2012, 28 state governments had independent public health departments, while 20 included public health functions under a larger umbrella agency with other responsibilities (Association of State and Territorial Health Officials, 2014). Figure 2.2 shows variations of responsibilities across umbrella health agencies.

Local Public Health Agencies

Local public health agencies operate at the front lines of public health and meet many of the most fundamental needs in public health administration. Local public health agencies take their authorities directly from the state. States have widely varying systems of public health governance, spanning the range from "decentralized," with largely independent local public health agencies, to "centralized" authority, where the state appoints local health officials, sets local agency budgets, and shares local public health decision-making. State statutes typically dictate whether local governments have broad authorities to act, as in Oregon, or whether state employees run localities centrally, as in South Carolina. In either case, or even where there is a mixed or shared system of governance, local public health agencies are responsible for administering a range of public health activities.

Local public health agencies of every type monitor population health and investigate disease outbreaks; conduct inspections; provide education, counseling, and connections to healthcare; and—more often than state public health departments—provide testing and other preventive services directly to individuals. Some agencies also provide particular treatment services, especially for sexually transmitted diseases and other communicable diseases like tuberculosis. These services are funded from a wide variety of sources, including health insurance, local taxes, fees and fines, state government transfers, and federal government programs. In many

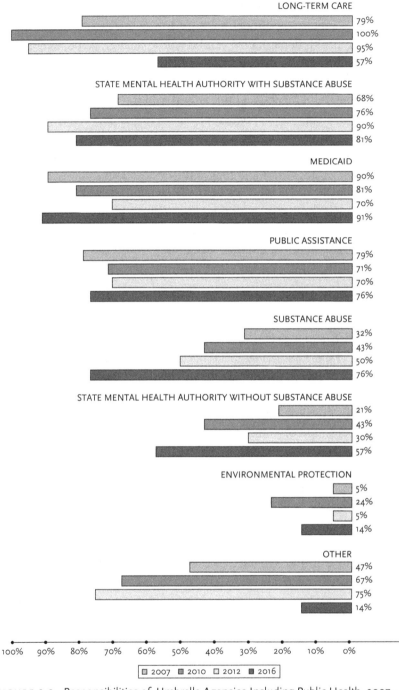

LONG-TERM CARE
79%
100%
95%
57%

STATE MENTAL HEALTH AUTHORITY WITH SUBSTANCE ABUSE
68%
76%
90%
81%

MEDICAID
90%
81%
70%
91%

PUBLIC ASSISTANCE
79%
71%
70%
76%

SUBSTANCE ABUSE
32%
43%
50%
76%

STATE MENTAL HEALTH AUTHORITY WITHOUT SUBSTANCE ABUSE
21%
43%
30%
57%

ENVIRONMENTAL PROTECTION
5%
24%
5%
14%

OTHER
47%
67%
75%
14%

100% 90% 80% 70% 60% 50% 40% 30% 20% 10% 0%

☐ 2007 ▣ 2010 ☐ 2012 ■ 2016

FIGURE 2.2. Responsibilities of Umbrella Agencies Including Public Health, 2007–2016 (N = 19–21).

Association of State and Territorial Health Officials. ASTHO Profile of State and Territorial Public Health, Volume Four. Arlington, VA: Association of State and Territorial Health Officials. 2017. http://www.astho.org/Profile/Volume-Four/2016-ASTHO-Profile-of-State-and-Territorial-Public-Health/ (page 19).

cases, funding is inadequate, and local public health agencies are sometimes limited in their capacity and unable to fully support the Ten Essential Public Health Services.

Local public health agencies may serve cities, counties, combined cities and counties, or larger regional areas. There are an estimated 2,800 city and county public health agencies across the country. The number of local public health jurisdictions varies from zero in Hawaii and Rhode Island to 352 in Massachusetts. Some agencies function with as few as four employees and serve fewer than 10,000 people, while others have as many as 450 employees and serve more than 1 million people (National Association of County and City Health Officials, 2017). Regardless of the structure or size of local public health agencies, their functions may necessitate cross-agency collaborations with housing authorities, emergency responders, and public works departments, as well as sharing resources with neighboring localities to maximize their efficiency.

An Ebola example illustrates how agencies typically collaborate to manage a public health threat. Consider a case first identified at a city hospital. That hospital is also in a state, and within national borders, so that three levels of government would have to work together to treat the affected individual and prevent an outbreak. The local public health agency would be first to arrive. Local health department and law enforcement agencies, as well as emergency response and fire departments, can stabilize and isolate new patients (and seek quarantine orders for others exposed), monitor individuals for symptoms and trace contacts, and issue warnings or health communications to surrounding communities. Local public health agencies will contact the state health department to support the response to a potential outbreak.

The state public health department may often have a greater capacity to manage public communications and notify healthcare facilities, coordinate logistics among facilities and government agencies, and secure funding and services from neighboring jurisdictions or the federal government when needed. State or regional public health laboratories will be involved in testing and reporting potential cases of disease and training healthcare workers to prepare for new cases. If the state with an outbreak declares a health emergency, federal emergency funds can be used to equip and guide healthcare entities and state and local health department workers to use best practices in treatment and prevention.

The federal government can support state and local public health activities through funding, logistical support, and disseminating information quickly. For Ebola in 2014–2015, U.S. Customs and Border Patrol and the

CDC exercised federal authority to secure the borders from international threats by implementing screening of travelers from affected areas for Ebola symptoms and quarantining exposed individuals. The Department of Defense has equipped public health laboratories for testing with FDA-approved assays and can help to transport American patients in affected areas overseas back to the United States for treatment. Going forward, the National Institutes of Health works to develop vaccines and support research on Ebola in preparation for future outbreaks.

Tribal and Territorial Public Health Activities

Given the historical and socioeconomic toll of colonization, subjugation, and discrimination on Native Americans over the last five centuries, it is not surprising that their life expectancy and disease burden in this country are worse than those of other Americans. The federal government has granted some tribal governments land and US citizenship, but only 567 tribes are federally-recognized and receive healthcare from the Indian Health Service (IHS). Many more are state-recognized or organized as non-profit or corporate organizations not served by IHS and so obtain health services through contractual or other relationships with state or local public health and healthcare entities. The long-standing health disparities of Native American populations are still fed by infrastructural public health law problems and lack of resources.

The public health system is a patchwork for many tribal populations, whose public health services come from a variety of tribal, state, and US public health agencies. For instance, CDC funding supports tribal epidemiology centers to conduct disease surveillance and outbreak investigations, whereas the IHS provides preventive health services to federally recognized American Indian and Alaska Native citizens. Because the Constitution recognizes tribes as sovereign entities, relationships between federal, state, local, and tribal governments fall under federal Indian law, which rests on a large body of case law recognizing tribes as "domestic dependent nations" with similar powers as state governments.

Tribes also have separate tribal law that their governments use to codify, implement, and enforce public health laws and support internal infrastructure. Where tribal governments can independently conduct broad public health activities, they may undertake prevention and control of communicable diseases, support for environmental health, motor vehicle safety, and health education for tribal populations. Even so, public health challenges often cross tribal boundaries, just as individuals can leave villages and reservations, so that many tribal public health issues may involve states, localities, other tribes, and the federal government (National Congress of American Indians, 2017).

Territorial public health departments also face unique challenges in the public health system. While territories exist completely outside US borders and have distinct governmental systems, they can still receive direct funding from states and the federal government for public health issues. The Commonwealth of Puerto Rico, Guam, the Northern Mariana Islands, the U.S. Virgin Islands, and American Samoa have public health agencies that are independent or fall under umbrella health agencies. Territorial public health priorities mirror those on the mainland as related to noncommunicable disease prevention and infrastructural or technological improvements, but they sometimes face differing health issues. For example, American Samoa has been working over the past few decades to eliminate Lymphatic filariasis, a tropical disease caused by parasitic worms that has been absent from mainland United States since the early 20th century. Because of their proximity to and relationships with the US public health system, territorial and tribal public health entities fulfill critical roles in prevention and health promotion even though their populations may not fall under any single state or federal jurisdiction.

The Private and Voluntary Sectors

The government is not the only element of public health infrastructure. From the 19th-century work of Nobel Peace Prize Laureate Jane Addams, whose public education campaigns challenged housing and sanitation issues in industrializing Chicago, to the 21st century organizing and advocacy by Gay Men's Health Crisis in response to the HIV epidemic, nongovernmental actors have identified, addressed, and supported public health needs in every jurisdiction. To this day, volunteers and private foundations share a history of developing, funding, and implementing the most critical public health programs.

Private entities can often be more responsive, efficient, and effective in communities than governmental agencies. For example, non-profit organizations may support health department activities and are often funded by governmental public health agencies to provide timely services and education to specific communities or individuals. Private contracting companies (both for- and non-profit) also receive funding from governmental agencies to conduct research and evaluation activities, develop educational materials, and, in some cases, perform inspections.

In some jurisdictions, public health services can be provided entirely by nongovernmental entities. Federal reimbursement programs have pushed public health initiatives to the private sector, including some healthcare providers and insurance companies. Although privatization of public health can pose conflicts when the private interest does not conform to the public needs, such as for environmental or occupational health issues, many community-based organizations can understand and adapt to local needs faster and more efficiently with private funding. Businesses also contribute to public health through their charitable donations. For instance, Wal-Mart, Office Depot, General Electric, and other companies made sizable in-kind and monetary contributions to support recovery efforts after Hurricane Katrina. More recently, the Million Hearts Initiative, led by HHS, has garnered financial and organizational support from professional organizations, healthcare facilities and providers, pharmaceutical companies, insurers, and faith-based organizations in a broad-based effort to prevent heart attacks and strokes.

National professional organizations also receive funding to support the training and development of the public health workforce and lead key initiatives in public health promotion that government cannot perform as well or at all. Public health practitioners receive continuing education and opportunities for professional development and collaboration through the American Public Health Association and the Council for State and Territorial Epidemiologists. Similarly, the Association of State and Territorial Health Officials and the National Association of City and County Health Officials support, train, and connect health officials and their staff on issues of public health importance. Each of these organizations receives federal funding to perform research and evaluation and provide timely recommendations on cutting-edge public health issues. Separately, each also advocates for the role and functions of public health professionals and resources to fund the public health system overall. For attorneys, the Network for Public Health Law, the American Bar Association's Health Law Section, and the American Health Lawyers Association provide opportunities to maintain up-to-date public health knowledge and build capacity as an integral part of the public health workforce.

The Healthcare System

No discussion of the public health system would be complete without reference to the US healthcare system. The healthcare system and public health system overlap in the populations they serve, but have different orientations. Health care focuses on treating individual patients, while public health focuses on preventing disease and improving health at the population level. The public health system allows everyone to benefit from population-level prevention programs, but not everyone can readily access all healthcare services without a way to pay for them.

This is because the US healthcare system is based on a mixed public-private financing model where individuals or the companies that insure them pay for discrete healthcare services, rather than a single-payer model where taxes to a central government support all healthcare entities and services. US spending for this healthcare delivery system reached $3.0 trillion in 2014, more than 17% of the gross domestic product—the highest expenditures of any country in the world (The Commonwealth Fund, 2017). Some of this increase is attributable to the rising cost of services, including everything from standard daily medications to complex surgical procedures, which has often become the target of legal or policy action and attention nationwide.

The federal government influences many aspects of the healthcare system, including healthcare facilities, healthcare providers, and insurers. Large government-sponsored Medicare insurance healthcare plans can negotiate lower premiums for beneficiaries than most employer-based health insurance or private insurance coverage programs that are left to market forces. Federal law is currently instrumental to shaping the future of the healthcare system through increasing access to care, allocating targeted funding for efficiency and innovation, and supporting consumer protections. Most significantly, the Centers for Medicaid and Medicaid Services (CMS) regulates national healthcare practices through reimbursement mechanisms for treatment and incentive programs for using healthcare technology, improving efficiency, and supporting multisector collaborations. The federal Department of Labor also prescribes the information and protections that employer-based health insurance companies must provide to the government and public through the 1974 Employee Retirement Income Security Act. HHS regulations require providers and insurers to comply with the 1996 Health Insurance Portability and Accountability Act to protect patient privacy, as well as the 2009 Health Information Technology for Economic and Clinical Health Act to expand the use of electronic health records and health information exchange.

State laws also shape the practice and delivery of healthcare through licensure of all types of facilities and providers that seek to accept patients and practice in the jurisdiction—or that provide telehealth services to expand access to treatment and preventive services. States also regulate and monitor insurance companies to ensure fairness and reporting of health-care usage and access. Finally, state courts accept cases of malpractice and fraud to compensate victims and deter future abuses in the healthcare system. Together, federal and state laws support the functioning of health-care in the United States today.

In recent years, some legal structures have been put in place to encourage more collaboration between the healthcare and public health sectors. At this writing, the 2010 Patient Protection and Affordable Care Act (ACA) continues to incentivize this collaboration (Longthorne, Subramanian, & Chen, 2010). The ACA required non-profit hospitals to conduct a community health needs assessment (CHNA) and develop an associated imple-mentation strategy to support their federal tax-exempt status every three years. In preparing CHNAs, hospitals must consult with governmental public health entities in their communities, as well as with members of underserved, low-income, and minority populations in the community. This mandated planning process facilitated cross-sector collaborations be-tween healthcare and public health, and it has led some healthcare entities to consider how they can play a role in addressing the social determinants of health in their communities. For example, a CHNA conducted by healthcare systems in Sonoma County, California, led to a community-wide action plan that focuses not only on health but also on educational attainment and economic security (Sonoma County Department of Health Services, 2012).

Funding and Public Health Programs

Public health has always been a good social investment: health outcomes often improve when public health spending increases. Cuts in the work-force and resources for health agencies cannot be called good planning or efficiency. Indeed, investments in public health are often remarkably cost-efficient. The Trust for America's Health (2016) has estimated that "an in-vestment of $10 per person per year in proven evidence-based community prevention programs that increase physical activity, improve nutrition and prevent smoking and other tobacco use could save the country more than $16 billion annually within five years—a return of $5.60 for every dollar invested."

Despite such a clear connection between spending and benefit, public health activities account for less than 3% of the US spending on health, and that spending has declined in recent years as state and local governments have faced budget cuts (Himmelstein & Woolhandler, 2016). Although jurisdictions vary in the amount they budget for public health adminis-tration, the National Center for Health Statistics (2015) estimated that per capital public health spending (federal, state, and local) averaged $248 per person in 2014. By contrast, per capital healthcare expenditures the same year averaged more than $9,000 per person (National Center for Health Statistics, 2015). The gap is growing, and the overall health status of Americans is not rising.

Some novel funding methods for public health show promise in supporting public health functions. CMS regulations are gradually incentivizing prevention in healthcare services, such as through "value-based purchasing" that only reimburses providers who do not make medical errors. CMS also certifies accountable care organizations that bring healthcare providers together with mental health, social work, and other prevention-based disciplines, although the reimbursement is based on dollars saved, rather than improved health status. Seventeen states support social impact bonds, financing mechanisms that pay organiza-tions for successful public health outcomes, such as chronic disease man-agement (The Rockefeller Foundation, 2017). States and localities are implementing wellness trusts, using pooled public and private funding to provide prevention and wellness interventions to a community. As shared, pooled, or aligned models for financing public health initiatives increase, so will the evidence for sustained funding and development of public health initiatives.

Improving the Public Health System

Over the last two decades, various national and state organizations have fo-cused on developing and implementing performance standards for public health agencies to assure the delivery of the Ten Essential Public Health Services. Broadly speaking, these efforts have focused on accreditation, governance, and evaluation.

Accreditation is a process through which state, local, tribal, and territo-rial health departments demonstrate—and are recognized for—compliance with "a set of nationally recognized, practice-focused and evidenced-based standards" (Public Health Accreditation Board, 2013). Nearly 180 public health agencies that meet established standards for performance and fulfill related documentation requirements are accredited by the Public Health Accreditation Board (PHAB), a non-profit organization that was formed in 2007. PHAB's standards are built around the Ten Essential

Public Health Services. One of these services is to "enforce public health laws that protect health and ensure safety," with respect to which PHAB's standards require health departments to (a) carefully evaluate how well current laws and regulations are aligned with evidence-based public health recommendations and (b) proactively consider how existing laws could be modified and strengthened. Although public health agencies may lack the legal authority to directly change their laws or regulations, they are required to play a role in educating policymakers about needed updates and changes to current governance or practices. Accreditation shows promise in improving capacity in and coordination between health department functions, including policy development, and improved communication with governing entities like boards of health (Kronstadt et al., 2016).

Governance impacts the way public health agencies are administered. Public health laws structure public health agencies in a variety of ways across the country. Depending on a state's law, for instance, local health agencies may be overseen by a director (or commissioner), a board of health, or both, and the qualifications to be a director or board member vary considerably between jurisdictions. These governance structures can make a difference. For example, in one study, local boards of health made up of both public officials and health professionals (where neither had a majority) were associated with better public health outcomes than boards comprised of health professionals alone (Hays et al., 2012). While public health agencies have little power to change their governance structure, the PHAB standards require public health agencies to document close collaboration between agency staff and governing boards/commissioners, so that policymakers are well informed and able to ensure accountability.

Finally, *evaluation* is needed to demonstrate whether existing programs, implementation strategies, and policies are having the expected results. Evaluation is particularly critical for informed decision-making in the context of competing priorities and limited budgets. PHAB requires that public health agencies either have the ability to conduct rigorous evaluations or have links to academic institutions or other entities with the capacity to do so. As discussed further in Chapter 21, research on the impact and effectiveness of public health laws and policies is a relatively new field, but it is essential to better understanding how the public health system operates and how it can be improved.

Conclusion

This chapter has described the public health system in the United States. In our federal system, important health services are delivered by agencies at all levels of government. Coordination between agencies and between governmental and nongovernmental parts of the public health system is crucial to success, especially in an era when funding has been steadily declining. We now turn to the idea of "transdisciplinary public health law," a concept meant to capture the importance of collaboration across the disciplines of public health and law.

Further Reading

Centers for Disease Control and Prevention. (n.d.) Ten Essential Public Health Services and How They Can Include Addressing Social Determinants of Health Inequities. Available from https://www.cdc.gov/stltpublichealth/publichealthservices/pdf/Ten_Essential_Services_and_SDOH.pdf

Kaiser Family Foundation. (2017). Health Reform. Available from https://www.kff.org/health-reform/

Levi, J., Segal, L. M., Gougelet, R., & St. Laurent, R. (2013). Investing in America's Health: A State-by-State Look at Public Health Funding and Key Health Facts. Trust for America's Health. Available from http://healthyamericans.org/assets/files/TFAH2013InvstgAmrcsHlth05%20FINAL.pdf

3 | A Transdisciplinary Approach to Public Health Law

Learning Objectives

- Explain the transdisciplinary model and the distinction between public health law practice and legal epidemiology.
- Understand the distinction between interventional, infrastructural, and incidental public health law research.
- Grasp the fundamentals of policy surveillance.
- Apply the concept of mechanisms of legal effect to develop hypotheses about how laws influence health.

Introduction

Public health law's primary mission is to support the design, implementation, monitoring, evaluation, and wide application of laws that improve public health and the performance of health systems. Ideally, as an integral part of this mission, public health law protects human rights and affirms values of justice, fairness, and self-governance. Public health law deploys traditional legal functions, like advising health officers on legal options or drafting legislation for policymakers. But it also includes many law-related activities—policy development, analysis, advocacy, enforcement, monitoring, and evaluation—that are performed by people without formal legal training, sometimes in collaboration with lawyers and sometimes not. This diversity of activities and actors makes public health law a "transdisciplinary" field.

To understand what we mean when we write that the field is transdisciplinary, think about something as apparently simple as car safety belt laws. Today, every state has one, and most of us would feel uncomfortable in a car without safety belts. They have saved tens of thousands of lives. But 50 years ago, many vehicles did not even come with them, and most people in cars that included them as features never used them. Law played a big part in bringing about a huge change in care design and human behavior, but there was more to it than just passing a law. To begin with, people had to start seeing driving as an activity that was causing far more deaths and injuries than necessary. Consumer activist (and lawyer) Ralph Nader led the way with his 1965 book, *Unsafe at Any Speed*. The book told a dramatic story about the unnecessary dangers of the cars Americans drove. He was a compelling advocate, but his book was built on government statistics that made the toll unmistakable: in 1965, 47,000 Americans died in crashes, a rate of 5.3 deaths/million vehicle miles traveled (Longthorne, Subramanian, & Chen, 2010). Once Nader helped start the public conversation on road safety, a government bureaucrat named William Haddon was at least as important in figuring out what could be done to address it. As the head of the National Highway Transportation Administration (NHTSA), he developed a comprehensive matrix of the human, machine, road, and environmental factors that contributed to crashes and their toll. (We discuss the Haddon matrix more in Chapter 7.) Safety belts were in the first instance a technical fix, and those famous crash dummy tests showed they were effective. But to work, the technology had to be in every car, and people had to use it. This is where law naturally came in. It was not the only way to get the work done—one can always try education and voluntary approaches—but it turned out to be the best way. After a period of policy experimentation, scientists, lawyers, and regulators working together arrived at the approach that still works today: federal regulations requiring that manufacturers install the belts and state laws that require drivers and, in most states, all passengers to wear them.

Of course, those laws did not write or enact themselves; putting these regulations and laws into place was no simple task. Lawyers were called upon to work closely with NHTSA scientists to develop federal auto safety regulations and shepherd them through the lengthy administrative process through which regulations are promulgated. At the end of this regulatory process, some of these regulations then became the subject of lengthy legal battles. At the state level, safety belt requirements had to be drafted, and once draft bills were on paper, they had to be passed. That required advocacy in all its forms, from public and policymaker education about the science to overcoming manufacturer resistance. As accepted as they are today, in the 1960s and 1970s, many people called safety belts an unjustified government intrusion on citizens' freedom to drive as they saw fit. Mandatory safety belt laws did not pass everywhere right away, but two things turned out to be very important to their ultimate spread across the country: first, enforcement by the police, which overcame much of the initial resistance to using them, and second, a parade of studies that showed the laws—and safety belts—were working. By 2014, due in part to safety belts and other legal interventions, like strict drunk-driving laws and rigorous safe highway and vehicle design standards, the rate of road deaths had fallen by almost 500%, to just 1.07/million vehicle miles traveled (NHTSA, 2015). (Sadly, road deaths are increasing again, apparently due to the rising prevalence of distracting devices in the car, a new job for public health law.)

The safety belt story shows just how public health law is a transdisciplinary field. There were certain things that only lawyers could do, like drafting sound legal documents and defending new laws in court. But there was also collaboration across disciplines, where lawyers were part of a team with scientists, lobbyists, and researchers to build, pass, or test a law. Haddon and his engineers came up with the general policy idea of expanding safety belt use; lawyers and scientists had to work together to figure out the best way that technological and behavioral change could be instigated. In the fight over whether to enact the rules, lawyers took part as litigators, experts, lobbyists, legislators, and staffers, but many non-lawyers played critical roles, too. Enforcement—key to the success of the policy—was the work of police. Scientists led the research that showed that the laws worked, though lawyers were often part of the research team. Public health law, in this story, was not just the work of lawyers. Other kinds of people played important roles and needed the skills and training to do their particular piece of the legal process.

The essence of a transdisciplinary model is true integration of theories, methods, and tools. The transdisciplinary model of practice and research is not merely lawyers and scientists pursuing the same public health goals in an independent or interactive manner. Rather, in a transdisciplinary model, professionals "representing different fields work together over extended periods to develop shared conceptual and methodologic frameworks that not only integrate but also transcend their respective disciplinary perspectives" (Stokols, Hall, Taylor, & Moser, 2008). In the auto safety story, lawyers and engineers had to understand each other's worlds well enough to devise changes in road standards or other laws that could be mandated using legal tools. As they worked on policy options, they had to think about politics, public attitudes, and which of their ideas were most likely to pass and be enforced. They had to interact with policymakers and advocates—it was a collaborative process.

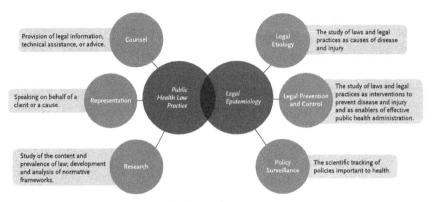

FIGURE 3.1. Transdisciplinary public health law.

Reprinted, with permission, from the Annual Review of Public Health, Volume 37 ©2016 by Annual Reviews, http://www.annualreviews.org.

Figure 3.1 depicts a transdisciplinary model of public health law, which includes both the kinds of functions we have long associated with the work of lawyers in public health and also the scientific research and analysis of law-related matters that we now recognize as integral to healthy public policies.

The Transdisciplinary Model of Public Health Law

Public Health Law Practice

The usual definitions of public health law for nearly a century have focused on the part of the work that lawyers do. In 1961, for example, an article by Robert Hamlin in the *American Journal of Public Health* defined *public health law* as "the application of general legal principles to the practice of public health." What we call *public health law practice* is the basic legal work Hamlin was referring to: "the application of legal skills in the development of health policy and the practice of public health." This work falls into three broad categories: counsel, representation, and research.

In practice, the public health lawyer's role as a *counselor* is broadly conceived. Within a strictly defined lawyer-client relationship, lawyers provide legal information, analysis, and advice. Government lawyers provide counsel to health officials and other organizational clients. Some lawyers provide technical assistance, rather than formally representing a client. They provide legal information, including interpretation of the law, training, and strategic consultation. They often draft model laws, ordinances, regulations, or policies. Their goal is to build the capacity of public health practitioners and other community leaders to use the law to solve problems and improve population health outcomes. Even further along the spectrum are lawyers who could best be described as working for the cause—whether it be tobacco control, a human rights approach to public health, or controlling obesity. Their counseling role centers on strategy and tactics to further specific legal and policy goals.

Representation, speaking for a client in legal and other fora, also takes many forms in public health law practice. For lawyers representing health agencies or other actual clients, it includes conducting litigation. Litigation to enforce or defend public health laws and regulations is a staple of contemporary public health practice. Cause lawyers and academics also take part in litigation, typically by filing amicus curiae ("friend of the court") legal briefs to bring relevant information before a court that the actual parties to a case may not be willing or able to supply. Some also initiate "impact litigation"—lawsuits designed to improve public health by forcing industries or government entities to change their practices—although opinion and evidence are mixed on the value of such litigation as a public health tool. Lawyers appear before legislative committees, regulatory agencies, or other policymaking entities to provide information or lobby as the client's status and wishes dictate. Cause lawyers often take leading roles in advocating for policies in their domains, engaging in community organizing, lobbying, and other activities to advance the cause.

Research in public health law practice is diverse. In public health practice settings and academic work, legal research often takes the form of the collection and analysis of law to characterize the conduct it prescribes ("What are the rules?"), or to answer specific legal questions ("Can x do y?"). Legal research is conducted to map the content and distribution of law across jurisdictions. Lawyers in both practice and academic settings help develop policy; lawyers conceptualize new regimes, such as the Framework Convention on Tobacco Control (an international treaty), develop model laws, and draft the statutes and regulations that give policies their form. Lawyers, particularly those in academia and non-governmental public interest organizations, take on the job of normative framing and analysis, offering ideas about what the law *should* be in the interests of justice or public health impact. As the Institute of Medicine (2011) observed, "Discussing the law and public policy is not possible without addressing the societal context—the national and community values, norms, and popular attitudes (i.e., toward government, toward public health) and perspectives that influence American policymaking and Americans' understanding of the 'good life.'"

As shown in Figure 3.1, we call all this public health law practice and note the need for legal training and experience in carrying out these functions. That said, however, it is also important to recognize that there are non-lawyers taking part in some of this work, too. Clients, like public health officers, often take an active part in the development of legal strategy; non-lawyers from academia, government, and the community take part in advocacy efforts and offer their expertise to the policy process. They often have powerful visions of what justice and fairness requires of the system. Many of the staffers at health agencies who enforce public health laws are not lawyers themselves. It is important to see that even core legal work is collaborative and transdisciplinary: lawyers and their clients and allies will do better work if they link perspectives and skills.

Legal Epidemiology

The work of conceptualizing, implementing, and evaluating laws to change behaviors and environments requires the same scientific skills and methods used generally in public health. This work is an integral part of public health law, which we call *legal epidemiology* and define as "the scientific study and use of law as a factor in the cause, distribution, and prevention of disease and injury in a population." Legal epidemiology has three components.

Legal prevention and control is the study and use of laws and legal practices that are designed to prevent disease and injury or enable effective public health administration. Using legal tools as interventions to change unhealthy behaviors and environments is routine. Examples range as widely as mandatory vaccination laws and cigarette warning labels. In public health, however, it is not enough to deploy an intervention; we also have to make sure it works as intended and does not have harmful side effects. The scientific literature is rich with studies that evaluate the impact and implementation of interventional public health laws or that study the factors that influence their enactment. We see the importance of this work in domains such as alcohol, auto safety, and tobacco control. Although not every legal intervention is evaluated in a timely and rigorous manner, there is no question of the feasibility and impact of this kind of research.

Legal prevention and control includes research on the impact of laws establishing the powers, duties, and jurisdiction of health agencies. Researchers can map differences in this legal infrastructure from jurisdiction to jurisdiction and use the variation to assess the influence of legal infrastructure on health agency activities and outcomes. Legal analysis can help agency staff better understand how their powers compare with the authority of peer agencies. Whether and how actors in public health agencies understand and apply the law, and have the resources they need to do it, will influence the agencies' outputs and outcomes.

Most laws are proposed, enacted, and enforced without any health-related intent or purpose behind them, but general law can have unintended health impact. *Legal etiology* is the study of *how* non-health law contributes to disease or injury. For example, minimum wage laws are intended to set the minimum hourly wage certain employers can pay within a jurisdiction, and zoning laws are intended to provide a systematic way to organize the development of communities. Despite being designed and implemented with little or no thought to health, many laws and policies can have powerful effects on health. Minimum-wage levels may influence maternal and child health (Komro, Livingston, Markowitz, & Wagenaar, 2016), and zoning may determine whether consumers can conveniently buy fresh fruits and vegetables (Mayo, Pitts, & Chriqui, 2013). Understanding that a wide range of laws and policies can have unintended and unexpected health consequences is foundational to addressing the social determinants of health. Legal etiology encompasses law's structural role in shaping the level and distribution of health in a community; its contribution to cultural beliefs about how health is produced, protected, and distributed; and the ways changes in general law can be used to improve health and health equity.

Policy surveillance is the third component of legal epidemiology. Surveillance in public health is the means by which people who are responsible for public health track the occurrence, antecedents, time course, geographic spread, consequences, and nature of disease, injury, and risk factors among the populations they serve. Policy surveillance is the ongoing, systematic, and scientific tracking of laws of public health importance. Policymakers, officials, and the public need basic information about what law requires and where it applies, and researchers need data on laws for evaluation. Scientific coding procedures, combined with modern information technology, allow the efficient publication of digitized legal data to the Internet. Publication supports the rapid diffusion of policy information to health professionals, policymakers, and the public. Because they are created in a scientific way, the data are readily used by researchers in studies evaluating the impact of laws. An example of a policy surveillance website is www.LawAtlas.org.

Mechanisms of Legal Effect

One of the most important ways a transdisciplinary perspective can promote more effective public health law is inculcating an empirical approach to *how* law works. The conventional view that people obey the law because they fear punishment (deterrence) is correct in many instances but is just one way that law works. Virtually all American smokers respect no-smoking rules, even though there is little or no risk of a fine. Some may be responding to a fear of social punishment (irritated glances or requests to quit from others in the area), which is a kind of deterrence, but many others are obeying the law because they believe obeying the law is the right thing to do (a mechanism called "legitimacy"). Laws express social values, which over a surprisingly short time can be internalized by people in the society. For example, there was widespread grumbling about mandatory safety belt laws when they were first passed—the classic complaints about government overreach. Pretty soon, however, buckling-up became habitual, and reassuring, to most drivers, and now most of us probably think someone who does not wear a safety belt is behaving irresponsibly. The law has changed from an external rule enforced by police to an internal rule enforced by ourselves.

Understanding how law works is crucial for anyone trying to develop innovative interventions aimed at newly recognized problems. Requiring calorie counts on restaurant menus can change behavior by providing information. Drunk-driving laws threatened punishment, but they also reflected and advanced a long-term effort to change the social view of drinking and driving from "normal" to "bad." Sometimes even a law that never goes into effect can change attitudes and behaviors: New York City, for example, never was able to implement a ban on large soda cups but generated a lot of discussion and publicity that some credited with reducing soda consumption in the city.

A scientific approach to understanding *how* law influences health is crucial to assessing *whether* it does so. Theories of how law influences structures, behaviors, and environments are used in implementation and outcome research. This enables researchers to know where to look, at what point in time we might expect to see effects, how effects might evolve over time, and what sort of intended and unintended effects to look for. Data on how law works helps to identify potential cause-and-effect relationships by providing evidence of plausible mechanisms to explain an observed association between a rule and an outcome. Theory also helps unpack a law into regulatory components that may have varying contributions to the overall effect and helps identify dose-response relationships between specific legal components or dimensions and health-related outcomes. This kind of evidence can guide reform and implementation, showing how specific practices can increase the impact and reduce side effects. In this and other ways, a transdisciplinary approach helps get the best from lawyers, researchers, policymakers, and community advocates.

Conclusion

This chapter has presented a transdisciplinary model of public health law that will frame the rest of the book and that captures a vision of public health as a cooperative enterprise among many different kinds of experts and forms of knowledge. Public health is technical, scientific, professional—and moral. The whole structure rests on the value of human thriving and the social imperative to help each other. Questions of moral and professional ethics are central to public health practice, and we discuss them next.

Acknowledgments

Some passages of Chapter 3 are taken, with permission, from the *Annual Review of Public Health*, Volume 37 ©2016 by Annual Reviews, http://www.annualreviews.org.

Further Reading

Burris, S., Ashe, M., Levin, D., Penn, M., & Larkin, M. (2016). A Transdisciplinary Approach to Public Health Law: The Emerging Practice of Legal Epidemiology. *Annual Review of Public Health*, *37*(1), 135–148.

Burris, S., & Wagenaar, A. (2013). Integrating Diverse Theories for Public Health Law Evaluation. In A. Wagenaar & S. Burris (Eds.), *Public Health Law Research: Theory and Methods* (pp. 193–214). San Francisco: John Wiley. Available from http://publichealthlawresearch.org/resource/integrating-diverse-theories-public-health-law-research

Burris, S., Wagenaar, A. C., Swanson, J., Ibrahim, J. K., Wood, J., & Mello, M. M. (2010). Making the Case for Laws That Improve Health: A Framework for Public Health Law Research. *The Milbank Quarterly*, *88*(2), 169–210.

4 | Ethics in Transdisciplinary Practice

Learning Objectives

- Define three basic meanings of *ethics*.
- Explain the distinction between deontology and consequentialism in ethical analysis.
- Understand the basic history of professional ethics in public health.
- Distinguish between the principles and procedures in medical ethics, research ethics, legal ethics, and public health ethics.
- Identify ways in which ethics are supported or enforced through law.

Ethics and Professional Ethics

Ethics has at least three important meanings for practitioners working at the intersection of public health and law. First, ethics is a field of philosophical inquiry aimed at defining the "Good"—what is moral, what is decent, what is right. Ethics differs from law or religion or social norms in its how it does so: the Good is defined not through sacred texts or divine revelation but rather an explicit process of reasoning. Although ethical principles may be influenced or derived from laws, religious beliefs, or conventional values, the distinctive quality of ethics is to justify ethical principles through reasoned argument rather than divine will, democratic deliberation, or custom.

Ethics is also the label for the set of basic principles that emerge from ethical deliberation. We discuss several codes of ethics or ethical systems in this chapter. These codes display ethics as objective statements of the good that people who adhere to a given profession or field are expected to accept and practice, unless they can use the ethical reasoning process to convince others that these principles are in some way incorrect. These codes are not developed or written like laws. They are nonetheless enforced, as we discuss, at the very least through some form of professional sanction but sometimes through legal mechanisms like regulations or private lawsuits.

An ethical code sets out basic principles of good conduct at a fairly abstract level. In life, people (and the organizations they belong to) are confronted with particular situations that pose ethical dilemmas but for which ethical principles may not supply an immediately obvious resolution. Ethical principles are meant to be a guide to virtuous behavior, so it is also important to understand the term *ethics* as naming an individual's commitment to a moral course of conduct in life. The commitment to ethics in this sense consists of a desire to know what the good is in any particular moment of decision, to actually do the good thing, and to integrate all of this in a lifelong practice of reflection and learning. Although professional ethical codes can entail sanctions, an ethical person regulates his or her own behavior, motivated by the desire to be virtuous rather than fear of punishment or hope of reward.

Ethics has a long history in all these forms. Defining the good, and the personal struggle to pursue it, were central preoccupations of the classical Greek philosophers like Plato and Aristotle and has been pursued by philosophers ever since. The idea of "professional ethics" traces back to the oath of Hippocrates that is still sworn by new doctors beginning their careers. Medicine also led the development of modern professional ethics: Thomas Percival, an English physician, published a code of professional ethics at the turn of the 19th century, and the American Medical Association (AMA) adopted the first national code of medical ethics at its founding in 1847. The American Bar Association (ABA) adopted its first Canon of Ethics in 1908, and they were quickly adopted by nearly all state and local bar associations. Codes of professional ethics have proliferated in the last half-century, so that most professions or professional societies, from architecture to zoology, have one (just Google it!).

Ethics are not just about clean hands and pure hearts. Professional ethics have been a matter of interest to sociologists seeking to understand how professions define themselves, gain authority, and evade outside interference in complex modern societies. Ethics are obviously a way that professions can regulate their members, including in ways that have little to do with virtue: codes of ethics have often, for example, limited the extent to which a professional can do business in collaboration with a nonprofessional. Ethical codes support professional expertise in the argument for self-regulation over government regulation. Ethics and professionalism can be seen as a *third way* or *third logic* (between the market and government bureaucracy) for organizing and regulating individual behavior in society: markets incentivize behavior with the promise of wealth; bureaucracies depend on external oversight and the threat of punishment; professionalism and ethics mobilize internalized values and a personal commitment to proper conduct (Freidson, 2001). The rise of ethics has made the profession of ethicists a powerful group, appointed to committees and called upon by the media to act as arbiters in public and private matters. As we will see, codes of ethics have also become bound up with law in subtle and important ways.

What Is Good?

Philosophers will generally agree that ethics entails defining the Good; they just cannot agree on how, exactly, to do it. For those entering transdisciplinary public health practice, it is useful to understand two powerful approaches that are still in use in professional and research ethics in our various fields. In the *deontological approach*, we judge our actions by their fidelity to the applicable moral rule or principle, which we are expected to obey without regard to consequences. For example, "thou shalt not kill" is a binding rule, as stated, even if we could save innocent people by killing a marauding desperado. Moral reasoning works by identifying the applicable rules and deriving through reason an understanding of the conduct those rules require. The end, no matter how nice, cannot justify the means if the means entail violating an ethical principle. By contrast, in the *consequentialist* or *utilitarian approach*, the goodness of an action is assessed by the consequences the action is expected to produce. Killing a murderer to save the innocent may not just be permitted; it may be a duty. Beneficial ends can justify costly means, as long as the benefit/cost ratio is positive.

Deontology is the dominant mode of reasoning in medical, professional, and research ethics; public health ethics tend to be consequentialist. The difference may be less in the kind of values espoused as in the kind of ethical conundrums the different fields encounter. In medicine, law, and other helping professions, ethics focus on relationships with patients or clients, one at a time. In public health, the "client" is the democratically elected government and the "patient" is a population. Trade-offs between ends, and imperfect means, are assumed. Research ethics has links to both a population and individual perspective but historically developed out of biomedical ethics and still retains its individualistic cast. These differences in approach have continued importance in practice, which we can illustrate with a famous thought experiment.

In the "trolley dilemma," a man is standing on a bridge above a rail yard. He sees that a runaway trolley car is heading toward a group of five workers who are making too much noise to notice or be warned. They will surely be killed unless the watcher runs and turns the switch to direct the car onto another track where one person is working and will surely be killed. What should the man do? In consequentialist theory, this should be easy: kill one to save five. But that feels wrong to many people, because we have a strong rule against killing and an instinctive discomfort with treating a person as merely a means to an end. The deontologist has an equally easy answer: thou shalt not kill, even if the consequence is five preventable accidental deaths. Yet the deontologist, too, is uneasy: are we just going to watch those people die? And it gets worse as the stakes get higher: what if we replace the five workers with a group of 100 and make them schoolchildren? What if the issue is whether or not to mandate a vaccine that will prevent hundreds of thousands of deaths but will also cause a dozen deaths due to side effects?

The Many Flavors of Professional Ethics

Codes of ethics differ because the kinds of professional or other work they govern differ and because they have emerged at different times for different reasons. Legal ethics have deep historical roots in the regulations that judges and legislators set for the emerging practice of law in medieval England. Concerns of competence, and honest dealing with clients and the court, predominated. In the ABA's 1908 Canon, and the subsequent ABA ethical models through the present Model Rules of Professional Responsibility, legal ethicists addressed these issues but within a larger attempt to understand the role of a lawyer who was at once an officer of the court (with duties to the system), a servant of the client (with duties to the client), and an expert practitioner of the law (with an obligation to exercise independent moral and professional judgment). Present Rule 2.1, for example, states

> In representing a client, a lawyer shall exercise independent professional judgment and render candid advice. In rendering advice, a lawyer may refer not only to law but to other considerations such as moral, economic, social and political factors, that may be relevant to the client's situation.

Rule 1.2 requires the lawyer, within certain limitations, to follow the client's wishes in a matter, but Rule 3.3 sets out in detail situations in which the lawyer may have to balance or even abandon complete fidelity to the client in order to ensure that the court is not mislead. There are many interesting and challenging moral questions embedded in the polydirectional duties of a lawyer, but the Model Rules also deal with more prosaic issues, like the sale of legal practice, advertising, and "Firm Names and Letterhead." These are more than professional rules enforced by the disapproval of the professional's peers. Every US state has adopted the rules as statutes or otherwise binding and enforceable rules of conduct for lawyers, who can be disciplined and lose the right to practice for violating them.

The AMA's (2016) ethical code includes some self-protective professional rules (affirming the right of a physician to be "free to choose whom to serve, with whom to associate, and the environment in which to provide medical care") but carry forward the key ideas of professional competence, pursuit of the patient's welfare (beneficence), and the foundational Hippocratic command to "first, do no harm" (nonmaleficence). Doctors were also intimately involved with the development of research ethics. Research has always been an important component of medicine and medical practice. Doctors and the rest of the world were shocked by the atrocities of Nazi doctors, who conducted torturous and murderous experiments on concentration camp prisoners, outrages detailed in the Nuremberg trials after World War II. In the trial verdict, the court listed 10 basic principles of legitimate medical research (subsequently referred to as the "Nuremberg Code"), including the primacy of voluntary participation, protection of the research participants, and the value of the research in relation to risks. It took a while, but by the 1960s, American and British doctors had noticed that the record of our own research on patients, while not as quite as racist and callous as the Nazi record, left much to be desired (Beecher, 1966; Pappworth, 1967). Nor was public health research immune: perhaps the single most infamous study in modern American history was the Tuskegee Study of Untreated Syphilis in the Negro Male, funded by the Public Health Service, which followed 600 black men for 40 years without ever treating the ones who had the disease, even after the discovery of penicillin.

Medical ethicists took this on and applied their evolving ideas of medical ethics to the research enterprise. The World Medical Association, meeting in Helsinki in 1964, adopted a declaration setting forth basic ethical principles for medical research with human subjects based on the Nuremberg Code. Outrage at the Tuskegee Study and other instances of unethical medical research led to a national commission and a document called the Belmont Report, which laid the groundwork for the ascendance of four basic ethical principles in research: respect for persons, beneficence, nonmaleficence, and justice in the conduct of research and the distribution of its benefits. These ethical principles essentially became law when they were made the foundation of federal regulations governing the ethical conduct of research conducted by entities receiving federal funds. The federal regulations known as the Common Rule require recipients of federal funds to promise that research they conduct, whether or not funded by government, will be reviewed by an institutional review board and found to be consistent with these four principles. Detailed requirements for informed consent are also set out, along with other specific requirements pertaining to common research issues like research on vulnerable populations such as children or prisoners, use of inducements for participation, and record-keeping. The Office for Human Research Protections in the Department of Health and Human Services enforces compliance with the Common Rule, and sanctions can range from training to suspension from research funding, which may be applied to individuals or institution-wide.

The Common Rule is now a significant regulatory system. All universities doing any significant amount of research employ full-time staff to manage compliance, ensure proper training of researchers, and keep track of studies. Over the years, the system has been criticized for its bureaucratic burden on the research process, for arbitrary decisions, and for a chilling effect on certain kinds of research (like research with children) that require more intensive oversight. Perhaps the most enduring criticism of the system was that it was devised by doctors and medical ethicists on a biomedical model and so is unsuited to guide or regulate research in other fields like anthropology, sociology—or public health. Ethnographers, for example, complained that requiring detailed protocols setting out the questions that would be asked of subjects was impossible in studies in which researchers would be living for an extended period of time in a community as participant observers. Oral historians, who could think of few ways in which their subjects could be harmed, asked why they were subject to the same rules as surgeons testing alternative invasive procedures. Public health researchers found that principles designed with clinical research in mind did not capture the range of duties, considerations, and dilemmas they faced.

Public Health Ethics, Human Rights, and the Law

To provide better guidance targeted at public health work, a working group of public health experts from both governmental and nongovernmental entities developed an ethics code, introduced in 2002 (Thomas et al., 2002). The current version sets out 12 principles:

1. Public health should address principally the fundamental causes of disease and requirements for health, aiming to prevent adverse health outcomes.
2. Public health should achieve community health in a way that respects the rights of individuals in the community.
3. Public health policies, programs, and priorities should be developed and evaluated through processes that ensure an opportunity for input from community members.
4. Public health should advocate and work for the empowerment of disenfranchised community members, aiming to ensure that the basic resources and conditions necessary for health are accessible to all.
5. Public health should seek the information needed to implement effective policies and programs that protect and promote health.
6. Public health institutions should provide communities with the information they have that is needed for decisions on policies or programs and should obtain the community's consent for their implementation.
7. Public health institutions should act in a timely manner on the information they have within the resources and the mandate given to them by the public.
8. Public health programs and policies should incorporate a variety of approaches that anticipate and respect diverse values, beliefs, and cultures in the community.
9. Public health programs and policies should be implemented in a manner that most enhances the physical and social environment.
10. Public health institutions should protect the confidentiality of information that can bring harm to an individual or community if made public. Exceptions must be justified on the basis of the high likelihood of significant harm to the individual or others.

11. Public health institutions should ensure the professional competence of their employees.
12. Public health institutions and their employees should engage in
collaborations and affiliations in ways that build the public's trust
and the institution's effectiveness.

Consideration of this code reveals several basic ethical tensions in public
health practice. For example, principle 7 refers to the "mandate" given
public health. From a legal perspective, this refers in part to the fact that the
agencies and activities that do core public health work are of the government, given powers by legislation and regulation, and even constitutions.
In democratic theory, governments rest on the consent of the governed, and
policy decisions are subject to voter approval at least indirectly in regular
elections. Yet the Code also calls for communities to have a chance to give
"informed consent" to programs. If a government agency decides to use its
authority to require aerial mosquito spraying to control Zika virus, residents
in the community to be sprayed have a practical interest and a moral right in
being consulted, and the wise agency tries to convince people of the need for
controversial actions. Ultimately, the agency is carrying out a legal mandate
of the government; it has consent in that sense. Does the code really give the
community a veto? Should it? Similarly, what is the ethical thing for a health
worker or agency to do if the city council or the legislature has not provided
the resources or authority to "work for the empowerment of disenfranchised
community members"?

The complex relationship between ethics, law, and public health shows
up in other interesting ways. International law and the law of many nations
includes forms of a right to health and obligations to respect, protect, and
fulfill other rights that clearly relate to health, like education, housing,
workplace safety, and gender equity. Commentators have argued that a
human rights perspective helps ethics broaden its gaze to encompass population-level problems of inequity and injustice, while ethics can in turn
strengthen legal claims in human rights litigation (Nixon & Forman, 2008).
Law also steps in to provide definitive answers to matters that continue to
be questions in ethical discussion. Medical ethicists, for example, may debate whether hospitals have an ethical duty to treat all patients that show up
for treatment, regardless of ability to pay. In practice, many US hospitals
by the 1980s were declining to treat emergency patients, including women
giving birth, if they could not pay, leading to a practice of shunting patients
to charity providers, known as "patient dumping." Congress barred this

practice as a matter of law in 1986, passing the Emergency Medical Treatment and Active Labor Act (42 U.S.C. § 1395dd), which required hospitals to provide obstetrical services to women in active labor and to at least stabilize other emergency patients before transferring or discharging them. Finally, the law sometimes indirectly enforces ethics. In a notable example, the Maryland Court of Appeals held that the informed consent document created an enforceable contract between the research participant and the research institution under which the participant could sue for damages based on insufficient disclosure of research risks (*Grimes v. Kennedy Krieger Institute,* 2001).

Conclusion

We have looked at the differing forms of ethics a public health practitioner will be likely to encounter in day-to-day work as if they were distinct and separate. But all of these systems are operating at the same time: a lawyer and a doctor working together on a vaccination project in a public health agency will bring their professional ethics with them and may find themselves dealing with research ethics and public health ethics. These systems of thought, though they can all be called "ethics," come with different histories, perspectives and concerns that do not always complement each other and may conflict. Nor, in real life, are ethics purely a matter of the individual or cooperative pursuit of virtuous behavior. Some, maybe most, of our ethical principles are now also legally enforceable rules.

So ethics are not simple, and they do not live purely in an abstract realm of philosophy. Failure to follow ethical principles when they are actually operating as legal rules or standards of reasonable behavior can lead to serious trouble for clients, lawyers, researchers, and practitioners in public health. But ethics also represent and support each person's internal drive to do the right thing. Indeed, a danger of making ethics into enforced rules is that it can lead to people working to the rule: they do what is required and do not do or think about any more. The contemporary public health professional is challenged to develop a personal commitment to professional and public health ethics, while understanding and maintaining fidelity to the rules as they stand in professional codes and the law, and to do this in cooperation with people from a range of professional backgrounds. As we practice public health law, we run into dilemmas of real weight that cannot be answered to the complete satisfaction of everyone, or that pose tragic choices for everyone. A shared commitment to ethical behavior, careful collection and assessment of the facts, and a strong understanding of applicable law are crucial to effective decision-making.

Further Reading

Halpern, S. D. (2004). Medical Authority and the Culture of Rights. *Journal of Health Politics, Policy and Law, 29*, 835–852.

II | Policy Development

SOLVING PROBLEMS WITH LAW

5 | Identifying Public Health Problems

Learning Objectives

- Understand basic concepts and methods used in epidemiology to define, describe, and investigate population health problems.
- Define *surveillance* and identify the primary measures of disease and injury it produces.
- Describe the types of studies that epidemiologists can conduct to identify public health problems.
- Name two kinds of limitations to epidemiological studies and explain ways to address them.

Introduction

This chapter introduces the methods of *epidemiology* to show readers how public health professionals describe, quantify, and investigate public health problems in practice. The chapter uses the story of a real outbreak to explore how epidemiologists work and how law fits in. Chapter 6 will then discuss the range of potential policy options that can be used to address these problems, and Chapter 7 presents strategies for deciding which interventions, or solutions, have the best chance of being effective in a particular situation.

Epidemiology

Epidemiology is the study of the causes (or "determinants") and distribution of disease and injury in a population. Epidemiology helps us identify public health problems and evaluate the effectiveness of responses, including legal solutions. *Descriptive epidemiology* aims to gather data to answer the most basic population health questions: Where and how often is disease or injury occurring? How is disease transmitted? Who is at risk? What behaviors or environmental conditions are associated with higher risk or the distribution of the problem in the population? And are disparities, or differences, in the problem based on race, social status, or gender? *Analytical epidemiology* aims to use data from descriptive epidemiology to develop and assess solutions to public health problems by revealing causes, causal processes, and effects of interventions. A basic understanding of epidemiology provides everyone in public health with a common language for describing disease in a population and a scientific foundation on which to build policy solutions.

The process of epidemiological investigation is exemplified in Chapter 1's story of how John Snow helped stop a cholera epidemic in London by tracing its origin to a single public water pump. He *observed* the characteristics of a disease, *conducted surveillance and mapping* to track exposures in real time, developed a *hypothesis* to explain the cause, and designed an *intervention* to test his hypothesis and prevent the disease from spreading further. Almost two centuries later, these tools remain the foundation of epidemiology. Less dramatically, the story also shows law's place in public health: Snow needed the approval of local government to implement his recommended solution, removing the handle from the Broad Street pump.

Descriptive Epidemiology's Measures and Tools

Epidemiologists use case studies like Snow's to form hypotheses about unusual health outcomes, but individual events must ultimately be put into population context for epidemiological work. *Morbidity* (illness) and *mortality* (death) are the core measures of descriptive epidemiology. Common epidemiological calculations compare who is sick with who is healthy in order to understand the origins of diseases and their impacts. These measurements can be expressed as numbers of cases, but to understand trends over time in a changing population, and between large and small groups, it is typically more useful to express morbidity and mortality as a rate (usually a rate per 1,000 or 100,000 people). For example, in 2015, about 122 in 1,000 US adults were living with diabetes, and approximately 6.7 new cases were diagnosed per 1,000 people per year. The comparison of the number of people living with diabetes (i.e., the *prevalence* of diabetes) and the number of newly diagnosed cases during a given year (i.e., the *incidence* of diabetes) shows that most people with diabetes live for a long time, as most cases were not diagnosed during the past one year. Data can also reveal important inequities. The prevalence of diabetes among non-Hispanic white adults is about 74 per 1,000, compared to 127 per 1,000 among non-Hispanic blacks and 151 per 1,000 among Native Americans (Centers for Disease Control and Prevention, 2017). By calculating how the burden of disease differs among different groups in the population, epidemiologists can show where we can most effectively—and equitably—invest public health resources to reach those in greatest need.

Detecting an Outbreak

One of the most fundamental tools of epidemiology is *surveillance*, the "ongoing, systematic collection, analysis, and interpretation of health-related data needed for the planning, implementation, and evaluation of public health practice" (World Health Organization, 2017a). Surveillance can be applied to environmental toxins in water or air, cancers, health-related behaviors like physical activity or dieting, marketing of products such as alcohol or tobacco, and more. The word "ongoing" tells us that surveillance is not just a matter of data snapshots at a particular moment in time; surveillance systems collect data consistently over time. "Systematic" tells us that surveillance data are collected with a standard protocol that can be described and repeated regularly. "Passive" surveillance systems define conditions or syndromes that healthcare providers, laboratories, or other sentinels are required to report as they occur; these are efficient but tend to underreport events. In "active" surveillance, epidemiologists contact healthcare providers, labs, or others potentially in possession of case information. Health departments can use both types of surveillance to detect and respond to outbreaks. An *outbreak* is generally defined as the occurrence of cases of disease in excess of what would normally be expected in a defined community. Consider this example from actual practice (Kim et al., 2010):

> *In fall 2014, healthcare professionals at Ronald Reagan UCLA Medical Center in Los Angeles observed severe bacterial infections among a cluster of hospital inpatients. Blood tests confirmed that the patients were infected with carbapenem-resistant* Klebsiella pneumoniae, *a strain of bacteria in the category of Enterobacteriaceae that is resistant to the carbapenem class of antibiotics. Carbapenem-resistant Enterobacteriaceae (CRE) live*

in most people's intestines without causing harm, but can cause serious infections if they spread to other body systems. Because it is resistant to most antibiotics, CRE has been referred to as a "superbug."

Although CRE is on the rise, it is still rare, fewer than 5% of U.S. hospitals reported a case in 2012. The UCLA hospital's infection prevention team, comprised of infectious disease physicians and staff with training in nursing and public health, detected the cluster and notified the municipal health department. Los Angeles County epidemiologists, in collaboration with hospital staff, promptly began a disease investigation.

Surveillance is the basis for addressing public health issues: interventions cannot be designed for problems that are undetected or unmeasured. Without regular data collection and review, clusters of disease might not be recognized. Confirming, or ruling out, a disease cluster is not possible without baseline population data for comparison, which depends on a history of consistent surveillance. Competing priorities limit how much data is collected: surveillance requires financial and human resources, both of which are limited in public health organizations. For these reasons, public health agencies (and legislatures) often face difficult decisions about which data to collect and analyze and whether to employ expensive, but more reliable, active approaches. In the CRE case, health department surveillance was passive, but many state statutes and regulations now require providers to report new cases of CRE to agencies as they are diagnosed.

As for diabetes, surveillance has demonstrated that poor health outcomes are unevenly distributed in populations. Vulnerability to disease and injury are associated with a variety of social determinants of health, including geographic and socioeconomic factors such as gender, race, and economic status. Surveillance can identify problematic health disparities that can be mapped to reveal patterns of disease and disparities in populations, which can in turn inform public health efforts that allow everyone to share a high level of health (Penman-Aguilar et al., 2016).

Determining the Source

Verifying that an outbreak has occurred is the first milestone for an epidemiological investigation. The urgent work then turns to finding the cause.

Health department and hospital staff in Los Angeles examined the medical records of infected patients to identify exposures that could be associated with their CRE infections. These included antibiotic use, duodenoscopy, and procedures patients underwent. Patient records also provided demographic information, the location of patients in wards, the clinicians involved, and even the food patients ate. In this case, all CRE-infected patients had a common exposure: a procedure called ERCP that inserted one of the hospital's two duodenoscopes into patients' digestive systems.

On January 28, 2015, the team successfully traced the outbreak to a source, a patient with active CRE who had first undergone duodenoscopy on October 3, 2014. One hundred fifteen patients had subsequently been exposed to the devices, which are notoriously difficult to clean. UCLA discontinued the use of both duodenoscopes immediately, and contacted the patients to test them for CRE and treat any resulting illnesses.

This part of the story captures the role of epidemiologists as "disease detectives" who identify the origins of outbreaks and figure out how disease spreads. Findings from descriptive epidemiology studies—such as the UCLA case report—help define pathways for disease. From the work of epidemiologists and other scientists over the years, we know that CRE is most commonly acquired in healthcare settings. The bacteria are particularly dangerous because they can survive on surfaces for an extended time. The source is typically an invasive tube or device inserted into the body, though CRE can also be acquired from exposure to the bodily fluids of someone with a related bacterial infection.

For some diseases, tracking an outbreak back to its source may be much more complex. For newly emerging diseases, testing may not be available or reliable, or the mode of transmission may be poorly understood. Sometimes the problem is finding the cause hidden in a haystack of possible sources of illness. For example, identifying the culprit in food-related outbreaks is challenging because meals have many ingredients. In 2008, the Food and Drug Administration (FDA) issued warnings attributing a large, multi-state *Salmonella* outbreak to US-grown tomatoes that many patients ate at Mexican restaurants. After further investigation, the FDA revised its assessment and concluded that jalapeño and serrano peppers from Mexico were the source. Tomato producers later sued the FDA (unsuccessfully) for compensation because its incorrect attribution severely damaged the market for their tomatoes (*Dimare Fresh, Inc. v. United States*, 2015).

Determining the Extent of the Outbreak
and Preventing New Infections

Once a likely source is identified, an effective response can be devised, including follow-up with those exposed.

> *UCLA staff cleaned and disinfected the contaminated duodenoscopes and surrounding areas with health department guidance. Repeated bacterial cultures ensured the equipment remained CRE-free over time. The FDA also issued new guidelines on preventing CRE transmission via duodenoscopes. Among the 115 patients contacted for testing, 11 were "lost to follow-up" and did not submit samples or contact staff. Of the remaining 104 patients, 89 remained uninfected, while 15 acquired CRE (14.4%) and required treatment. Their average time between exposure and acute symptoms was 44 days, though some patients became sick as early as four days after exposure, and as late as 90 days. Seven of the 15 CRE patients (6.7%) did not develop symptoms. Three patients died during the outbreak.*

Accurately quantifying trends allows epidemiologists to characterize public health problems, identify changes in population health, and help develop appropriate responses. *Prevalence* measures a proportion of the population experiencing a long-lasting disease or condition during a specified period of time, expressed per 1,000 or 100,000 people. For example, in 2015, the prevalence of diabetes among US adults was 94 per 1,000. Prevalence gives a good picture of the ongoing burden of disease in a given population, including endemic conditions. In our CRE example, however, epidemiologists needed to calculate changes in the occurrence of new cases of disease, called an *incidence rate*, to quickly identify fluctuations or patterns in the occurrence of disease. Incidence rates are expressed as the number of new cases of disease occurring per the number of people who are at risk for that disease, measured either at the beginning of a time period or as a factor of the amount of time each person was at risk during the time period. As a simple example, in 2015 there were an estimated 1.5 million new cases of diabetes among US adults. After excluding the number of existing diabetics in the United States, the corresponding incidence rate of adult diabetes is 6.7 per 1,000 people (Centers for Disease Control and Prevention, 2017). Whereas prevalence captures the potential for survival once a patient has contracted a disease and the number of deaths from it, incidence rates quantify the risk of new cases occurring in populations.

Defining Priorities: Mortality and Morbidity

Mortality and morbidity, measures of the proportion of a population that dies or suffers from a given condition, are universal concerns. Epidemiologic tools can be used to define public health priorities and compare the effectiveness of potential interventions. The *case-fatality rate* of a disease or condition demonstrates its severity by measuring the proportion of diagnosed cases that result in death during a specified period of time. The case-fatality rate for the UCLA CRE outbreak was 20%, which was better than the generally reported CRE case-fatality rate of 50% in healthcare settings (Jacob et al., 2013). In contrast, the case-fatality rate of seasonal influenza is less than 1%, but with annual prevalence and incidence rates that are orders of magnitude higher than CRE, it poses a much larger public health impact. In other words, a disease with a high case-fatality rate may still be a low priority if it occurs rarely.

Years of potential life lost (YPLL, also called YLL) ranks public health impacts by measuring the cumulative number of years lost to premature death in a population. This statistic is computed by aggregating the difference between average life expectancy and actual ages at death from a condition. In 2015, premature death from heart disease in the United States resulted in 1.35 million YPLL, while homicide resulted in fewer than 560,000 YPLL (Centers for Disease Control and Prevention, 2016). These estimates represent 11.8% and 4.9% of YPLL for all conditions that year. Using YPLL as a measure, however, highlights conditions that tend to cause death earlier in an expected average lifespan; heart disease caused nearly 40 times as many deaths as homicides in 2015 but fewer than three times as many YPLL, because homicide victims tend to be much younger than people who die of heart attacks (National Center for Health Statistics, 2016).

Death is not the only thing that matters to public health. *Disability-adjusted life years* (DALYs) and *quality-adjusted life years* (QALYs) combine measures of the length and the quality of life to quantify the burden of disease more comprehensively than simple mortality statistics. DALYs quantify the years that disability and premature death shorten the lifespan in a population, assuming that meeting the standard life expectancy means full health. By comparing the difference in age of standard life expectancy and potential early death due to a disease with the impact of disease or disability during those years, DALYs indicate where overall health is diminished in a population. Because life expectancy and burden of disease differ by country and condition, DALY metrics are standardized by the World

Health Organization every few years (World Health Organization, 2017b). QALYs assign scores for differing states of health caused by disease or injury in a population. Each year in perfect health is scored 1.0, with this value decreasing for conditions resulting in less-than-perfect health down to 0.0 for death. By calculating the number of years a person is likely to live at a given state of health and comparing that to the cost of preserving that state, QALYs show how effectively resources can be used to influence various health conditions.

Each of these measures illuminates values and choices for improving public health. Even when surveillance is consistently maintained to provide accurate estimates of morbidity and mortality in a population, there is no single correct or value-free allocation of resources. YPLL gives greater weight to conditions that kill younger people; DALYS and QALYS take into account not just life versus death but the impact of disability, and so point to more investment in preventing causes of morbidity. Once descriptive data has been analyzed, epidemiologists use analytical studies to assess the impact of interventions and learn what works best. The next section describes these methods and how they are best utilized.

Analytical Epidemiology's Study Types

Analytical epidemiologists use a range of study designs and methods to identify the *etiology*, or cause, of public health problems and test potential *interventions*, or solutions, to prevent them. Differentiating between *causation*, where an exposure contributes directly to an outcome, and *correlation*, where an exposure and outcome simply exist together in time, is crucial to this endeavor. Understanding the two kinds of epidemiological study designs helps consumers of research, including those who design legal and policy solutions to health issues, know which data suggest the need for action.

In *experimental* studies, participants are exposed to different interventions or treatments and then the researchers observe the outcomes to study causation. *Observational* studies measure health events without manipulating the circumstances in which people experience diseases or injuries to reveal correlations. These study designs provide valuable information about public health problems and how to address them, but understanding their strengths and weaknesses allows us to decide how much weight to give their results when making public health decisions.

Experimental Studies

Randomized controlled trials (RCTs) can test the effectiveness of drugs, devices, and public health interventions. In RCTs, a defined population is randomly assigned to two groups: one receiving the new intervention being tested (the treatment group) and one receiving a standard treatment or no treatment at all (the control group). Outcomes such as morbidity and mortality are recorded, and results are analyzed according to each person's grouping. *Double-blind* RCTs are a study variation in which neither the participants nor the researchers know which group any given participant is assigned to.

Experiments are the most reliable study designs for causal inference because randomizing participants provides confidence that the only difference between cases and controls is their exposure to the intervention being tested, so no unmeasured factor is the hidden cause of different outcomes among cases and controls. Randomization allows the results of the study to be generalized or interpreted broadly because each group approximates characteristics of the overall population. Studies can become poorly randomized at any point; for example, when participants become lost to follow-up (meaning they "drop out" or stop participating) or, for example, when women are more represented in a treatment group than a control group, results might show that women respond to that treatment better than men. This skewed data may affect study methods, potentially requiring researchers to start over, or may be reflected as limitations when interpreting the results.

RCTs are commonly used to test clinical interventions, but they are a challenge to implement in public health practice. Studies providing a benefit to treatment groups, such as increasing access to services that provide lifesaving treatment only to some parts of a population, may be ethically problematic. Depriving some groups of that access could be illegal. Public health laws and policies usually cannot be implemented experimentally by, for example, randomizing some cities to adopt a law restricting gun purchases and others to be in a control group. We can, however, usually evaluate differences in outcomes between jurisdictions with or without certain policies as "natural experiments" that use *quasi-experimental methods.* As described in Chapter 21, the quasi-experiment is the gold standard study design for legal epidemiology because it uses tools to mimic the benefits of a RCT without the problematic aspects of actively randomizing legal and policy interventions in populations.

Observational Studies

Cohort studies and case-control studies are used to examine *etiology*, the causes of health problems, by studying the relationship among exposures, diseases, and injuries. Just as they examine correlations among a risk factor of disease, morbidity, and mortality, observational studies can measure the impacts of specific interventions on health status. A law can be a cause of disease and so an exposure for etiological purposes: researchers comparing patients "exposed" to a law or a hospital policy requiring duodenoscope sterilization to those "unexposed" can evaluate whether the law or policy influenced the likelihood of developing the infection.

Cohort studies compare at least two groups of people, or cohorts, with different exposures and observe their health outcomes over time. Cohort study designs can be *prospective* or *retrospective*, collecting different kinds of data for different purposes. Prospective cohort studies follow a cohort of people from a point in time into the future to observe a single or several related health outcomes downstream, or later in time. These studies can track incidence, making them useful to showing causality, particularly when studying large cohorts. The Framingham Heart Study recruited 5,000 residents of Framingham, Massachusetts in 1948 to participate in physical examinations and interviews that were analyzed for markers and patterns in developing cardiovascular disease. The study continues today among descendants of the original participants and new, diverse area residents, relying on geographic and generational similarities to identify risk factors for disease. Studies like these can cost enormous amounts of time and money, but the benefits are compelling: This study has generated much of our current understanding of treatment and prevention for cardiovascular disease.

Retrospective cohort studies assemble a cohort of people to learn about historical risk factors that may be associated with a common condition among them, such as foodborne illness or other disease outbreaks. Researchers examine patients' medical records or ask about prior exposures to assess whether certain characteristics or vulnerabilities (such as underlying disease, age, or sex) relate to the eventual condition. Obtaining accurate historical data from interviews poses a significant challenge when people's memories of the past have faded or changed, and studying uncommon conditions may not be possible if few people with the condition are alive and willing to participate. However, retrospective cohort study results are usually less time- and resource-intensive than other study designs and may indicate important correlations between exposures and outcomes when study populations reflect the composition of the target or overall population.

Other study designs compare two groups of participants to identify potential risk factors. In these *case-control studies*, epidemiologists compare prior exposures among patients who became sick or died from a disease (cases) with those who did not (controls). This study design was selected by the team studying the CRE outbreak to compare similar people in a single environment who differed in exposure or disease: patients in the hospital who contracted CRE and those who did not. Their analysis showed that recent antibiotic exposure, active inpatient status, and a history of bile duct cancer were patient characteristics associated with CRE infection. As with cohort studies, case-control studies also suffer from challenges in obtaining historical data that can also skew results.

Cross-sectional studies examine outcomes and exposures among people at the same point in time. For instance, a researcher might look at CRE diagnoses (the outcome) and pre-existing medical conditions (exposures), to see if individuals with chronic conditions appear to be particularly vulnerable to acquiring antibiotic-resistant infections in healthcare settings. A study could collect detailed data about a population (e.g., all patients in the hospital), separating the group into exposed individuals with disease, exposed individuals without disease, unexposed individuals with disease, and unexposed individuals without disease. Because this method only looks at data collected at one point in time, it can discover associations but cannot prove cause and effect.

Interpreting Data and Identifying Limitations

Epidemiology is, ultimately, concerned with causes of disease. In supporting inferences of causation, all study designs have inherent limitations. The way that researchers address them determines whether and how the results can be used in future studies, health communication, and designing interventions. Successfully interpreting data requires addressing limitations to the interpretation. We focus here on four: support for causal inference, generalizability, statistical significance, and bias.

Confusing correlation with causation in study results can be a problem for both researchers and the public. Be aware that exposures, interventions, and disease can be chronologically linked but not causally linked. This means that a pre-existing event, such as a drop in outdoor temperatures, may not be the cause of a later event, such as acquiring the flu, though they may seem very related based on the large increase in flu rates each winter. Associating these two events ignores other causes of flu, such as the origins and virulence of influenza strains in circulation each year, and even individual behaviors such as touching the face after shaking hands. The *ecological fallacy*, incorrectly interpreting the results from a population-level study to make inferences about individuals, can affect all observational studies.

A powerful example was a 1998 paper by Wakefield et al., which described cases of children who both had autism and had received the measles, mumps, and rubella (MMR) vaccine. The study included only 12 children referred to a gastroenterology clinic with similar symptoms; it used no controls, blinded diagnostic tests, or systematic data collection. Nonetheless, lead author Wakefield claimed in public statements that he had proved vaccination could cause autism. Whether he was sincerely convinced of this or was just trying to get attention, his assertions, reported widely by the media, raised concerns among parents worldwide about the safety of vaccines. The paper was eventually retracted and Wakefield, accused of fraud and scientific misconduct, was stripped of his medical license (Mnookin, 2011).

A 2002 study exemplifies a valid epidemiological approach to the autism-vaccine connection and highlights why Wakefield was so reckless to suggest one based on his research. Madsen and colleagues conducted a retrospective cohort study of all children born in Denmark between 1991 and 1998. They had virtually complete information on vaccination, autism diagnoses and a range of other possible confounders from Danish medical records and surveillance datasets for more than half a million children. They found no association between the onset of autism and vaccination age, the time of vaccination, the time since vaccination, or the date of vaccination (Madsen et al., 2002). Although the study was observational, the large number of subjects, observed over seven years, and the careful analysis of possible confounders, provide strong support for the epidemiological consensus that there is no link between vaccines and autism (Institute of Medicine, 2012).

As this example shows, the limitations inherent in observational studies do not mean that they cannot help epidemiologists understand the causes of disease or the impact of interventions. *Causal inference* becomes stronger as the weight of evidence—the number of well-designed studies with large numbers of subjects and long time periods—increases. Causal inference also becomes more confident when other contextual factors are consistent with a causal relationship. Bradford Hill's Criteria of Causation (discussed in Chapter 21) is another useful tool, setting out nine factors (such as whether there is a plausible biological or social mechanism by which the cause could produce the effect) that tend to support an inference of causation.

Generalizability is the extent to which study findings can be applied more broadly, requiring a study population that reflects the population from which it is drawn. Results can be generalized to a population when the study uses a random sample, as with RCTs, or when the data capture nearly all the cases of disease that exist in the population, as in a national disease registry. Conversely, when the number of persons studied (the "n") is small or not randomly selected, findings will not be generalizable to the overall population. Wakefield's 12 participants are less likely to represent the entire population receiving the MMR vaccination than the Madsen study of all children born in Denmark. Likewise, a study that looks at the impact of a policy change in a few cities may not be generalizable to communities in other parts of the country or to more rural communities.

Data analyses place great weight on whether or not studies have *statistical significance*, which indicates that the probability of the results occurring by chance is small. A *p-value* is a fractional value calculated to represent the probability that the magnitude of the study results occurred by chance alone. A p-value of less than 0.05—meaning that the likelihood of the reported results occurring by chance is less than 5%—is usually considered the cut-off for a statistically significant finding. Although a p-value of 0.05 or less is a well-established standard in the scientific community, it is a convention, and studies with somewhat higher p-values can still be informative for decisionmakers and can be presented as evidence in courts.

Finally, it is critical also to consider *study bias*. Bias is a systematic error that causes a study to misrepresent or incorrectly capture results. It can happen when researchers make decisions in any element of a study, from initial design to the interpretation of results. Investigators can initially introduce *selection bias*, a nonrandom inclusion or exclusion of people that means the study participants misrepresent the overall population. Bias is usually unintentional and unconscious. A researcher may introduce *information bias* when asking more extensive and probing questions about health of an "exposed" cohort than of an "unexposed" cohort after hypothesizing that those exposed are likely to suffer adverse health effects, resulting in data of different quality or amounts among the groups. Other forms of bias include *recall bias*, when individuals asked about their past activities are more likely to recall certain events than others, and *volunteer bias*, when those who agree to participate in studies differ in attitudes, health status, educational background, or other characteristics from those who do not. Using a combination of different study designs can help avoid some of these biases, and it is important when evaluating a study's results to carefully consider what biases may have influenced research findings.

Using Epidemiology to Inform Policy Decisions

Both the Wakefield study and the UCLA outbreak offer important lessons for how scientific research can influence decisions and, ultimately, policy— for good and for ill. Misinformation about the link between MMR vaccine and autism persists today, and many people opposed to vaccines rely on that study's discredited findings when advocating for broad exemptions or to eliminate vaccine mandates altogether. The problem of "superbugs" in healthcare facilities also continues. The deaths and illnesses during the CRE outbreak led to lawsuits, and the FDA, which regulates medical devices, held hearings in 2015 over the use and risks associated with duodenoscopes. The UCLA case-control study and others like it have identified prior antibiotic use as a factor associated with CRE infection, and curbing excessive antibiotic-prescribing practices remains a national priority. Several states have considered and adopted new laws requiring the reporting of infections like CRE to the state and local health departments, and healthcare facilities have instituted policies requiring infection prevention and antibiotic stewardship training for hospital staff.

Conclusion

This chapter has discussed the use of epidemiologic studies to identify the source of public health problems and inform policymaking. Epidemiology is a powerful tool for identifying public health threats, examining risk factors, prioritizing problems, and assessing options for prevention and control. We next discuss the various types of policy approaches that can be used to respond to public health challenges and how findings from epidemiologic studies can be used to help inform what type of policy response is most appropriate in a given situation.

Further Reading

Berkman, L., Kawachi, I., & Glymour, M. M. (Eds.). (2014). *Social Epidemiology*, 2nd ed. New York: Oxford University Press.

Briss, P. A., Zaza, S., Pappaioanou, M., Fielding, J., Wright-De Aguero, L., Truman, B. I., . . . Task Force on Community Preventive Services. (2000). Developing an Evidence-Based Guide to Community Preventive Services–Methods. *American Journal of Preventive Medicine, 18*(1 Suppl.), 35–43.

Rose, G. (1985). Sick Individuals and Sick Populations. *International Journal of Epidemiology 14*, 32–38.

Rothman, K. J., Greenland, S., & Lash, T. L. (Eds.). (2008). *Modern Epidemiology*, 3rd ed. Philadelphia: Wolters Kluwer Health/Lippincott Williams & Wilkins.

6 | Choosing a Legal Approach

Learning Objectives

- Understand the range of ways law can be used to influence behavior and environments for better health.
- Recognize the potential for innovation and complementary action in the United States' system of federalism.
- Understand the drawbacks and limitations of the main tools of public health law.

Introduction

Public health researchers use epidemiology to study the causes and distribution of disease and injury. But once a public health problem is identified, what should be done? This chapter turns to the wide range of legal strategies that can be used alone or, as is more often the case, in combination, to address public health challenges. Law can be used to set specific standards of conduct, change social norms, and structure the default choices available in everyday life. Law can do this through many legal devices, including statutes, regulations, orders, guidelines, and taxes, and it can be invoked at the local, state, and federal levels. This complex matrix of legal options and actors invites innovation, creativity, and sophistication.

The example of motor vehicle injuries provides a clear example of the many different ways law can be used to influence behavior and environments for better health. Federal law includes dozens of safety-related regulations that govern new car manufacturing, from obvious requirements like airbag and safety belt mandates to less visible rules setting standards for brake performance and "crashworthiness." Federal law also sets standards for safe road design. At the state level, a license is required to drive, and drivers must reach a certain age and pass a competency test before receiving a license. State laws also prohibit driving under the influence of alcohol and other intoxicants. State tort law allows people injured by negligent driving and dangerous motor vehicle products to sue for damages. State and local traffic codes require drivers to obey the speed limit, stop at stop signs, signal turns, and yield to pedestrians. Other laws require periodic vehicle safety inspections and require that information about a vehicle's safety profile and history be disclosed to used-car buyers. Some jurisdictions use tolls to reduce traffic congestion.

This chapter describes the most important ways law can be used in public health. Law can specify the conduct required—or prohibited—generally or in specific circumstances. Licensing laws limit who can engage in a behavior that requires special qualifications to assure quality and reduce risk. Law can be used to influence the cost of behaviors, providing an incentive to be healthier. In public health, law is often used to shape the information and built environments in a way calculated to promote healthier behavior. This breadth of strategies makes law a highly adaptive tool for improving health.

Setting Behavior Rules and Performance Standards

Prohibitions ("you must *not* do X") and mandates ("you *must* do X") are among the most fundamental—and most commonly used—forms of law. Mandates and prohibitions may be directed at individuals or organizations. In the example of safety belts, manufacturers must install them (a mandate), and individuals must wear them (another mandate). Mandates are often used to instigate the adoption of a new behavior, and they are most successful when the behavior becomes a custom or a habit. A mandated regulatory standard was required to get proper three-point restraints (the modern safety belt) into all cars, but now well-designed safety belts are an industry standard. A law requiring safety belt use, enforced with fines, was needed to dramatically increase the rate of safety belt use, but over time the rule has helped to make wearing a safety belt the natural and sensible thing for people in cars to do—a habit and a social norm.

Mandates typically require consistent enforcement to be optimally effective. Even today, safety belt laws supported by "primary enforcement," meaning that a driver can be stopped and get a ticket for not wearing the belt, are more effective than "secondary enforcement" laws that only authorize a safety belt ticket if the driver has been stopped for another offense. Primary enforcement with higher fines is the most effective approach of all (Nichols, Tippetts, Fell, Eichelberger, & Haseltine, 2014). Similarly, evidence suggests that a ban on texting while driving has a positive public health impact in the short term, but if it is not consistently enforced, people return to their previous patterns of conduct (Abouk & Adams, 2013). Even apparently simple legal mandates can be complex to implement or enforce or may have unintended consequences. Compliance with a safety belt law is reasonably detectable by a police officer; it is much harder to detect illegal cell phone use. Primary safety belt laws are effective in preventing crash deaths, but, as a side effect, they can be used as instrument for racial profiling.

Complex, detailed mandates and prohibitions are a key tool of the modern regulatory state. Codes for food safety set specific standards for everything from kitchen lighting to the proper temperature of a freezer. Medical marijuana laws prescribe rules for packaging, marketing, advertising, and the kinds of products that may be sold. Detailed environmental laws, supported by even more detailed regulations, require facilities to install technology to manage pollutant outputs, use chemical motoring systems to ensure that maximum contaminant levels are not exceeded, and make regular reports to regulators. Complex processes in global economic systems require complex rules, but they can be expensive for the regulated community to follow and for government to implement, monitor, and enforce. Moreover, complexity may give rise to unintended loopholes and opportunities for evasion. By "grandfathering" existing air pollution sources from new regulatory requirements when it amended the Clean Air Act, for example, Congress created a perverse incentive for businesses *not* to upgrade their facilities or build more modern, environmentally-friendly plants—the opposite of what was intended. Health and safety regulation—essential for public health—is also technically challenging and politically charged.

Licensing

Licenses are another way for government to set standards. Licensing schemes prohibit individuals or businesses from engaging in specified conduct unless they first receive permission (in the form of a license) from the government. There may be qualification requirements that must be met before receiving a license; for example, to obtain a medical license, aspiring physicians must complete years of training and a medical board exam, and these requirements may serve important public health goals: health professional licensure influences and supports high standards of training, competency, and conduct. Facility licensure helps ensure that hospitals, restaurants, and other operations with serious health implications are configured and maintained according to the current understanding of healthy practice. In a broader sense, we can consider the process of drug approval by the U.S. Food and Drug Administration (FDA), in which pharmaceutical makers must demonstrate safety and effectiveness through clinical trial, to be a form of licensing.

Licenses can also be used to regulate where an activity can take place. For instance, a jurisdiction may prohibit businesses near schools from holding a liquor license or limit the types of businesses that can hold a liquor license. It could also limit the overall number of licenses in a neighborhood. Licenses can also provide a powerful mechanism for ongoing supervision. Food service licenses come with a long list of compliance conditions related to food storage, handling, and preparation. Food service licensees are regularly inspected by health officers, and violations of license requirement lead to warnings, fines, or, in more severe cases, the suspension or revocation of a license. Similarly, even after FDA approval, drug companies must track and report adverse events, and if the facts warrant, the FDA can withdraw its approval of a drug.

Licensing systems can have drawbacks as well. In some cases, licensing of health professionals, occupations, and healthcare institutions has been used as a tool for discrimination or limiting economic competition. Recently, the U.S. Supreme Court found that North Carolina's licensing requirements for dentists were being used to unfairly keep non-dentists from providing teeth whitening services, in violation of antitrust law (*North Carolina Board of Dental Examiners v. Federal Trade Commission*, 2015). Although program costs can be offset by charging licensing fees, licensing systems can be costly for government to implement, and the application process and ongoing compliance can be expensive for people and businesses. If not designed appropriately and targeted where there are true public health risks, these systems can have negative impacts on local economies and discourage investment in new businesses and industries.

Litigation

Civil litigation is a basic legal tool for making and enforcing legal standards. The courts offer both governments and individual citizens an opportunity to make claims for compensation for wrongful or negligent harms they have suffered and to seek behavior change from those who have caused the harm. From a public health point of view, litigation can be a powerful tool for enforcing healthy standards of individual and especially corporate behavior, and for placing the cost of legal but risk-creating activities on those who profit from them. It has even been a vehicle for funding public health programs.

Mass tort litigation involves lawsuits brought on behalf of numerous individuals who have been harmed by the same unsafe product or negligent course of conduct, such as the sale of food tainted with a bacterial agent. Such lawsuits serve to provide compensation to those who have been harmed and to punish wrongful conduct. These lawsuits can also serve a public health purpose if they lead businesses to redesign their products, modify their practices, or otherwise alter conduct detrimental to public health. The threat of significant monetary damages can lead business to practice "preventive corporate law" that tries to prevent injuries or disease from occurring in the first place (Koenig & Rustad, 2001). For example, the threat of litigation is one reason that "motor vehicle manufacturers routinely provide greater safety than the standards require" (Vernick, Rutkow, & Salmon, 2007).

States and cities have used litigation as a means to secure behavior change from risk-creating industries and to be compensated for the costs they incurred while providing services to people injured by dangerous products or practices. The most prominent example of this use of litigation is the Master Settlement Agreement (MSA) that ended lawsuits by multiple states against the major tobacco companies. The MSA, described in more detail in Chapter 8, secured billions of dollars in compensation (at least some of it dedicated to support health programs) and reforms in tobacco marketing. In recent years, dozens of states and cities have followed this model in suits against makers of opioid analgesics, which have taken a huge toll on lives and health services budgets.

Litigation typically ends in compromise, so deals like the MSA usually have critics on all sides. As a mode of dispute resolution, litigation also suffers from high cost and slow pace. Cases can cost millions or hundreds of millions of dollars to prosecute, and an award of damages may not come until years after the wrongful conduct, especially if there are repeated appeals. These factors can make the process less like a deterrent and more like a cost of doing business: despite the MSA, and the billions the companies still pay every year, "Big Tobacco" is still a big, and profitable, business. Nor are all cases as straightforward as tobacco, where the evidence that smoking caused disease was ironclad. In toxic exposure cases, the harm may have unfolded over a long period of time in a context with many other possible causes, and there may be limited or no evidence of the biological mechanism that links exposure to harm. Even if a plaintiff has strong epidemiological evidence that the defendant's actions increased the risk of developing a certain disease, the evidence may not convince a jury that it was "more likely than not" that the defendant's conduct *did* cause the disease.

Changing Economic Incentives

Regulatory rules and licenses can raise the cost of an activity, but that is not their primary intended purpose. Sometimes policymakers use legal devices with the primary goal of directly raising the costs of unhealthy activities or providing economic incentives for healthy ones. Taxes are the most obvious tool, but public health has also used insurance requirements as a means of requiring people or businesses to "internalize" (i.e., pay) the costs of their unhealthy or risky conduct.

Taxes increase the cost of unhealthy behaviors and have the added benefit of generating revenue for the government. "Sin" taxes on products like alcohol, cigarettes, and now marijuana are a venerable and effective tool for public health. State and local tobacco taxes reliably produce lower smoking rates. Raising excise taxes on alcohol reduces excessive consumption and related harms, like motor vehicle crashes. The positive public health effects of raising tobacco and alcohol taxes are predictably proportional to the size of the tax, so making sure that taxes are crafted to keep up with inflation is an important legal consideration and political challenge.

A tax is a simple thing in itself, but using taxes for public health is no simple matter. Though taxes can lower consumption of harmful products, they can also have a disproportionate economic impact on poorer people, and especially on people who are pathologically dependent on a product such as alcohol, tobacco, or marijuana. With the collective harms associated with tobacco, alcohol, and marijuana, stretched governmental budgets, and political opposition to new taxes, using tax law to influence public health today puts policymakers on difficult terrain.

Requiring individuals to purchase insurance is another policy mechanism to force individuals and organizations to internalize the costs their conduct creates. Car insurance, which drivers are legally required to buy, is a way to spread the cost of accidents across all drivers, but experience rating is typically used by insurance companies to make drivers with worse records pay more. An even more interesting example are laws that permit riding a motorcycle without a helmet, but only if the rider obtains a specified amount of medical coverage for motorcycle-related accidents. The goal of this policy approach is to preserve the freedom to choose a riskier option while ensuring that medical costs that would be otherwise imposed on others (hospitals, doctors, other insurance carriers) in the event of a motorcycle accident are instead borne by the person engaging in the risky behavior. The higher costs also serve as a deterrent to not wearing a helmet, and they force the rider to, at least in part, confront the reality of the risks that he or she is taking on.

The economic policy options outlined here all focus on *discouraging* unhealthy or dangerous conduct. An alternative approach is to *encourage* individuals and businesses to make decisions that promote public health. For instance, to increase access to healthy foods, some states and localities provide financial incentives in the form of loans, grants, and tax incentives for grocery stores and other healthy food retailers located in underserved communities ("food deserts"). Some states provide tax credits to companies that incentivize healthy behavior through employee wellness programs, and the federal government allows the costs of such programs to be deducted as a business expense. Unlike taxes that raise prices, the use of tax mechanisms to fund incentive programs reduces government revenue and so is limited by the availability of public funding.

A more subtle way of incentivizing health behavior is to modify the default options that people are presented with, sometimes referred to as *nudging*. This approach draws on research from the field of behavioral economics, which rests on psychological research showing that people's decisions are not driven by economic rationality but instead are prejudiced by unconscious biases and mental shortcuts. One of these is the tendency to make the easy choice: to stick with the option initially offered (the "default") rather than make the effort to investigate another one. Changing the default can be an effective public health intervention. Making HIV testing the default, and making people who do not want to be tested affirmatively opt out, increases testing rates (Montoy, Dow, & Kaplan, 2016). Similarly, New York City issued a regulation limiting the size of sugary drinks. The regulation is based on the theory that people generally consume whatever portion they are given, and so requiring smaller portions would stimulate a reduction in consumption and obesity. (A court struck down the rule based on issues unrelated to its effectiveness, as discussed in Chapter 14.)

Changing the default option is often presented as an alternative to more "coercive" or "paternalistic" public health regulations, like direct mandates. Nonetheless, some still object to this approach as being an ethically questionable form of covert government manipulation. Others point out that the default is often created by profit-seeking companies with manipulative purposes of their own and have expressed concern that such approaches do not go far enough. On this view, behavioral approaches like this may put too much a focus on individual decision-making, downplaying the role of corporations whose deliberate actions contribute to poor health.

Changing the Informational Environment

Policymakers can alter the *informational environment* by creating disclosure requirements, regulating marketing and advertising, and conducting government education programs. Some of the policy options in this category raise First Amendment issues that will be discussed further in Chapter 13.

Disclosure Requirements

Disclosure requirements operate from the premise that transparency can better inform individual choices and will also push manufacturers and businesses to make healthier decisions about their products and activities. For instance, laws requiring the disclosure of the calorie content in food may prompt consumers to buy lower-calorie foods while simultaneously nudging producers to reformulate their products to reduce the number of calories.

These disclosure requirements rest on assumptions about individual and corporate behavior that may not be correct. For example, there is little evidence that current warning labels on alcohol have had any significant impact on consumer decision-making (Kersbergen & Field, 2017), and rather than change corporate conduct, warning labels on tobacco products have had the unintended effect of insulating the industry from legal liability (see Chapter 8). Moreover, almost by definition, mandated disclosures put the onus for behavioral change on the individual receiving the message, ignoring the broader social, economic, and cultural forces that shape behavior. This accounts for the repeated research finding that "the simple act of conveying information to an individual seldom suffices to change that individual's behavior" (Parmet & Smith, 2006).

Marketing and Advertising

Restricting marketing and advertising raises complicated First Amendment issues but is likely a more powerful approach to countering promotional tactics that threaten public health. Such regulations can help address problematic aspects of the informational environment that subtly and, often unconsciously, influence consumer behaviors. For instance, the large tobacco product displays found behind the counter in many retail outlets (sometimes referred to as "powerwalls") shape consumer decisions in little-noticed ways. The displays take advantage of what psychology refers to as the "mere exposure" effect: the phenomenon that "[s]imply being exposed to something will cause you to like it more" and to underestimate its dangers (Arkush, 2008). Rather than being based on considered reflection, these attitudes develop subconsciously as a result of exposure to tobacco product displays over and over again. In response, jurisdictions around the world (though not in the United States) have prohibited the display of tobacco products in retail stores, requiring them to be placed under the counter or otherwise out of view.

Marketing restrictions can help to counter the persuasive power of large corporations with powerful advertising budgets. But in addition to First Amendment concerns, such restrictions may be criticized as excessively paternalistic, and they may be ineffective if they simply cause companies to divert their advertising dollars to other types of marketing activities. Instead of restricting advertising and marketing, another policy option is for the government to "speak" on its own behalf. For example, instead of limiting the advertising of sugar-sweetened beverages, the government could instead launch a public education campaigns about the health harms of sugary drinks.

"Government Speech"

A mandated label can be understood as a form of governmental speech, but because the labels appear on commercial products, there may be First Amendment limitations on their form or content. The First Amendment does not apply when government speaks directly through information products it produces itself. Laws themselves can be understood as a form of speech that work by highlighting a problem. The New York soda portion law is a good example: it never went into effect, but health experts attribute a major decline in soda consumption in part to the widespread publicity and public awareness the controversy generated.

Running large-scale public education campaigns is obviously much more expensive than mandating information for others to spread. Even more problematically, the evidence of effectiveness of such educational campaigns is quite mixed, especially when dealing with complex behaviors such as diet and exercise. Among other challenges, "pervasive marketing for competing products or with opposing messages, the power of social norms, and the drive of addiction frequently mean that positive campaign outcomes are not sustained" (Wakefield, Loken, & Hornik, 2010). Thus public education campaigns are most effective when they are one part of a more comprehensive policy approach to a problem.

Changing the Built Environment

Law can be used to shape the physical environment where we live, work, and play. Building and housing codes, for example, require commercial and residential property to incorporate a wide range of evidence-based standards that make the buildings safer. These provisions ensure that buildings are structurally sound, can withstand predictable stresses like high winds or earthquakes, have electrical wiring that does not create a fire risk, and have plumbing systems that deliver clean water and safely dispose of human waste. For many public buildings, these codes also ensure that structures are accessible to individuals with disabilities. Zoning laws and urban design policies are two additional types of policies that shape the built environment and impact health.

Where houses, schools, business, and industrial facilities are located in a community significantly impacts the health of the local population. Zoning ordinances empower local governments to create geographic "zones" in which defined activities can be located. For example, a local planning department may create residential areas where people are allowed to build and occupy homes; commercial districts that contain businesses such as office buildings, grocery stores, and other retail establishments; and industrial zones where manufacturing, mining, and other pollution producing activities are allowed to occur. These zoning ordinances can further public health goals by, for example, ensuring a safe distance between residential areas and industrial plants. Zoning ordinances can also incorporate specific standards and rules that affect health. For example, some zoning laws have density standards that restrict the number of alcohol or fast food retail outlets per square mile. Likewise, zoning ordinances can be used to facilitate activities—such as the creation of farmers' markets—that may promote health.

Urban design has recently begun to address the fact that too often our communities are designed with only cars in mind. This contributes to obesity, pollution, car crashes, and congestion. "Complete Streets" policies can help cure these problems by requiring or encouraging community design elements and transportation options that provide safe, efficient, convenient, and comfortable travel for all individuals, no matter how they get around. Although Complete Streets policies vary in their specifics, they generally include the creation or expansion of sidewalks, bike lanes, bus lanes, frequent and safe crossing opportunities, median islands, and accessible pedestrian signals.

Although zoning and urban design can be powerful tools to promote health, most of these systems were not created with public health as a focus, and ordinances may be written and implemented in many jurisdictions without taking health outcomes into account. Zoning can also be a problem for health and health equity. A primary effect (and, evidence suggests, a purpose) of zoning in the past hundred years has been to create barriers to racial and socioeconomic integration (Rothstein, 2017). Indeed, some experts argue "[d]ensity zoning is now the most important mechanism promoting class and racial segregation" in the United States (Massey, Albright, Casciano, Derickson, & Kinsey, 2013). Segregation is unhealthy as well as unjust, forcing people to live in communities with lower opportunities for health and a greater exposure to unhealthy environmental conditions (Matthew, Rodrigue, & Reeves, 2016).

Conclusion

This chapter has provided an overview of legal approaches that can be used to promote public health and address specific health problems. Policymakers can restrict or mandate conduct, create and enforce licensing schemes, increase the costs of unhealthy conduct, incentivize healthy conduct, change the informational environment, or modify the built environment. Though any given legal lever may come with constitutional or practical limitations, and law rarely provides the sole solution, there is almost always one or more suitable legal tools available to public health problem-solvers.

Further Reading

Burris, S. (1997). The invisibility of public health: population-level measures in a politics of market individualism. *American Journal of Public Health*, *87*(10), 1607–1610.

Fung, A., Graham, M., & Weil, D. (2007). *Full Disclosure: The Perils and Promise of Transparency*. Cambridge: Cambridge University Press.

Mello, M. M., Wood, J., Burris, S., Wagenaar, A. C., Ibrahim, J. K., & Swanson, J. W. (2013). Critical Opportunities for Public Health Law: A Call for Action. *American Journal of Public Health*, *103*(11), 1979–1988.

Sunstein, C., & Thaler, R. (2008). *Nudge: Improving Decisions about Health, Wealth, and Happiness*. New Haven, CT: Yale University Press.

7 | Using Evidence and Knowledge Critically in Policy Development

Learning Objectives

- Identify sources of policy recommendations and evidence of policy impact.
- Learn to identify biases and indicators of research credibility.
- Acquire tools for "educated guessing" about policy options in matters where evidence is incomplete or lacking.
- Understand the "health in all policies" approach and the use of health impact assessments.

Introduction

The best advice to anyone undertaking a campaign to address a public health problem through legal action is: Be as sure as you can be that your policy idea is a good one, because you will be spending a lot of resources of all kinds to get the measure passed into law and then implemented. Predicting what is likely to work is easier said than done, but it *can* be done and is always worth the effort. In this chapter, we offer some practical ideas about using evidence in devising legal solutions for public health problems. We introduce some good resources for policy evidence and advice, and suggest some criteria that you can use to assess the credibility of research studies without becoming a researcher or statistician yourself.

There will definitely be instances in a public health law career when you will be able to push for a policy that has already been proven to work. A lot of the time, however, you will have to come up with policy solutions to health threats without a well-developed evidence base to stand on. There is a simple reason why people grappling with new or newly recognized health problems will not have evidence-based solutions to apply: new problems, by definition, rarely have existing, well-tested solutions. The whole point of innovation is that one is trying something new. Accordingly, we speak of "evidence-informed" policy, not "evidence-based" policy. As the term "evidence-informed" suggests, expertise, research knowledge, and analogous evidence can go a long way to helping policy innovators make good choices.

Managing Bias

The first and most dangerous source of error is almost always our own lying brains. We start any assessment of policy options with beliefs and goals. Some of us will start with ideological doubts about government programs, while some of us will be ideologically suspicious of market-based solutions. Along with adopting ideologies, we usually become members of groups who think the same way, so our personal beliefs, and our allegiance to our social and professional "teams," conspire to obscure the facts before us. Nobel-prize winning research has shown that we think faster than we realize, and reach conclusions in ways that are often invisible to us. For example, we are prone to "confirmation bias," which means that we are more likely to notice and accept assertions (and research) that support our pre-existing beliefs. Similarly, we instinctively value our group identities and loyalties highly and may unconsciously pick loyalty over accuracy when weighing conflicting evidence. When all that happens, our "reasoning" brains become advocates, cherry-picking the facts and making arguments that support our more or less unconscious intuitions. We are all at risk of pursuing a policy because it *feels* right in light of our pre-existing beliefs, and because our colleagues and friends like it.

This is just human nature. We cannot overcome it, but we can try to correct for it. One method is to cultivate humility about our judgment; be skeptical of first reactions, and consciously try to keep an open mind until all the facts are accounted for, avoiding the impulse to massage the facts toward the conclusion we want. Training in law can help—lawyers learn to separate facts from arguments and legal conclusions and to question unsupported assertions.

In public health, there is an even more powerful way to fight our inborn biases: science. The scientific method—using well-developed theory to pose hypotheses that are then tested against evidence using transparent, reproducible methods—is designed to minimize bias. Public health depends upon scientific research to define problems epidemiologically, examine the risk factors (including social and behavioral risk factors), and evaluate interventions. Science, of course, does not fully eliminate bias either. Scientists are people with biases, including ideological commitments or funding sources that may shape their results—or the research questions they choose to ask—in subtle ways. Scientists may have professional incentives to find "significant" results, and, like everyone, they may be reluctant to come to conclusions that will be unpopular with their peers. These are not defects in the scientific method but a condition of human life. Each viewer and each process of learning has limitations, which are manageable if we recognize them. All of this boils down to a three-pronged approach when it comes to interpreting information about public health problems and possible legal solutions: be skeptical, consciously assess the methodological strength and limitations of any source of information, and triangulate multiple sources.

The kind of evidence you will be able to draw upon will depend a lot on the problem you are trying to solve. In Chapter 5, you learned about how epidemiology helps us understand health problems. In Chapter 6, you were introduced to a variety of legal strategies that are available to change behaviors and environments. That is where public health policymaking starts: with a more or less well-defined sense of a problem and the ways law might respond. If the problem you are facing has been recognized for a long time, and one or more legal responses have been launched and evaluated, you will be in the lucky position of being able to quickly find a lot of evidence and evidence-informed recommendations. As the problem gets newer, and experience shorter, the evidence base is thinner, and there will often be studies with conflicting results. When you are among the first to be dealing with a new problem, your challenge moves from interpreting research findings and sifting through expert advice to making the most educated guesses you can in a process of public health policy innovation.

Finding and Interpreting Evidence about Well-Tested Interventions

Systematic Reviews

When you are dealing with a well-known problem that others have already addressed, you may be lucky enough to be able to find a *systematic review* of the impact of current responses. A systematic review synthesizes the results of many studies using explicit, rigorous, and transparent methods. Systematic reviews assess the effectiveness of an intervention based on the overall weight of the evidence available, taking into account study results and the strengths and limitations of each study's methods. Many systematic reviews use statistical techniques to integrate the results of included studies, a method called *meta-analysis*, which entails pooling and reanalyzing data from many studies. Finding one or more credible systematic reviews is always a happy moment for a busy public health law practitioner.

Several organizations support and publish systematic reviews of recognized high quality. The Cochrane Collaborative currently offers more than 5,000 systematic reviews on a wide range of health interventions. The Campbell Collaboration provides a similar service with systematic reviews covering a broad range of social science subjects including, among others, education and criminology. The Community Guide for Preventive Services publishes the findings from the U.S. Preventive Services Task Force, which was created by the US government in 1996 to systematically identify effective and economically efficient public health interventions. All of these reviews follow standard protocols, and they are valuable sources of predigested evidence on the effects of legal interventions on health. Systematic reviews, including those prepared under the auspices of these organizations, are often published in peer-reviewed journals, so you can find them by going to the organizational websites or searching in PubMed (the free research database maintained by the National Library of Medicine). (See Box 7.1.)

Cochrane, Campbell, and Community Guide reviews are credible because they are conducted according to transparent and tested methods under the auspices of respected scientific organizations. You may also find systematic reviews conducted by researchers unaffiliated with these institutions. The credibility of such reviews is a bit more difficult to discern, but properly done reviews should all have certain basic elements that you can look for and evaluate critically, even without statistical training:

- Is there a clearly stated research question (e.g., "what is the effect of a minimum legal drinking age of 21 on fatal and nonfatal crashes?")? If the question is unclear, or seems to confuse legal concepts or mechanisms, you may be cautious about accepting the results.

BOX 7.1 RESOURCES FOR PUBLIC HEALTH LAW EVIDENCE

Cochrane Library, http://www.cochranelibrary.com/: Library of systematic reviews in health and healthcare

Campbell Collaboration, https://www.campbellcollaboration.org/: Library of systematic reviews of social interventions

Guide to Community Preventive Services (The Community Guide), https://www.thecommunityguide.org/: Collection of evidence-based findings of the Community Preventive Services Task Force

Healthy People, https://www.healthypeople.gov/: Science-based, 10-year national objectives for improving health, including specific recommendations and evidence for public health laws

County Health Rankings and Roadmaps, What Works for Health, http://www.countyhealthrankings.org/roadmaps/what-works-for-health: Collects and rates evidence for policies and programs to improve population health and health equity

Center for Public Health Law Research, www.phlr.org: Research results and evidence briefs summarizing knowledge base for public health law

LawAtlas, www.lawatlas.org: Interactive access to key public health laws

National Library of Medicine (PubMed), https://www.ncbi.nlm.nih.gov/pubmed: World's largest database and repository of biomedical research literature, with links to published studies

Prevention Status Reports, https://www.cdc.gov/psr/: CDC's status report on state public health policies and practices designed to address 10 important public health problems

Winnable Battles, https://www.cdc.gov/winnablebattles/: CDC's guide to measurable impact on major health threats

- Does the review provide explicit, sensible criteria for including or excluding studies? If no criteria are given, or you have reason to doubt that the criteria make sense, you may suspect bias.
- Does the review tell you what databases were searched and what search terms were used? Did the researchers check the references in the studies they found to find others? You can reflect on your own research experience to consider whether the search strategy might be at risk of missing important studies.
- How current is the review? Leading review organizations typically update reviews periodically as new studies become available. If a review is more than a decade old, it may not reflect the current state of the literature.

- Does the review follow an explicit protocol, like that of the Cochrane Collaboration or the PRISMA standards (Moher, Liberati, Tetzlaff, Altman, & Prisma Group, 2009)?

You may also come across *narrative reviews*. In a narrative review, the authors summarize qualitatively the findings of many studies. Narrative reviews are not intended to synthesize results and typically do not follow an explicit protocol. These can be very informative as a way to get a sense of what is known, but the author's bias is less constrained. As with systematic reviews, however, a critical reader can assess the clarity of the topic as stated and how studies were found. Since narrative reviews rarely use sophisticated statistical methods, even a non-scientist reader can assess the logic and consistency of any inferences the authors draw from the studies they review.

"Expert" Policy Recommendations

Another way to get good ideas fast is to look to one of the many sites that provide policy recommendations. The federal government has several. The Healthy People series, produced by an interagency workgroup spanning multiple government agencies, is revised every 10 years and makes recommendations for policy on many health topics. The Centers for Disease Control and Prevention also tries to highlight good policy ideas in advisory products like Winnable Battles. The recommendations are developed by experts, usually through some consultative process. Recommendations are also made by many professional organizations, advocacy groups, and academic projects, such as the County Health Rankings and Roadmaps project (funded by the Robert Wood Johnson Foundation). The critical reader can evaluate the rationale and evidence base provided with the recommendations. The fact that experts or government agencies are making the recommendation is an important factor, but if there is no research evidence or clear rationale, skepticism is in order.

Models

Models are another form of information you may encounter when a problem and potential policy responses have already been studied to some degree. Researchers use existing data to build mathematical models that can predict the impact of different legal inventions or examine counterfactual scenarios ("what would have happened if . . . ").

With modern computing and sophisticated methods, modelers can incorporate an immense amount of data and test millions of different possible scenarios. For example, *agent-based models* create whole communities of computer-generated individuals with diverse preferences and then explore the outcomes produced by their interactions in a given environment over time. Policy changes can then be introduced into that environment to model their effects. In a 2016 study, researchers built a model of two communities with different vaccination rates to estimate the impact of a rule that requires unvaccinated kids to be sent home during a measles outbreak (Getz, Carlson, Dougherty, Porco Francis, & Salter, 2016).

No matter how sophisticated the techniques or how much data is crunched, models are only as valid as the assumptions upon which they rest. These days, modeling can be dauntingly sophisticated to the consumer, but they all boil down to a set of assumptions about how prior evidence can be used to predict future results and about what assumptions should be plugged into the model in areas where we lack data. These assumptions should be clearly laid out in any paper reporting modeling results. The authors of the measles study provide a detailed explanation of why they chose the modeling approach they used and how they defined key variables like the rate of transmission between students. The nonexpert reader will not be able to assess the methodological validity of these methods—that is what peer review is supposed to do—but even someone with no modeling or statistical expertise can understand (and question) the factual assumptions and logic underlying the model.

Cost-Benefit Analysis

In a world of hard choices and trade-offs, it makes sense to ask what a new legal intervention will cost and to compare that cost to an estimate of the benefits the law will produce. *Cost-benefit analysis* (CBA) is an approach to answering this question in economic terms. "Costs" of a law can include things like salaries for law enforcers, direct compliance costs for those who are obeying the law, and even "hedonistic" costs—lost pleasure associated with giving up a prohibited behavior. "Benefits" can include the value of lives saved or injuries prevented, as well as things like decreased worker absenteeism. The resulting estimates can be powerfully persuasive to policymakers, and it is widely said in advocacy circles that CBAs are an essential tool for making the case for a law.

CBAs must be treated with caution. Like other models, they are built on assumptions about costs and benefits that should be confronted and questioned. It might have already occurred to you that one of those assumptions is the dollar amount to attribute to a lost (or saved) human life. Conducting a CBA also typically requires placing a monetary value on injuries or the pleasure lost to, say, drinking less sugar-sweetened soda. Economists have "objective" tools they can draw on to value these things (like standard calculations of YPLLs or DALYs—see Chapter 5), but that does not change the fact that the "cost" or "benefit" of life or health is a matter of values that goes beyond the dollar. In practical terms, choices about these dollar amounts may determine whether the cost-benefit ratio is positive or negative, and these choices can be consciously or unconsciously biased.

There are many other assumptions and (implicit) value judgments that must also be made in conducting a CBA. In a CBA of a medical marijuana law, for example, the researcher would have to decide whether to treat the pleasure of marijuana use that is not necessary to its therapeutic effect as a benefit or a cost to society. If the law, as in California, did not legalize all steps in the supply chain, should the researcher include the profits of the growers and distributors as economic benefits or ignore them as the fruits of crime that create no social benefit? Or, consider a study of a regulation requiring healthcare workers to get flu shots. Most people who die because of the flu are elderly. If the researcher computes the benefit using standard life expectancies and a constant value per life-year, this intervention will have a lower benefit than others that save younger people—in effect assigning a lesser value to older lives. This is a value choice, not science, and so the CBA consumer must keep points like this in mind to use the tool intelligently.

Individual Studies

When problems and legal solutions are newish, it is likely that the evidence, if any, will be in individual studies of various kinds, often looking at the effects of the law in just one or a few jurisdictions. A good place to search for these studies is on PubMed, the National Library of Medicine's free online database. PubMed uses an elaborate tagging system so that when you find a study that is relevant, it will help you by suggesting others on the same topic. Often it has links to the full text, and if there is a review you have missed, it will often point to that as well.

The credibility and usefulness of any study depend on the methods. A qualitative study using a dozen interviews and a 30-respondent survey to explore the implementation of a new health law cannot tell you whether the law is actually achieving its goals. A study of outcomes one year before and one year after a new law in one place may find that the law is associated with better health, but it is not strong support for inferring causation or assuming that the law would work somewhere else. This is where triangulation helps judgment: Are the findings among several studies consistent? Are the study findings consistent with our understanding of causal factors, and with experience? Are places that have the policy doing better in the outcome than places that do not? Is the study "controlling" for factors other than the new policy that could be responsible for the changes being observed? Do the people implementing or experiencing the policies perceive them to be working?

Policymakers cannot wait for perfect evidence. Rather, at its best, evidence-informed policymaking is a learning process, in which initial educated guesses are tested in practice and evaluated in a timely way. As time passes, there is more evidence and more opportunity for more rigorous evaluation. As the evidence accumulates, policymakers can revisit earlier judgments and amend, repeal, or steam ahead as the accumulating evidence warrants.

Using Evidence and Expert Knowledge to Understand and Solve "New" Problems with Law

New problems do not come with evidence-based solutions, but we can be smart about how we innovate. When a new threat to health emerges on to the legislative agenda as a "problem," lawmakers and advocates who are sincerely looking for a promising intervention face several common challenges. First, they have to get a good grip on the problem for both political and practical reasons. Problems, after all, define solutions. Second, they have to choose a legal approach to address the problem. The set of intervention options is likely to emerge quickly and reflect a variety of interests, political constraints, and ideological and psychological factors. The trick is to rely on the kinds of scientific knowledge about the problem we looked at in Chapter 5 and to use that knowledge in conjunction with expertise in how law works generally (see Chapter 6) to make "educated guesses" for policy. Even when it is not possible to anticipate whether a legal change will work, it is possible to avoid obvious mistakes. We discuss two helpful tools that you can use once you have assembled as much information as you can. These work particularly well when you bring together people with diverse expertise and perspectives on the problem you are addressing.

To illustrate, we use a real policy problem. In the early years of this century, Americans became aware that the forms of traumatic brain injury we loosely refer to as "concussions" could be a serious threat to long-term health. Football was at the heart of the matter, and football was not the sort of activity that politicians and public health advocates thought they could or should interfere with lightly. While it might be logical to ban tackle football for kids, or substantially change the rules of the game, neither the evidence nor the political will were sufficient for so drastic an intervention. Instead, some smart people defined the "problem" as how to prevent repeated concussions among student athletes. There was strong evidence that having one concussion increased the risk of another (especially if kids returned to play before they were fully healed), and secondary prevention put the focus on changing what happened to kids who were hurt, rather than changing the game.

Causal Mapping

A consensus on how a problem unfolds—i.e., the causal chain from risks to harm—the slate on which legal solutions can be written. If we can agree on the likely chain(s) of events, we can often see opportunities for interventions to reduce or eliminate risks or to change how people manage them—and often law is a way to do it. *Causal mapping* is a practical way to create this picture. We use the term *mapping* here to embrace any visual tool that purports to depict how one variable influences another or changes over time. In public health policymaking, causal maps or diagrams "can help to describe ("how things are now"), classify ("why things go together"), explain ("how things really work"), predict ("what will happen if . . . "), and decide ("what you should do now") (Swanson & Ibrahim, 2013). Pictures are a well-established tool for simplifying the complicated, and the *exercise* of trying to complete a picture is itself a useful way to question and clarify our assumptions about how things interrelate. Figure 7.1 depicts the kind of model the youth concussion stakeholders (including doctors and social scientists who understood the psychology of sports participation, parents, coaches, educators, and politicians) might have used.

The heart of the model depicts the chain of events that leads from an initial concussion to a repeat concussion and, ultimately, long-term harm. The outer boxes identify the evidence that supports each link in the chain. Given this model, we can readily see how to break the chain: Make sure that kids leave the game when they have suffered a possible concussion

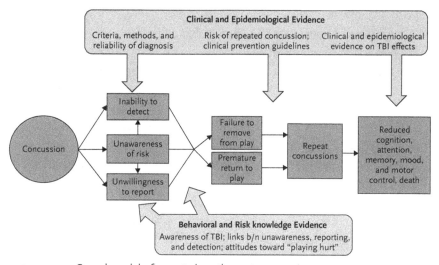

FIGURE 7.1. Causal model of repeated youth sport concussions.

This figure originally appeared in Anderson, E., & Burris, S. (2014). Researchers and Research Knowledge in Evidence-Informed Policy Innovation. In T. Voon, A. D. Mitchell & J. Liberman (Eds.), Regulating Tobacco, Alcohol and Unhealthy Foods: The Legal Issues (pp. 36-63). Abingdon, UK: Routledge.

and that they do not come back before they are healthy. In theory, one could just make rules that required those steps, but lawmakers went further by directly using legal tools to deal with the "risk factors" for failing to leave the game or coming back too soon: unawareness of the risks posed by concussion, inability to detect a concussion, and unwillingness to report a concussion. Laws in all the states now also require that coaches, athletes, and parents get some form of education about the harms of concussion and how to detect it, information that, it is hoped, will also make kids and coaches more willing to report concussions.

The Haddon Matrix

In the case of these concussion laws, the initial political instinct to focus on preventing repeat concussions made sense. As time has passed and the evidence of risk has increased, however, there may be more willingness to consider the full spectrum of risks and points of interventions. This is where a tool like the Haddon matrix can come in. William Haddon, the pioneer in the science of injury prevention whom we have already mentioned, recognized that all harms could be considered in terms of the interaction between a host, an agent, and the social and physical environment over time. The resulting typology supports a matrix of approaches to addressing population harms. A completed matrix helps identify what to target (hosts, agents, and environments) and when (before, during, and after the event).

Figure 7.2 is a representative Haddon matrix for youth sports concussion. The host is the athlete who suffers the head injury, and the agent of harm is participation in sport. The matrix points to some of the same points of intervention as the causal model we saw earlier, but it also identifies possible interventions at the preinjury phase. Can you think of ways that the rules could be changed (mandated by law if necessary) to make sure that kids of very different body sizes are not facing off against each other? What about ways law or rules could be used to make sure that the more dangerous maneuvers are taken out of the game? The matrix also gets us thinking (and hopefully doing more research) on the protective effects of equipment and field conditions, which could lead to new regulatory mandates in the same way Haddon's work led to safer road designs and air bags. Trying to assemble important possible points of intervention in this way is an extremely helpful approach to selecting the most plausible and feasible points of intervention to try.

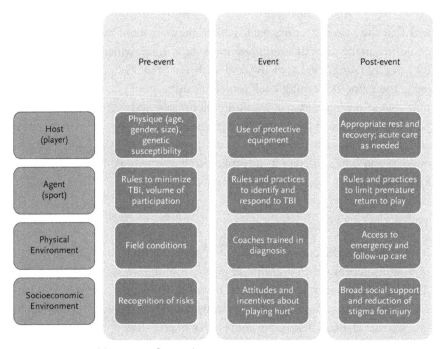

FIGURE 7.2. Haddon matrix for youth sport concussions.

This figure originally appeared in Anderson, E., & Burris, S. (2014). Researchers and Research Knowledge in Evidence-Informed Policy Innovation. In T. Voon, A. D. Mitchell & J. Liberman (Eds.), Regulating Tobacco, Alcohol and Unhealthy Foods: The Legal Issues (pp. 36-63). Abingdon, UK: Routledge.

Causal models and the Haddon matrix help you identify possible points of intervention and possible types of interventions. Epidemiological research allows us to see risk factors and causal processes. Knowledge of how law works, and of the many types of legal intervention available, gives us options. Sometimes law has been used, and thoroughly evaluated, in analogous ways, even if it has not yet been applied to a new problem. For instance, evidence that alcohol taxes reduce consumption of booze supports the hypothesis that taxes on sugar-sweetened beverages will reduce consumption of obesogenic sodas. Together, all of these tools can help us see that we often know more about how to tackle a "new" problem than we think.

Considering Broader Impact and Cross-Sectoral Cooperation: Health in All Policies and Health Impact Assessment

So far in this chapter, we have been focused on the relatively simple case of devising a specific legal intervention for a discreet, well-defined, and finite problem like brain injuries in sports. This is important work, but, in a broader perspective, we still have to deal with two other, related issues in policy development. The first issue is that many of our most significant health problems, like obesity, actually require a response coordinated across many policy domains. Obesity results in part from individual food options and preferences, but its prevalence in a given population is influenced by a wide variety of factors including the transportation and recreation options people have and even whether it is safe to go out and play in their neighborhood. Thus comprehensive responses to obesity require cross-sector collaborations that involve officials and policy experts involved in transportation, recreation, public safety, zoning/land use, education, housing, and more. That points to the second issue, which is that many non-health policies have important health effects that may not be considered in the policymaking process. Decisions about zoning, for example, influence the location and amount of affordable housing in a community, and housing is a basic determinant of health. Yet health considerations have not historically been central to zoning decision-making.

Health in All Policies (HiAP) is defined as "is an approach to public policies across sectors that systematically takes into account the health implications of decisions, seeks synergies and avoids harmful health impacts in order to improve population health and health equity" (Tang, Ståhl, Bettcher, & De Leeuw, 2014). It is both a way of thinking and, its proponents hope, a way of doing business in government. The two are linked. It is important for more people in more parts of the government and the community to understand the social determinants of health and realize that health is a lot more than going to the doctor. That understanding will not help much, though, unless it is built into policymaking and enforcement. HiAP works if transportation and housing and law enforcement officials in a city take on the promotion of health as part of their jobs and are willing to work together to develop and implement healthy policies. There are numerous examples of successful HiAP efforts across the country; for example, the HiAP task force in the Seattle area has led to "the inclusion of health-based metrics and objectives in city and county land use and transportation plans" (Wernham & Teutsch, 2015).

An important tool in a HiAP approach is the health impact assessment (HIA). Modeled on the more familiar environmental impact assessments, HIAs use a variety of relatively rapid methods (including literature reviews, modeling, qualitative research, interviews with stakeholders and experts, and compilation and analysis of existing data) to systematically identify possible health effects of proposed policies and assess their severity. For example, researchers in Atlanta conducted a two-year HIA on the proposed Atlanta BeltLine project, a multibillion-dollar redevelopment scheme incorporating transit, trails, parks, retail, and housing. Its recommendations, most of which were incorporated into the project plan, included prioritizing construction of trails and greenspace rather than residential and retail construction, making health an explicit goal in project priority setting, and ensuring that affordable housing was included (Ross et al., 2012). HIA results can be used to enhance positive results, as the Atlanta story shows, but also to avoid or mitigate negative effects—or to support a decision to abandon the proposal altogether. A few states have even mandated the use of HIAs in certain situations.

Conclusion

In public heath, the difference between an effective intervention and an ineffective one is measured in injuries and deaths. The stakes are high. Policymakers and advocates cannot see into the future, but we can think carefully and use the best available evidence and knowledge. "Evidence-informed" policy requires that all participants in the policy process, including community advocates, government officials, legislators and their staffs, and even the media, take facts seriously. It is the business of policymakers to make policy without the benefit of complete data to solve problems that cannot wait. Doing so effectively requires affirmative efforts of the kind we have outlined here to understand the problem being addressed, to explicitly define how law might influence that problem, to look at actual evidence that informs the definition of the problem or solution, and to test and tweak policy proposals. It is good to learn from our policy mistakes, but it is even better to learn *before* we make them.

Further Reading

Anderson, E., & Burris, S. (2014). Researchers and Research Knowledge in Evidence-Informed Policy Innovation. In T. Voon, A. D. Mitchell, & J. Liberman (Eds.), *Regulating Tobacco, Alcohol and Unhealthy Foods: The Legal Issues* (pp. 36–63). Abingdon, UK: Routledge. Also available at http://publichealthlawresearch.org/sites/default/files/downloads/product/PHLRBetterGuessing_2014March_0.pdf

Haidt, J. (2012). *The Righteous Mind: Why Good People Are Divided by Politics and Religion*. New York: Pantheon Books.

Kahneman, D. (2013). *Thinking, Fast and Slow*. New York: Farrar, Straus and Giroux.

Miller, T. R., & Hendrie, D. (2013). Cost-Effectiveness and Cost-Benefit Analysis of Public Health Laws. In A. Wagenaar & S. Burris (Eds.), *Public Health Law Research: Theory and Methods* (pp. 347–378). San Francisco: Jossey-Bass.

Pew Charitable Trusts/Robert Wood Johnson Foundation Health Impact Project. (n.d.). Available from http://www.pewtrusts.org/en/projects/health-impact-project

III | The Power to Act
LEGAL AUTHORITY AND
ITS LIMITATIONS

8 | The Constitution, Federalism, and Federal Preemption

Learning Objectives

- Understand the role of the US Constitution in setting the framework for the federal government.
- Define *federalism* and explain how the Constitution allocates power between the federal and state governments.
- Explain the difference between express preemption and implied preemption and understand the role that preemption plays in public health policy.

Introduction

A new public health law should be rooted in the best available evidence, but it must also be legally sound. The city council, legislature, or agency enacting a law must have the legal *authority* to do so, and the law must not *exceed the limits* imposed by any higher law, like the state or federal constitution. It does not matter how effective a suggested policy would be if it is struck down in court.

This chapter focuses on the constitutional division of lawmaking authority in our nation's complicated federal system, in which states and the federal government share governmental authority. The chapter starts with some background on the US Constitution, legal authority, and governmental structure before diving into the issue of *federalism*—the relationship between the federal government and the states. It particular, it examines the legal doctrine of *federal preemption*—the ability of the federal government to limit the authority of state and local governments—using the example of tobacco regulation to provide context. We explore how the legal authority to engage in any particular public health action depends on both what level of government (federal, state, or local) and what branch of government (legislative or executive) is considering the action.

The Constitution

Under our system of government, questions of legal authority—questions about who has the power to do what—ultimately track back to the national Constitution. The US Constitution allocates power between the federal (national) government and state governments, sets limits on the government's powers, and defines the roles of the three different branches of the federal government.

Drafted at the Constitutional Convention of 1787, the Constitution was designed to remedy some of the problems with the Articles of Confederation, the first compact binding the newly independent states. Under the Articles of Confederation, the powers of the national government were quite limited; reacting to the abuses of the British government, the states zealously guarded their own authority. The national government was authorized to conduct diplomacy with foreign governments and engage in war, but, critically, it had no authority to raise money through taxation. Instead, it was dependent on voluntary contributions from the states, which were not reliably forthcoming. And even in the narrow areas where the Articles of Confederation granted the national legislature some lawmaking power, the national government had no ability to enforce its decisions. (The national government consisted solely of a legislature; there was no executive branch and no permanent court system.) As a result, Alexander Hamilton (1787) lamented that the country was left with the "the extraordinary spectacle of a government destitute even of the . . . power to enforce the execution of its own laws."

When this design proved unworkable, the delegates to the Constitutional Convention sought to establish a much stronger federal government while still leaving broad swaths of authority to the individual states. As discussed in Chapter 9, the Constitution gave the newly designed legislature, Congress, far broader powers than those set out in the Articles of Confederation, including the power to "lay and collect taxes." The Constitution also set up an executive branch headed by the president to implement and enforce the law and a judicial branch headed by the Supreme Court to resolve disputes. Division of the government into three separate branches—legislative, executive, and judicial—was "designed to create a system of checks and balances and lessen the possibility of tyrannical rule" (Chemerinsky, 2015).

When the Constitution was sent to the states for ratification, several states insisted on the addition of clearer protections for individual rights. This led to the creation of the Bill of Rights, consisting of 10 amendments that were quickly added to the newly ratified Constitution. The Bill of Rights includes some of the fundamental protections—for freedom of speech and religion, for due process of law, for trial by jury in criminal cases—that are commonly associated with the Constitution. Importantly, the protections in the Bill of Rights only apply to actions by the *government*, not by private parties. For example, the government cannot fire an employee for engaging in political activity outside of work, because it would violate the First Amendment's protections for free speech. But private-sector employees do not have similar protection against being fired for expressing their political views, unless a state law provides it. (While the Bill of Rights was originally thought to place limits only on the *federal* government, most of those same protections now also apply to state and local governments as a result of later court decisions.)

In many cases, the meaning of a constitutional provision is not self-evident. The Constitution consists largely of somewhat vague pronouncements (like the Eighth Amendment's prohibition of "cruel and unusual punishment") that can be interpreted in many different ways. Writing in 1787, the authors could not possibly have anticipated all of the issues that might be raised more than 200 years later. Thus, judges need an explicit, defensible method of interpreting the Constitution and applying its provisions to modern-day concerns. Methods of interpretation are hotly contested because they inform how Supreme Court justices and lower court judges make decisions. For example, some judges believe that that Constitution's meaning was fixed in 1787 and is essentially un-changing. In this view, the role of judges is to seek out and implement that pre-existing meaning. Others contend that the meaning of the Constitution must change as society evolves and that the Constitution's adaptability is the source of its strength. Table 8.1 encapsulates the leading approaches and their challenges.

Legal Authority for Public Health Measures

With that background in mind, we move to some general principles of legal authority to enact public health measures. When considering

TABLE 8.1. Theories of Constitutional Interpretation

INTERPRETIVE METHOD	DEFINITION	CHALLENGES
Textualism	Follow the "plain meaning" of the Constitution's words.	Many questions are not clearly answered by the text; words are subject to multiple meanings.
Originalism	Follow either the "original intent" of the Framers or the "original public meaning" of the Constitution (what it was understood to mean at the time it was written)	Framers could not foresee all issues; original intent/meaning often not known; Framers did not agree with each other on all issues
Constitutional Principles	When meaning is unclear, draw upon the structure and core principles/values of the Constitution (e.g., protection of minorities, self-governance)	Disagreement about what the core principles are; principles may be in conflict; may not be clear which way principles cut in any given case
Pragmatism	When meaning is unclear, look at the consequences of a decision and consider its effects	Consequences may be unknown or unknowable; gives judges considerable power to impose own views and biases
Precedent/ Tradition	Follow the way courts have interpreted an issue in the past	Sometimes courts get it wrong; society changes its views on issues over time

whether a government entity (e.g., a local city council) can enact a particular public health measure, there are two essential questions to ask: (a) Does the government entity have the authority to regulate in this particular area? and (b) Does this measure violate the Constitution or conflict with any other higher laws? The federal government, state governments, and local governments all have broad authority to regulate in order to protect public health, so the answer to the first question is usually yes. The second question arises because even if the government entity has authority to pass the law in question, the law may still be void because it conflicts with a "higher" law. The Constitution is the supreme law of the land (and the state constitution has the same pride of place within each state's law), and, generally, state laws cannot conflict with federal ones and local ordinances cannot conflict with state laws.

When considering both of these questions, the courts have traditionally given governments significant leeway. More often than not, they uphold public health measures even if they impose some limitations on personal autonomy or private business interests. This is at least in part in deference to democratic decision-making; if tough choices are to be made about how to protect the public, courts generally prefer that democratically elected officials make the call. Additionally, judges recognize that they are not scientific experts, and therefore they rely on legislatures and specialized agencies to review the evidence and choose a course of action when there is scientific debate. As we will see, however, there are plenty of cases in which public health measures have been struck down by the courts on constitutional or other grounds. These cases are interesting and important because they touch on the meaning and importance of values such as free speech, liberty, and freedom from racial discrimination.

Although courts are generally deferential to governments' efforts to address public health concerns, the specifics of the legal authority to pursue public health measures and the procedures for doing so can vary considerably between differently situated policymakers. This is true with respect to both the *vertical* distribution of power between the federal, state, and local governments and the *horizontal* distribution of power between legislative bodies (such as state legislatures) and executive entities (such as state health departments).

The federal government and state governments have parallel structures. Each state has a legislative branch, an executive branch (headed by a governor), and a judicial branch (headed by the state's highest court). Municipalities, such as cities, also divide power between an executive (often a mayor) and a legislature (a city council), but they do not have their own judicial branches, and the separation of powers between the executive and the legislature may be more fluid (e.g., the mayor may also be a member of the city council). As we will discuss, the basis of legal authority is different for each level and branch of government—though the spheres of authority overlap considerably. Similarly, the procedures vary between levels of government. As a general rule of thumb, the processes for enacting a law or promulgating a regulation are less formal at the state level than the federal level and even less formal at the local level. Nonetheless, required procedural formalities must be observed, even at the local level. For example, local public health laws have been challenged on the basis that council members violated "open meetings laws" by conferring in private or failing to provide proper notice of upcoming meetings.

Federalism

The US government is organized on the principle of "federalism," meaning that power is shared between the federal government and state governments, with each having their own spheres of authority. The Constitution defines the relationship between the federal and state governments with two separate provisions. First, the Supremacy Clause provides that the Constitution and federal laws are the "supreme Law of the Land" (United States Constitution, 1787). In the event of any conflict, federal law takes precedence over state or local law. (We return to this momentarily.) Second, the 10th Amendment provides that "[t]he powers not delegated to the United States by the Constitution, nor prohibited to it by the States, are reserved to the States respectively, or to the people." This amendment, the last one in the Bill of Rights, expresses the principle that, absent a conflicting federal law, states retain the traditional powers that they possessed prior to the ratification of the Constitution. This includes the states' historic "police powers," discussed further in Chapter 10, to regulate for the health, safety, and welfare of their residents.

Assuming they are all acting within their legal authority, there is nothing that prohibits federal, state, and local governments from working to address the same public health issue in different ways. Indeed, this is often what occurs. For example, the federal government requires K-12 schools that receive federal funds to meet certain nutritional guidelines for food sold in the school. In addition, most states have their own guidelines for school nutrition, and these requirements may exceed the minimum requirements set by the federal government. At the local level, school boards are also able to set their own nutrition requirements—as long as they do not conflict with federal and state standards. Local school districts can also develop complementary policies and programs by, for example, prohibiting the advertising of unhealthy food and beverages on campus.

Historically, state and local governments have taken the lead in addressing issues of public health, and local health departments still carry out many of the critical day-to-day functions of public health. However, the federal government's role in public health has been increasing steadily over time. This is in large part due to the recognition that in an interdependent, industrialized, and globalized society, few issues of public health are truly local in nature. For example, the creation of the US Food and Drug Administration in the early 20th century was due in large part to the realization that the mass production and mass marketing of food and drugs across state lines necessitated a federal oversight role.

Despite the increasing role of the federal government in public health matters, state and local governments still play a critical role as "laboratories of democracy," testing out new policy approaches that can be studied and, if successful, shared with other jurisdictions. Indeed, many of the most critical innovations in public health, from smoke-free laws to water fluoridation, began as local experiments that only spread to other jurisdictions after their feasibility and efficacy had been established. In recent years, however, antiregulatory forces have waged a political and legal battle aimed at aggressively limiting state and local authority to innovate new approaches to public health (and other social and economic) problems.

Preemption

Different levels of government often work in parallel, and frequently in coordination with one another, to address the same public health challenge collaboratively. But sometimes the relationship is fraught, with the federal and state governments pursing different—or even opposite—approaches. As noted earlier, the Supremacy Clause elevates the Constitution and federal laws over other laws in the event of conflict. The same idea, in somewhat different legal form, applies to the relationship of state to local law, as we will explain in Chapter 10.

The doctrine of *preemption* implements this principle. It not only establishes that higher law prevails in the event of a conflict, but it also more generally empowers the higher-level government to block or override the actions of lower levels of government. Federal preemption comes in two forms: *express* and *implied.* Express preemption is implicated when Congress passes a law that specifically and directly limits state (and therefore also local) authority in some particular way. Implied preemption occurs when courts find that state or local regulations are inconsistent with a federal regulatory scheme created by Congress, even though such laws are not expressly preempted. The decades-long effort to reduce tobacco use provides a useful case study for exploring the interplay between state and federal regulation, particularly with respect to issues of preemption. This example highlights the ongoing legal and political struggle over where important health policy decisions should be made.

Tobacco Regulation: An Example

Tobacco regulation is often identified as one of the greatest public health success stories of the 20th century, but it is a story of incomplete success at best. In 1964, when US Surgeon General Luther Terry released his landmark report on the health consequences of smoking, more than 40% of American adults were regular smokers. Today, that percentage is around 15%, and experts estimate that tobacco control measures have prevented more than 8 million premature deaths since 1964 (Holford et al., 2014). However, smoking still kills more than 480,000 Americans every year, and it remains the leading cause of preventable death in the United States. Moreover, the impact on health-related disparities is stark. The smoking rate is gradually approaching zero for adults with graduate degrees, but it remains stubbornly high for adults without a college degree, living in poverty, or residing in rural areas.

In the 1950s, the scientific community came to a consensus that smoking was deadly, but instead of acknowledging the health harms of smoking, the tobacco industry vigorously denied that such harms existed. In a 2006 decision finding that the major cigarette companies had violated federal racketeering laws, Judge Gladys Kessler found a long pattern of deliberate deception:

> From at least 1953 until at least 2000, [cigarette manufacturers] repeatedly, consistently, vigorously—and falsely—denied the existence of any adverse health effects from smoking. Moreover, they mounted a coordinated, well-financed, sophisticated public relations campaign to attack and distort the scientific evidence demonstrating the relationship between smoking and disease, claiming that the link between the two was still an "open question." Finally, in doing so, they ignored the massive documentation in their internal corporate files from their own scientists, executives, and public relations people that . . . there was "little basis for disputing the findings [of the 1964 Surgeon General's Report concluding that smoking causes lung cancer]" (*United States v. Philip Morris USA, Inc.*, D.C. Cir. 2006).

Although tobacco companies now grudgingly concede that smoking is deadly, they continue to aggressively market their products, spending close to $25 million *each day* on advertising and promotion. Considerable evidence suggests that this marketing continues to make tobacco products more attractive to youth, despite restrictions imposed by the Master

Settlement Agreement (discussed later in this chapter). In seeking to limit regulation and protect itself from legal liability, the industry has used preemption as a key legal tool.

Express Preemption

The year after the 1964 Surgeon General's Report was released, Congress passed the Federal Cigarette Labeling and Advertising Act (FLCAA), requiring warnings on cigarette packages for the first time (these read, "Caution: Cigarette Smoking May Be Hazardous to Your Health"). Though this often presented as a public health success, it was actually the tobacco industry, which realized that some form of regulation was inevitable, that was behind this law. As historian Allan Brandt summarizes, "If the industry could not avoid government action, it could ensure that the action was taken in their preferred venue: the U.S. Congress" (Brandt, 2007). Working with Congress, the tobacco industry ensured that the law included a preemption provision prohibiting any state or local government from requiring its own warnings on cigarette packages or advertisements. This was an example of *express preemption*: the law was explicit (express) in limiting state and local authority.

Express preemption is often problematic from a public health perspective because it effectively means that the federal law sets a "ceiling" on regulation; states are barred from enacting laws that would provide greater protection for public health than the federal standard. Here, the effect of the FCLAA was to prevent the states from innovating by determining what types of cigarette labeling requirements would be most effective. Absent preemption, states could have required vivid graphics, for example, along with the federal textual warning. More troublingly, the FCLAA's preemption provision was not limited to warnings; it more broadly preempted state and local governments from engaging in *any* regulation of the advertising or promotion of tobacco products.

The tobacco companies, who had powerful allies in Congress, argued that such preemption was necessary to avoid "a multiplicity of State and local regulations pertaining to labeling of cigarette packages [that] could create chaotic marketing conditions" by requiring different labeling for cigarettes sold in different parts of the country (Senate of the United States, 1965). In nearly any context, the need for a uniform, consistent regulatory scheme is the most commonly asserted argument in favor of preemption. While uniformity and consistency do make it easier for businesses to operate, industry groups often advocate for federal preemption for an additional reason: the rules set in preemptive federal statutes are often less stringent that those that at least some states would otherwise set. That was surely the case with the FCLAA, which cut off state efforts to design their own health warnings and blocked state and local efforts to limit tobacco advertising.

When express preemption is involved, the extent of the preemption depends on an analysis of the specific wording used in preemption provisions, and there are often disputes about what exactly Congress meant. Usually, it is clear that Congress intended to preempt *some* state laws, but it may be unclear *which* laws fall within the preemption provision's reach. In the case of the FCLAA, two major disputes about the law's preemptive scope popped up decades after the law was first enacted. In both cases, public health advocates sought to work around the FCLAA's preemption clause to pursue tobacco measures that were not barred by federal law, but they were eventually stymied by the Supreme Court's broad reading of the FCLAA's preemptive scope.

In *Cipollone v. Liggett Group, Inc.* (1992), the Supreme Court considered whether the FCLAA preempted state court lawsuits against the tobacco industry. The relevant preemption clause of the FCLAA read: "No requirement or prohibition based on smoking and health shall be imposed under State law with respect to the advertising or promotion of any cigarettes the packages of which are labeled in conformity with the provisions of this chapter." The issue in *Cipollone* was whether the statute's language only preempted laws and regulations set forth by state legislatures and administrative agencies or whether it also barred *lawsuits* against the tobacco industry.

The Supreme Court concluded that lawsuits asserting that the tobacco industry had failed to adequately warn consumers about the dangers of smoking were indeed preempted by the FCLAA. It reasoned that judicial decisions imposing liability on tobacco companies in such cases would imply that the tobacco companies' "advertising or promotions should have included additional, or more clearly stated, warnings," and would thereby create the non-uniform standards that Congress sought to avoid.

Nearly 10 years later, in *Lorillard v. Reilly* (2001), the Supreme Court reexamined the same preemption clause in another context. In that case, the Supreme Court struck down a Massachusetts regulation that prohibited outdoor tobacco advertising near schools and playgrounds. Stressing that the regulation of land usage is a quintessential local power, Massachusetts had argued that the FCLAA preempted state law requirements relating to *what* could be said in tobacco advertisements but not laws about *where* such ads could be placed. The Supreme Court rejected this argument. Looking at the plain language of the preemption clause, the majority concluded that the FCLAA made no such distinction between location-based and content-based regulation and that the Massachusetts regulation was therefore preempted. It noted that a contrary holding would have permitted states and localities to use location-based restrictions to essentially eliminate outdoor tobacco advertising by very narrowly limiting the locations where tobacco advertising was permissible (an outcome that, in the Supreme Court's opinion, Congress sought to avoid).

There are two interesting postscripts to this story. The first is that although states were preempted from passing laws to regulate tobacco advertisements, they eventually succeeded in doing so indirectly. Starting in 1994, every state filed a lawsuit against the major cigarette companies in order to recover funds that the states were spending on treating smoking-related illnesses. (Since the legal claims at issue were not premised on the industry's advertising or its failure to warn of health risks, they were not preempted.) These lawsuits culminated in the 1998 Master Settlement Agreement (MSA) between the cigarette companies and 46 state attorneys general. In the MSA, the companies agreed to make major monetary payments to the states and to reform their marketing practices. For example, the companies agreed to end the use of cartoon characters in advertising, discontinue brand name sponsorships of most athletic events, and stop using billboards and other outdoor advertising (except at retail stores). Because these commitments were made as part of a voluntary settlement—and not imposed through state law—they were not preempted by the FCLAA.

Second, in 2009, Congress decided to revise the language of the FCLAA's preemption provision. In the Family Smoking Prevention and Tobacco Control Act (FSPTCA), it added language stating that "a State or locality may enact statutes and promulgate regulations, based on smoking and health, that take effect after the effective date of the [FSPTCA] imposing specific bans or restrictions on the time, place, and manner, but not content, of the advertising or promotion of any cigarettes." Congress changed the law to eliminate the preemption that *Lorillard* had found in the earlier version of the FCLAA. Although they still cannot regulate the content of cigarette advertisements, states and localities can now restrict where, when, and in what form they appear (subject to First Amendment limitations discussed in Chapter 13).

Implied Preemption

The second type of federal preemption is *implied preemption*, which takes several forms. Under this doctrine, even if Congress has not explicitly said that state law is preempted, state laws cannot stand if they are clearly inconsistent with federal law (*conflict preemption*), pose an obstacle to the fulfillment of Congressional objectives (*obstacle preemption*), or interfere with a comprehensive regulatory system set up by Congress (*field preemption*). The Supreme Court has repeatedly stated that in areas of traditional state authority—including public health—there is a "presumption against preemption." This means that if Congress's intent is not clear, the courts should lean against finding state and local laws preempted. As the Supreme Court has explained, "[this] approach is consistent with both federalism concerns and the historic primacy of state regulation of matters of health and safety" (*Medtronic, Inc. v. Lohr*, 1996).

Implied federal preemption has not played a major role in the story of tobacco regulation. However, in a recent case, a federal appeals court ruled that any state products liability lawsuit based on a theory that cigarettes are "inherently defective" would be preempted under the doctrine of obstacle preemption (*Graham v. R.J. Reynolds Tobacco Co.*, 2015). The court reasoned that (a) a court decision finding cigarettes to be "defective" would function, "in essence, as a ban on cigarettes," and (b) this would conflict with Congress's conclusion—expressed through the FCLAA and other statutes governing cigarette sales—that cigarettes should be regulated but not banned. The court wrote: "Congress has known about the dangers of cigarettes [and] has regulated cigarettes for many years. But it has never banned them. Indeed, regulation of cigarettes rests on the assumption that they will still be sold and that consumers will maintain a 'right to choose to smoke or not to smoke.'"

Although it dealt with whether or not lawsuits were preempted, the logic of the decision would suggest that if Congress has regulated (but not banned) any harmful product, states and localities may not prohibit its sale. If that logic were extended to other cases, it could strip states and local governments of a great deal of regulatory power. For example, communities around the country have banned (or strictly limited) the use of trans-fats in prepared foods. The federal government has not banned them but has instead regulated them with labeling requirements. Using the court's logic, the federal regulation of trans-fats could be read to presume their availability and therefore preempt local bans. As this suggests, preemption can be a powerful legal tool for industries fighting against regulation and seeking to shift legal doctrine in their favor.

The *Graham* decision was appealed, however, and it was vacated by an *en banc* panel (a panel consisting of all of the judges on the court) of the same appeals court two years later (*Graham v. R.J. Reynolds Tobacco Co.*, 2017). Contrary to the first appeals court decision, the *en banc* panel concluded that "[n]othing in [federal law] reflects a federal objective to permit the sale or manufacture of cigarettes." Rather, the FCLAA and other cigarette-related laws set the requirements that tobacco companies must follow *if* cigarettes are sold. According to this second opinion, Congress never sought to guarantee that cigarettes could be sold, and therefore the lawsuits at issue in *Graham* did not stand as an obstacle to the accomplishment of any federal objectives. The court closed by referencing the presumption against preemption, writing:

> We may not supersede the "historic police powers of the States" unless it is the "clear and manifest purpose of Congress." And "[t]hat assumption applies with particular force when Congress has legislated in a field traditionally occupied by the States."
>
> R.J. Reynolds and Philip Morris would have us presume that Congress established a right to sell cigarettes based on a handful of federal labeling requirements. We decline to do so. We discern no "clear and manifest purpose" to displace tort liability.

Although the implied preemption argument was ultimately rejected in the *Graham* case, it will certainly be raised again in challenges to other tobacco regulations or lawsuits.

Outside of the tobacco context, courts have found implied federal preemption in a variety of public health cases, including cases relating to state regulation of medical devices and automobile safety. As a general rule, however, courts have been more willing to find implied preemption in areas of law where the Constitution grants Congress the primary regulatory rule, such as in cases touching on immigration, foreign affairs, and maritime law.

Lessons Learned? Preemption Law and Politics in Public Health Today

This brief review of preemption in the context of tobacco shows the role that preemption plays in policing the blurry line between state and federal authority. It also suggests that preemption is usually tied up with issues of politics and power—in particular, with calculations by advocates about which level of government will be most amenable to their wishes. Those with influence in Congress can seek to use preemption as a way of staving off more aggressive regulation by states and localities. In the case of the FCLAA, the tobacco industry used its sway over Congress to insert a broad preemption provision into the law, and this provision continued to block attempts at state- and local-level regulation—as well as lawsuits—for decades. This bulwark did not protect the industry forever, though. States found creative ways to push back against the harm that tobacco use was causing their citizens, and in the 1990s the tobacco industry eventually yielded to the pressure of state lawsuits and agreed to major restrictions on its marketing practices. In the 2000s, as political dynamics shifted further, Congress rolled back much of the FLCAA's preemption of state and local authority.

Similar preemption dynamics continue to play out in a variety of other contexts. For example, when cities around the country started enacting ordinances requiring calorie information on restaurant menus, the restaurant industry began pressing for a federal law that would set minimum requirements but preempt more stringent local laws. In 2010, Congress included a menu labeling requirement in the Affordable Care Act—but also preempted states or localities from imposing any additional obligations on the chain restaurants subject to the federal law. To the consternation of public health advocates, the federal law sets the "ceiling," and local jurisdictions cannot require different or additional labeling.

As discussed in Chapter 10, industries seeking to avoid or minimize regulation also pursue favorable *state* laws that preempt local laws. This is currently one of the most active battlegrounds in public health policy, with ongoing efforts to preempt local laws relating to gun control, paid leave, fracking, obesity prevention, and more.

Conclusion

After providing some background on the Constitution and governmental authority, this chapter discussed *federalism,* which deals with the distribution of authority between the federal, state, and local governments. In particular, it focused on the legal doctrine of *preemption*, which is derived from the Supremacy Clause of the Constitution. Preemption empowers "higher" levels of government to override or block the actions of "lower" levels of government. From a public health perspective, preemption can be problematic if it limits the flexibility of local governments to address public health challenges, particularly because local innovation has historically been the source of key breakthroughs in public health policy.

Further Reading

Brandt, A. M. (2007). *The Cigarette Century: The Rise, Fall, and Deadly Persistence of the Product that Defined America.* New York: Basic Books.

Clinton, R. N. (1989). A Brief History of the Adoption of the United States Constitution. *Iowa Law Review, 75,* 891.

9 | Federal Public Health Authority

Learning Objectives

- Understand that Congress can only exercise the powers enumerated in the Constitution and the implications of this limitation.
- Describe how Congress's use of the Commerce Clause has evolved.
- List the three ways that Congress can use its taxing/spending authority to influence public health.
- Summarize the importance for public health of the Supreme Court's decision in *National Federation of Independent Business (NFIB) v. Sebelius.*
- Describe how Congress can delegate its authority to federal agencies.

Introduction: Federal Public Health Authority

The Constitution provides the general framework for the organization of the federal government and its powers in relation to state and local governments. In some areas, such as immigration and foreign relations, the federal government is paramount. In other fields, state and local governments have traditionally played the lead role. Traditional state fields include public health and healthcare but also a wide variety of others including education, criminal justice, and insurance regulation. Even in these areas, however, the federal government has extremely powerful levers it can pull to exert its influence and push policy in its preferred direction.

Take, for example, how Congress used its spending power to get states to raise the minimum age for alcohol sales. When the majority of states lowered their minimum drinking age from 21 to 18 in the 1970s, they experienced an increase in traffic fatalities caused by inebriated younger drivers. To address the problem, Congress wanted to raise the minimum drinking age back to 21, but it ran into a constitutional obstacle. Not only is public health a traditional area of state regulation, but the 21st Amendment to the Constitution, which repealed Prohibition in 1933, gave the states the primary authority to regulate alcohol sales and use within their borders. Thus Congress arguably lacked the legal authority to directly increase the minimum sales age. So, instead, it passed a law withholding some federal funding for transportation projects from states that would not raise their drinking age to 21. The Supreme Court upheld this indirect approach (*South Dakota v. Dole*, 1987).

Even though Congress can only exercise the limited number of powers allotted to it by the Constitution, those powers are, in practice, quite extensive. After introducing Congress's enumerated powers, this chapter focuses on the two that are most central to federal public health lawmaking: the Commerce Clause and the Taxing and Spending Clause. Neither speaks of health, but in practice Congress can pursue virtually any type of public health objective using one or the other of these constitutional tools. The chapter concludes with a discussion of how Congress can delegate its powers to federal agencies.

Enumerated Powers

Under the Constitution, the federal government is one of *enumerated powers*, meaning that Congress only has the authority specifically granted to it in the Constitution. Any law that Congress passes must be supported by one of its enumerated, or listed, powers. Beyond that, how Congress chooses to prioritize its actions is its prerogative: the federal government is one of limited powers, not affirmative duties. Because there is no constitutional right to health—or to housing, education, or other basic needs—Congress is not required to ensure that everyone has adequate health insurance or to prepare for infectious disease outbreaks. Instead, we rely on our democratic process to encourage our representatives in Congress to "promote the general welfare."

The powers allotted to Congress are primarily enumerated in Article 1, Section 8 of the Constitution (Box 9.1). If Congress is unable to sufficiently ground a law in one of these powers, courts can strike down that law if it is challenged.

In the seminal case of *McCulloch v. Maryland* (1819), the U.S. Supreme Court upheld the power of Congress to create the Bank of the United States, even though no enumerated power specifically mentions the creation of a bank. In an opinion by Chief Justice

BOX 9.1 CONGRESS'S ENUMERATED POWERS UNDER ARTICLE I OF THE CONSTITUTION

1. The Congress shall have power to lay and collect taxes, duties, imposts and excises, to pay the debts and provide for the common defense and general welfare of the United States; but all duties, imposts and excises shall be uniform throughout the United States;
2. To borrow money on the credit of the United States;
3. To regulate commerce with foreign nations, and among the several states, and with the Indian tribes;
4. To establish a uniform rule of naturalization, and uniform laws on the subject of bankruptcies throughout the United States;
5. To coin money, regulate the value thereof, and of foreign coin, and fix the standard of weights and measures;
6. To provide for the punishment of counterfeiting the securities and current coin of the United States;
7. To establish post offices and post roads;
8. To promote the progress of science and useful arts, by securing for limited times to authors and inventors the exclusive right to their respective writings and discoveries;
9. To constitute tribunals inferior to the Supreme Court;
10. To define and punish piracies and felonies committed on the high seas, and offenses against the law of nations;
11. To declare war, grant letters of marque and reprisal, and make rules concerning captures on land and water;
12. To raise and support armies, but no appropriation of money to that use shall be for a longer term than two years;
13. To provide and maintain a navy;
14. To make rules for the government and regulation of the land and naval forces;
15. To provide for calling forth the militia to execute the laws of the union, suppress insurrections and repel invasions;
16. To provide for organizing, arming, and disciplining, the militia, and for governing such part of them as may be employed in the service of the United States, reserving to the states respectively, the appointment of the officers, and the authority of training the militia according to the discipline prescribed by Congress;
17. To exercise exclusive legislation in all cases whatsoever, over such District (not exceeding ten miles square) as may, by cession of particular states, and the acceptance of Congress, become the seat of the government of the United States, and to exercise like authority over all places purchased by the consent of the legislature of the state in which the same shall be, for the erection of forts, magazines, arsenals, dockyards, and other needful buildings; and

18. To make all laws which shall be necessary and proper for carrying into execution the foregoing powers, and all other powers vested by this Constitution in the government of the United States, or in any department or officer thereof.

Note: Section 5 of the 14th Amendment also gives Congress the power to enforce the amendment's protections of due process and equal protection under the law.

John Marshall, the Supreme Court cautioned against an overly literal and narrow interpretation of the Congress's powers, writing that by its nature, a constitution provides only the "great outlines" of the government's structure. Congress, the Supreme Court reasoned, should be given leeway to determine *how* to carry out its enumerated powers. Establishing a bank was a permitted "incidental or implied" power that would help the federal government to collect taxes, borrow money, and support an army and navy (all powers that are enumerated). From that time onward, the Supreme Court has generally construed Congress's enumerated powers broadly. Thus, even though some of the powers Article I lists are quite specific, the list as a whole is interpreted by the courts to provide Congress with wide-ranging authority to address virtually any subject.

A number of specific powers, such as the power to enter into treaties or grant patents for inventions, have relevance for public health that will not be explored here. But as a general rule, two powers loom largest in public health and most other domestic policy contexts: the power to regulate interstate commerce and the power to tax and spend. In our interconnected national economy, most laws can be framed as an attempt to regulate interstate commerce. Even when this is not the case, the federal government can usually influence the conduct of individuals, businesses, and states through taxes or spending.

Commerce Clause Power

The Constitution's Commerce Clause gives Congress the authority to regulate "commerce . . . among the several States, and with the Indian Tribes." Deciphering the meaning of this clause requires figuring out what counts as "commerce," a question that has bedeviled the Supreme Court repeatedly for the past two centuries. The Supreme Court settled on its current approach in the late 1930s and 1940s, when it concluded that Congress was not limited to directly regulating the movement of goods and services between states but could also legislate with respect to anything that had a "substantial effect" on interstate commerce (*U.S. v. Darby Lumber Co.*, 1941). Thus, for example, Congress could set workplace safety standards, even though such laws did not directly regulate economic transactions crossing state lines. The Supreme Court also articulated a related *aggregate effects doctrine*, under which the Commerce Clause permitted Congress to regulate activities that, viewed in isolation, had a negligible impact on commerce, so long as those actions would substantially affect commerce if many people engaged in the same action (*Wickard v. Filburn*, 1942). This allowed Congress to regulate activity that occurred solely within state lines, like a single farmer growing wheat, so long as the cumulative effect of such activity could have substantial effects on interstate commerce.

Combined, these two doctrines gave Congress extremely broad authority to regulate economic activity, and it proceeded to base an exceedingly wide range of actions on its extensive Commerce Clause authority. These included civil rights laws, criminal laws, licensing requirements, laws regulating food and drugs, insurance regulations, and more. Indeed, the Commerce Clause has been referred to as "the principal constitutional foundation of the modern regulatory state" (Coan, 2012).

Between 1937 and 1995, not one law was struck down on the grounds that it exceeded Congress's Commerce Clause authority. For example, in *Heart of Atlanta Motel v. United States* (1964), the Supreme Court upheld the 1964 Civil Rights Act, which prohibited racial discrimination by private businesses open to the public. The Court rejected the argument that Congress's authority under the Commerce Clause did not extend to the regulation of local companies that did not conduct business across state lines. Alluding to the aggregate effects doctrine, it concluded that the "disruptive effect that racial discrimination has on commercial intercourse" in the economy as a whole provided the necessary link to the Commerce Clause. Similarly, in *Perez v. United States* (1971), the Supreme Court ruled that a federal criminal law prohibiting "loan sharking"—using violence or extortionate threats to collect a debt—was justified by the Commerce Clause, even though each individual case was typically local in nature (and not exactly your typical commercial transaction). The Supreme Court reasoned that loan sharking provided financing to organized crime, and organized crime in turn had substantial effects on interstate commerce.

As Congress based more and more actions on the Commerce Clause in the late 20th century, many scholars speculated that the Commerce Clause power was virtually unlimited, since nearly any type of activity could be characterized as impacting commerce in the aggregate. In 1995, however, the Supreme Court—for the first time in six decades—found that Congress had gone too far. In a 5–4 decision, the Supreme Court concluded that the Gun-Free Schools Act, which prohibited individuals from carrying guns in school zones, was unconstitutional (*U.S. v. Lopez*, 1995). The Court wrote that although Congress can regulate local economic activity that, in the aggregate, has a substantial effect on interstate commerce, "[t]he possession of a gun in a local school zone is in no sense an economic activity." Ruling otherwise, the majority wrote, would "authorize enactment [by Congress] of every type of legislation . . . at the expense of the Constitution's system of enumerated powers." Four dissenting justices, however, objected that this decision was contrary to earlier decisions such as *Perez*, since a logical line could be drawn between school violence and an aggregate effect on economic activity.

Later, in a 2005 case about medical marijuana, the Supreme Court appeared to return to an expansive interpretation of "commerce," holding that a federal law prohibiting individuals from growing marijuana for their own personal medical use (as authorized by state law) was justified by the Commerce Clause (*Gonzales v. Raich*, 2005). Even though no commercial activity was involved, the Supreme Court reasoned that some home-grown marijuana would likely find its way into interstate markets, and therefore Congress could regulate such cultivation and use. (This case highlights the intersection of the Commerce Clause and preemption; because the regulation of home-grown marijuana was within Congress's constitutional power, Congress also had the power to displace conflicting state law on the subject.)

As *Lopez* and *Raich* (as well as *NFIB v. Sebelius*, which is discussed later in this chapter) suggest, the Supreme Court continues to struggle with how to define what exactly "commerce" means for purposes of the Commerce Clause. The Commerce Clause supplies the legal foundation for much of what Congress does, but occasionally a case still arises that tests the outer boundaries of Congress's authority.

Power to Tax and Spend

In those few cases when Congress cannot use the Commerce Clause to accomplish its objectives, it has another very effective tool at its disposal: the power to "provide for the . . . general welfare" through taxing and spending (often called the Taxing and Spending Cause). These powers operate independently, so Congress does not need to demonstrate a nexus with interstate commerce in order to levy taxes or spend money on a particular project or program. Rather, it must only be able to demonstrate that its taxing and spending is "for the general welfare." In practice, this is not much of a limitation at all (and certainly includes efforts to further public health). Thus the taxing and spending power is a flexible tool that Congress can use in cases when the Commerce Clause (and Congress's other Article I powers; see Box 9.1) would not justify action.

Congress can use its power to tax and spend in three main ways. First, it can enact taxes to raise funds for public health efforts, to discourage unhealthy behavior, or to encourage healthy conduct. In addition to raising money, taxes and tax credits can influence the behavior of both individuals and businesses. The federal excise tax on cigarettes, for example, discourages smoking by individuals, while the Affordable Care Act's (ACA) tax credits incentivize small businesses to provide health insurance for their employees.

Second, Congress can appropriate funds to spend for the general welfare. This spending power underlies the federal bureaucracy that administers federal healthcare programs, conducts and funds health-related research, and supports state and local public health efforts. The government can also use its spending power to subsidize private conduct that it wants to encourage, such as the development of new vaccines. Notably, however, both the taxing and spending powers of Congress are also used in ways that may be antithetical to public health. For instance, federal agricultural spending likely contributes to the US obesity epidemic by artificially lowering the price of unhealthy foods, such as those produced with government-subsidized high fructose corn syrup (Franck, Grandi, & Eisenberg, 2013).

Third, the *conditional spending power* allows Congress to attach conditions to federal grants to the states, thereby influencing state conduct. As suggested by the *South Dakota v. Dole* case discussed earlier, this is a compelling way of getting states to do what Congress wants. Even though Congress lacks the ability to directly require states to adopt or enforce any particular law, money is a very powerful motivator. For example, the 1992 Synar Amendment provides that states that do not adopt and enforce laws prohibiting cigarette sales to minors face the risk of losing a portion of their federal funding for substance abuse prevention and treatment. Needless to say, every state submits a detailed annual report to the federal government demonstrating its compliance (or attempted compliance) with this requirement.

NFIB v. Sebelius

The Supreme Court's 2012 decision in *National Federation of Independent Businesses (NFIB) v. Sebelius* addressed the scope of Congress's power under both the Commerce Clause and the Taxing and Spending Clause. This case, which considered the constitutionality of key sections of the ACA, is one of the most well-known and controversial decisions of the past few decades. The Supreme Court's decision is consequential, regardless of whatever ultimately happens to the ACA, because it shapes (and arguably reshapes) the contours of Congress's Article I powers, which may have significant implications for Congress's authority to enact public health laws moving forward.

The Individual Mandate

The ACA included an "individual mandate," requiring most adults to demonstrate that they have health insurance that meets minimum federal standards or else pay a penalty. Congress considered the individual mandate essential to stabilize the health insurance market, given the ACA's requirement that insurance companies could no longer discriminate against people with pre-existing medical conditions. Soon after the law was passed, NFIB and other plaintiffs filed suit, arguing that the individual mandate exceeded Congress's power under the Commerce Clause. Eventually the case made it to the Supreme Court, and by a 5–4 vote the Court ruled that the Commerce Clause did *not* provide Congress with the authority to impose the individual mandate.

Writing for the majority, Chief Justice Roberts reasoned that while Congress has broad authority to regulate activity that affects interstate commerce, the Commerce Clause does not permit the government to require people to engage in economic activity or to purchase a specific product—in this case, health insurance. Roberts explained:

> [T]he Government's logic would justify a mandatory purchase to solve almost any problem. To consider a different example in the health care market, many Americans do not eat a balanced diet. . . . Under the Government's theory, Congress could address the diet problem by ordering everyone to

buy vegetables. . . . That is not the country the Framers of our Constitution envisioned.

Justice Ginsburg, writing in dissent, objected to this framing of the issue and to the majority's conclusions. First, she argued that it is quite clear that a program to reduce the number of uninsured Americans has substantial implications for interstate commerce—and that this alone should be enough to authorize Congress's action under the Supreme Court's Commerce Clause precedents, including *Heart of Atlanta, Perez*, and *Raich*. Second, she objected to the characterization that Congress was "compel[ling] individuals not engaged in commerce to purchase an unwanted product." Since virtually all Americans consume healthcare at some point in their lives, she argued that Congress was not forcing people into a market, but rather "defining the terms on which individuals pay for an interstate good they consume"—by, in effect, requiring them to pay in advance through insurance.

The Court's decision that the Commerce Clause did not provide authority for the individual mandate was, however, not the end of the matter. In a separate 5–4 opinion, Chief Justice Roberts joined with the Supreme Court's more liberal justices in concluding that the individual mandate could be upheld under Congress's taxing power. Because the mandate was enforced by a penalty collected through the tax system (i.e., the penalty is added to one's tax payment), Justice Roberts wrote that the mandate was effectively a tax on the choice not to carry insurance—and Congress was within its authority to impose such a tax.

The Supreme Court's decision to uphold the individual mandate as a tax was surprising to many observers who thought that the government's Commerce Clause argument was stronger than its Taxing and Spending Clause argument. But it reinforces the basic point that any Congressional action must be supported by just *one* enumerated power. In this case, the government argued that two enumerated powers supported the individual mandate. Although it lost its Commerce Clause argument, prevailing on the Taxing and Spending Clause argument was all that was needed to uphold this part of the law.

Medicaid Expansion

The other major provision at issue in *NFIB* was the ACA's "Medicaid expansion," which required states participating in the Medicaid program (which is all of them) to broaden eligibility for participation the program.

The Medicaid expansion was designed to enable most adults with incomes under 138% of the federal poverty level (FPL) to qualify for Medicaid. Before the ACA, low-income adults in most states were not eligible for Medicaid unless they possessed certain other qualifying characteristics, such as parenthood or disability, and the income limitation for most Medicaid groups was lower than 138% of the FPL.

Congress premised its authority for the Medicaid expansion on its conditional spending power under the Taxing and Spending Clause. Since Congress was providing funds to the states for Medicaid, it was entitled (it reasoned) to place conditions on those funds—similar to what it had done to encourage states to raise their minimum drinking age. But in *NFIB*, the Supreme Court found that the deal offered by Congress to the states was so "coercive" as to deprive states of autonomy over their own policy decisions. For the first time ever, the Court invalidated an effort by Congress to use its conditional spending power, concluding that Congress exceeded its constitutional powers (and raised federalism concerns) by disguising a legal command it could not issue as a monetary incentive.

Writing for a seven-justice majority on this point, Chief Justice Roberts noted that a state that refused to expand Medicaid was threatened with the loss of *all* of its Medicaid funding, which could amount to 10% of more of state's entire budget. This, he concluded, was "economic dragooning that leaves the States with no real option but to acquiesce in the Medicaid expansion." Although the Supreme Court did not spell out the exact point at which influence turns to coercion, it concluded that no state could realistically decline to participate in the expansion, and this made the program unconstitutionally coercive. Having concluded that the Medicaid expansion unduly pressured states in violation of the Taxing and Spending Clause, the Supreme Court had to determine the proper remedy. In yet another 5–4 split, it ruled that states must be given the option of whether or not to expand Medicaid. The four dissenting justices would have invalidated the Medicaid expansion program in its entirety.

Implications

The *NFIB* decision consisted of three main holdings (Table 9.1), all of which could have lasting implications for the scope of Congressional power to regulate for the public's health. First, the Supreme Court concluded that Congress had exceeded its Commerce Clause authority by

TABLE 9.1. Anatomy of the *NFIB v Sibelius* Decision

ISSUE	DECISION
Under the *Commerce Clause*, can Congress mandate that individuals purchase health insurance?	No (5–4)
Under its *Taxing Power* can Congress mandate that individuals purchase health insurance?	Yes (5–4)
Is the ACA's Medicaid expansion a constitutional use of Congress's conditional spending power?	No (7–2)
What is the appropriate remedy for the unconstitutional use of the conditional spending power?	The appropriate remedy is to make the Medicaid expansion optional for the states (5–4)

"forc[ing] individuals into commerce" with the individual mandate. It is too soon to determine whether this is the beginning of a broader push by the Supreme Court to more narrowly redefine what counts as "commerce" that Congress can regulate. But, as many public health laws are premised on the Commerce Clause power, this is an important issue to watch.

Second, the Supreme Court upheld the individual mandate under Congress's taxing power. This suggests that if the contours of Congress's Commerce Clause power remain uncertain (or are further restricted by future decisions), Congress could instead turn to the taxing power to further its public health objectives. Under *NFIB*'s reasoning, Congress appears to have broad authority to take virtually any regulatory action—even, perhaps, requiring everyone to purchase vegetables—so long as the penalty for noncompliance is enforced through the tax system. However, for political reasons, it is likely that Congress will not want to rely too heavily on its taxing authority to justify public health actions.

Finally, the Supreme Court concluded that Congress had "coerced" the states into accepting Medicaid expansion, exceeding its authority under the Taxing and Spending Clause. As we have seen, conditional spending—using federal funding to influence state conduct—is a tool Congress has repeatedly used to nudge the states into implementing public health initiatives. The exact bounds of the Supreme Court's coercion doctrine are unclear, but fear of future court decisions that build on the holding in *NFIB* may deter Congress from relying on its conditional spending power to promote public health goals.

Federal Administrative Authority and Delegation

So far we have looked at Congress's power to enact federal health laws, including measures that influence states to take action that Congress desires. We have noted that the Commerce Clause and the power to tax and spend enabled the growth of the modern regulatory state. While Congress sometimes enlists state governments in this undertaking, most of the national regulatory work in this country is assigned by Congress to federal administrative agencies. The doctrines of *preemption* and *home rule*, discussed in Chapters 8 and 10, address the vertical distribution of authority between levels of government. By contrast, the issue of *delegation*—which is central to public health law—addresses the horizontal distribution of authority between the legislative branch and the executive branch. And while we focus here on delegation within the federal government, similar rules and practices apply at the state level.

When Congress passes a law, it typically delegates (assigns) the authority to implement that law to a federal agency. These agencies are usually part of the federal executive branch. For example, the US Environmental Protection Agency (EPA) is tasked by Congress with implementing a wide array of federal laws relating to the environment. The EPA is part of the executive branch of the federal government, and the EPA administrator is part of the president's cabinet. Although legislatures typically select an existing administrative agency to implement a new law, they also have the power to create new administrative agencies.

Delegations of power relating to public health tend to be to be quite broad. For example, the Supreme Court has recognized that the Food and Drug Administration "has been delegated broad discretion by Congress in any number of areas" relating to the regulation of food and drugs (*Young v. Cmty. Nutrition Inst.*, 1986). Because public health authorities may be called upon to respond to unanticipated issues and diseases, flexibility in regulatory authority is essential. Statutes often grant agencies even broader authority in emergency situations, including the power to waive otherwise applicable procedural requirements.

One major task of administrative agencies is to promulgate *regulations*, or rules, that fill in the gaps of a broad statutory scheme and provide clearer direction to the entities they regulate. Congress may delegate general authority to federal administrative agencies to issue regulations, or it may provide detailed guidance and limitations on the scope of rulemaking authority. Congress could, for example, instruct an environmental agency to "issue regulations limiting emissions from new fossil fuel-fired power plants, taking into account health and environmental impacts, as well as technical feasibility," or it could instruct the agency more specifically to "issue regulations limiting emissions from new fossil fuel-fired power plants that set a maximum level of emissions no higher than 1,400 pounds of carbon dioxide per megawatt-hour." In either event, the instructions provided by Congress limit the federal agency's regulatory power. A more specific set of instructions means that the agency has less discretion or flexibility.

The Administrative Procedure Act (1946) governs the process through which federal agencies promulgate regulations. To issue a new regulation, agencies must generally provide for "notice and comment." That is, they must first issue a "Notice of Proposed Rulemaking" in the Federal Register (the official record of the federal government's activities). After a proposed rule is published, the public can provide comments to the agency about the planned action. While anyone can provide submit a comment through an online form at http://regulations.gov, it should be unsurprising that regulated industries tend to be the most active commentators and that such industries typically seek to reduce the stringency of proposed rules (West & Raso, 2012). The agency is required to review and respond to all comments before issuing a final rule, which may include modifications suggested by some of the comments. Once a final rule is promulgated by an agency, it carries the force of law. However, if Congress disapproves of any agency action, it can refuse to provide funding to implement the rule, or it can override it by passing a new law. Additionally, the Congressional Review Act (CRA; 1996) provides that Congress can void an agency rule by passing a joint resolution, signed by the president, within 60 days of the rule's issuance. The CRA was only used once to invalidate a rule between 1996 (when it was enacted) and 2016, but in 2017 it was used to override more than a dozen rules that had been issued during the final months of the Obama administration.

Conclusion

Federal public health authority is grounded in the Constitution's enumerated powers. Congress cannot take any action unless it can be linked to one of the powers listed in Article I of the Constitution. Congressional power is broad, which is consistent with our need as a nation for consistent and coherent laws, and Congress's power can be delegated to federal agencies that then regulate within their assigned domains. At least in the short term, cases exploring the outer limits of Congress's authority are likely to center on the meaning and implications of the *NFIB* decision, which addressed the reach of Congress's power under both the Commerce Clause and the Taxing and Spending Clause.

Further Reading

Huberfeld, N., Leonard, E. W., & Outterson, K. (2013). Plunging into Endless Difficulties: Medicaid and Coercion in National Federation of Independent Business v. Sebelius. *Boston University Law Review, 93*, 1–88.

Metzger, G. E. (2012). To Tax, to Spend, to Regulate. *Harvard Law Review, 126*, 83–116.

10 | State and Local Public Health Authority

Learning Objectives

- Define *police power* and explain the scope of state authority to regulate for public health.
- Understand the source of local public health authority and the difference between "Dillon's Rule" and "home rule" jurisdictions.
- Explain why regulated entities and public health advocates may have different preferences regarding what level of government engages in regulation.

Introduction

We next turn to the authority of state and local governments to engage in public health regulation. Unlike Congress, state governments are not limited to a set of enumerated powers. Instead, they have *plenary power*, or broad authority to regulate, except as limited by the US Constitution, federal law, or the state's own constitution. The scope of local government authority, by contrast, depends on the specifics of the state's law, which establishes the system of county and municipal government.

Under federalism, there is "competition" for authority. Lawmakers at each level—federal, state, and local—can be expected, all else being equal, to carve out more power for themselves. Advocates for a cause generally want power to be concentrated at the level where they are most likely to win: when your side has the support of the federal government, states' rights seems like a bad idea, and vice versa. Cities like New York City and states like California are hubs of policy innovation where public health advocates champion states' rights, while regulated industries often invest heavily in advocacy for blanket federal rules.

Aside from political considerations, there are enduring trade-offs in political economy between centralization and *subsidiarity*, the principle that decisions should be made at the most local level possible. The venerable idea that local and state governments, in their social and political variety, can serve as "laboratories of democracy" is countered by the principle that the affairs of regional and national markets should be governed by uniform rules. While the previous chapter explored federal public health authority, this chapter examines state public health authority and how it is apportioned to local governments and state administrative agencies.

State Public Health Powers

The 10th Amendment to the US Constitution provides that "[t]he powers not delegated to the United States by the Constitution, nor prohibited to it by the States, are reserved to the States respectively, or to the people." Among the historic powers that states possessed prior to the ratification of the Constitution, and which the 10th Amendment thereafter reserved to the states, was the "police power." In this context, the police power refers to states' far-reaching authority to regulate for the health, safety, and welfare of their residents.

The Supreme Court explained the outlines of the police power in the landmark public health law case, *Jacobson v. Massachusetts* (1905). In that case, Rev. Henning Jacobson challenged a law requiring members of the public to be vaccinated against smallpox—during a smallpox outbreak—or else pay a fine. The Court described the broad scope of the state's police power as applied to public health:

> The authority of the state to enact this statute [arises from] what is commonly called the police power. . . . Although this court has refrained from any attempt to define the limits of that power, yet it has distinctly recognized the authority of a state to enact . . . "health laws of every description." . . . According to settled principles, the police power of a state must be held to embrace, at least, such reasonable regulations established directly by legislative enactment as will protect the public health and the public safety. . . . The mode or manner in which those results are to be accomplished is within the discretion of the state, subject, of course, so far as Federal power is concerned, only to the condition that no rule prescribed by

a state, nor any regulation adopted by a local governmental agency acting under the sanction of state legislation, shall contravene the Constitution of the United States, nor infringe any right granted or secured by that instrument.

Under *Jacobson*, police power authority is not unlimited; states cannot "infringe any right granted or secured by" the Constitution. Nonetheless, police power authority is exceedingly broad. For example, there is no real question that states possess the authority to require individuals to obtain insurance coverage (an "individual mandate"), as Massachusetts did when enacting the 2006 health care reform law that served as a model for the Affordable Care Act. Unlike Congress, whose power to impose this requirement was sorely tested in *NFIB v. Sibelius* (see Chapter 9), states have no need to point to an enumerated power—they can instead rely on their broad police power. When the Massachusetts individual mandate was challenged, the state Superior Court quickly dismissed the suit, writing:

> The field for the legitimate exercise of the police power is coextensive with the changing needs of society. . . . The Legislature could have found that the Act bears a real and substantial relation to the health, safety, good order, comfort, and general welfare of the community because, by virtue of its mandate, more of those who fall ill will have insurance coverage and the burden of paying for such coverage will be more equitably distributed. As a rational basis of fact can reasonably be conceived to sustain it, the Act is a proper exercise of police power (*Fountas v. Com'r of the Massachusetts Dept. of Revenue*, 2009).

Judicial review of the exercise of the police power is typically deferential: so long as a state can identify a "real and substantial relation" between its law and improving public health, its law can be sustained under its police power. This means that the evidentiary bar is extremely low. As noted in *Fountas*, "legislation [based on the police power] may be struck down only if no rational basis of fact can reasonably be conceived to sustain it." While state authority to enact health laws is broad, we will see in later chapters that the exercise of that authority may also be challenged on federal constitutional grounds, such as the First Amendment, which entail more stringent review by the courts.

Local Public Health Powers

Local governments are, legally, administrative subdivisions of the state. In the Supreme Court's words, they are "convenient entities" established to manage affairs and preserve order at the local level (*Hunter v. City of Pittsburgh*, 1907). Since these entities derive their powers from the state, the state can decide how much of its broad police power it will share.

States vary considerably in how much authority they give to local governments, and the balance of power between state and local governments has shifted over time. In the late 19th century, *Dillon's Rule*, named for Judge John Forrest Dillon (author of an influential treatise on municipal law), became the general default rule. Under Dillon's Rule, a locality possesses only those powers expressly granted to it by the state, and the scope of those powers is to be construed narrowly. In other words, municipalities can only regulate in areas where the state has explicitly authorized them to do so, and if there is any question as to whether or not a municipality has authority to act, the presumption is that it does not. This approach, which sharply limited local government power, reflected Judge Dillon's "strong belief in private property rights . . . and skepticism of government in general" (Spitzer, 2015).

In the Progressive Era of the early 20th century, reformers took aim at Dillon's Rule. The "home rule movement" sought to "undo Dillon's Rule by giving localities broad lawmaking authority and to provide local governments freedom from state interference in areas of local concern" (Briffault, 1990). These reformers argued that cities needed the flexibility to address their own challenges, particularly as the importance of cities grew due to industrialization and urbanization. Local governments resented the frequent interference of state lawmakers, many of whom were from more rural areas and did not seem to understand or care about the needs of cities.

Over time, more states moved to adopt some form of home rule, often through amendments to state constitutions. Under its broadest form, localities in home rule states are authorized to exercise the full range of police power granted to the state, so long as their actions are not in conflict with state law. This full form of home rule provides a default rule that is the opposite of Dillon's: unless the state explicitly provides otherwise, municipalities possess the full range of police power, and their actions are presumed to be valid in the absence of a direct conflict with state law. Other states allow local governments to adopt "home rule charters"—often by popular vote—that specify the scope of the locality's powers. This is home rule in the sense that voters are able to define the scope of their own government's powers, but the local powers may not be as broad as in a full home rule jurisdiction.

The historic debate between proponents of Dillon's Rule and home rule carries on today in various forms. Should the default rule keep power at the state level, unless there is a deliberate decision to delegate it to local governments? Or should cities by default have broad authority to address public health issues and other local challenges? Public health advocates tend to support home rule, because local governments tend to be less subject to pressure from well-funded lobbying campaigns than state governments and correspondingly more open to taking on public health issues that may challenge entrenched interests. As Gorovitz, Mosher, and Pertschuk (1998) write:

> Most industries cannot afford to place lobbyists in every community, contribute to numerous local campaigns, nor even keep abreast of every proposed piece of local regulation which may concern them. Local representatives also tend to be responsive to individual citizens and community organizations more directly than state or federal legislators, because local lawmakers must live and work among their constituents. Conversely, trade associations and other industry representatives are seen as outsiders rather than as *bona fide* constituents.

By contrast, trade association and other industry groups often have more influence at the state level, where they can pool their resources to employ lobbyists and make strategic campaign contributions.

For similar reasons, industry groups—as well as organizations ideologically committed to limited government, as Judge Dillon was in his day—may push to limit local control. In the past few decades, there have been a number of industry-funded efforts to limit the scope of home rule. For example, California's broad home rule authority was limited by Proposition 26, approved by voters in 2010, requiring a two-thirds vote before a local government can impose a fee on businesses. Tobacco, alcohol, and fossil fuel companies all poured money into the campaign for this proposition (Rogers, 2010). Similarly, various conservative groups have successfully advocated for laws that limit the authority of local governments to impose taxes or increase municipal spending (Deller & Stallman, 2006). Such measures directly limit cities' ability to impose fees or taxes on businesses that harm public health. They also squeeze cities' budgets, decreasing their ability to support public health initiatives (particularly those that might invite costly lawsuits).

State Preemption

Chapter 8 discussed Congress's power to displace state laws through the preemption doctrine. States have a parallel ability to preempt local action, although it is not rooted in the Constitution. Rather, because local governments are subdivisions of the state and derive their powers from the state, the state retains the power to limit the scope of local authority, including by preempting local laws. The specifics of preemption law vary from state to state.

Ohio, for example, recognizes only *conflict* preemption. Under the state's strong home rule doctrine, it is not enough for the legislature to declare its intent to preempt local law; to find preemption, a court must determine that there is a real conflict between state and local law (in other words, that it is impossible to comply with both). In 2011, the city council of Cleveland, Ohio, enacted a "trans-fat ban," sharply limiting local restaurants' use of trans-fats in cooking. Shortly thereafter, the Ohio General Assembly (the state legislature) enacted a law prohibiting local governments from regulating trans-fat content in food, in an attempt to preempt laws like Cleveland's. Cleveland sued the state, and the state law was ultimately invalidated because, as the court wrote, it "[did] not set forth [affirmative] regulations but simply purport[ed] to limit municipal legislative power " (*Cleveland v. State*, 2013). Because the state had not itself regulated trans-fats in a way that conflicted with the city's rule, there was no preemption.

Other states, however, do not place the same emphasis on home rule and allow the state legislature to preempt local laws more easily. Texas law blocks a wide range of potential local gun control ordinances by simply stating that "a municipality may not adopt regulations relating to . . . the transfer, private ownership, keeping, transportation, licensing, or registration of firearms, air guns, knives, ammunition, or firearm or air gun supplies." ("Regulation of Firearms, Knives, and Explosives," 2017).

Like efforts to limit home rule, preemptive state laws—such as the Ohio law at issue in Cleveland's trans-fat litigation—are often pushed by industries or interest groups that seek to avoid local regulation. These groups often hold more sway at the state level, and so they prefer that decisions be made there. Industry arguments for these laws are often framed in terms of promoting "uniformity," "fairness," or "economic growth." These are legitimate considerations in the abstract. In practice, however, these laws "abrogate . . . local authority to adopt innovative solutions to public health problems, eliminate the flexibility to respond to the needs of diverse communities, [and] undermine grassroots public health movements" (Pertschuk, Pomeranz, Aoki, Larkin, & Paloma, 2013).

In the 1980s, when local governments started to prohibit smoking in bars, restaurants, and other workplaces, the tobacco industry responded by pushing state legislatures to preempt local ordinances—and several such preemptive state laws are still in effect. The National Rifle Association later pressed for state laws to preempt local gun control provisions and succeeded in almost every state. More recently, at the urging of industry-backed groups, state legislatures are going beyond preempting local laws and are "threatening to withhold resources from communities that defy them and to hold their elected officials legally and financially liable" (Badger, 2017). A recent Florida law provides that officials who enact or enforce preempted gun control laws can be held personally liable in court ("Fl. Stat. Ann.," 2017), and an Arizona law provides that a city that passes a preempted law can lose *all* of its state funding ("Ariz. Rev. Stat. Ann.," 2016).

State Administrative Authority and Delegation

As at the federal level, when state or local legislative bodies pass a law, they usually delegate the authority for its implementation to an administrative agency. Most states, for example, have their own environmental protection agencies that are tasked with carrying out environmental laws at the state level. Like federal agencies, state and local regulatory bodies derive their authority to act from the legislatures that created them. These authorities are limited by the applicable governing statutes and the extent of the delegation in each instance, but delegations of power relating to public health tend to be quite broad. For example, Wisconsin state law provides that the state Department of Health Service (the public health agency) has "general supervision throughout the state of the health of citizens" and possesses the "power to execute what is reasonable and necessary for the prevention and suppression of disease" ("Fl. Stat. Ann. 790.33," 2017) Likewise, many states have their own analogues to the federal Administrative Procedure Act, setting out the process that must be followed before an agency can issue an administrative rule.

Conclusion

This chapter completes our introduction of the sources of public health authority at the federal, state, and local level. As we have seen, the federal government is one of enumerated powers, while state governments have broad police power. The scope of local authority has been a point of tension between local and state governments for well over a century, and that debate continues today—with significant implications for public health.

Further Reading

Gostin, L. O. (2005). *Jacobson v Massachusetts* at 100 Years: Police Power and Civil Liberties in Tension. *American Journal of Public Health*, *95*, 576–581.

Pomeranz, J. L., & Pertschuk, M. (2017). State Preemption: A Significant and Quiet Threat to Public Health in the United States. *American Journal of Public Health*, *107*, 900–902.

Su, R. (2017). Have Cities Abandoned Home Rule? *Fordham Urban Law Journal, 44*, 181–216.

11 | Constitutional Limitations
| DUE PROCESS OF LAW

Learning Objectives

- Differentiate substantive from procedural due process.
- Provide examples of "fundamental rights" and explain why determining whether or not a right is "fundamental" is critical to any substantive due process analysis.
- Understand how the state action doctrine limits who can be held responsible for due process violations.

Introduction

Laws provide authority for public health action, but also set limits. The drafters of the US Constitution drew lessons from centuries of philosophy and governance to limit the authority of the federal government, aiming to prevent the abuses of colonial rule. Even with a government of limited powers, several states would not ratify the Constitution unless it expressly guaranteed basic civil liberties like freedom of speech, press, and assembly and freedom from unreasonable searches and seizures. The first 10 amendments to the Constitution, called the Bill of Rights, were drafted to guarantee these liberties; among these is *due process of law*. This chapter covers the right of due process as a limit on public health action.

The Constitution's Fifth Amendment provides that "No person shall . . . be deprived of life, liberty, or property, without due process of law." The Fifth Amendment, like all of the Bill of Rights, was originally interpreted by the Supreme Court as limiting only federal government actions. After the Civil War, the ratification of the 14th Amendment, which has its own Due Process Clause, expanded the guarantee to citizens harmed by state actions (*Twining v. New Jersey*, 1908). When individuals believe their due process rights are being abridged, they can challenge the government's actions in court. Because courts are left to decide whether these actions are appropriate to the circumstances, due process relies on standards that are not expressly written in the Constitution.

Due process embodies two core limitations on government action: the government must respect fundamental rights, and it cannot deprive people of "life, liberty, or property" without sufficient procedural protections. *Substantive due process* is a doctrine of fundamental rights. It provides that the government cannot violate certain rights unless it has a "compelling state interest." The Supreme Court has used substantive due process as a means of protecting rights that it considers vital elements of liberty in a free society, even though not all of these rights are actually spelled out in the Constitution. *Procedural due process*, by contrast, looks at how the law is applied. It requires basic safeguards of fairness, such as advance notice and an appropriate hearing, before a governmental action against a person's interest is carried out. These safeguards help balance the power of the individual against that of government and are thought to promote better, more accurate results.

This chapter starts by outlining the basic doctrines of procedural and substantive due process, including the legal tests that courts apply to decide whether due process rights have been violated. After reviewing the Supreme Court's struggle to define the scope of reproductive rights, we examine two cases where public health was raised as a justification for governmental action: one about involuntary sterilization and one about Ebola. The chapter concludes with a brief discussion of the *state action doctrine*.

Procedural Due Process

Where an individual's life, liberty, or property may be affected by a government's actions, procedural due process requires that it provide those individuals advance notice and a hearing conducted by an impartial decision-maker, as well as the right to appeal the decision in a court of law (*Zinermon v. Burch*, 1990). The requirements of procedural due process are flexible, taking into consideration that a fair and efficient legal system has to balance process with speed and affordability. Courts typically weigh four factors: the significance of the individual interest affected by the action (paying a small fine counts far less than going to jail, for instance), the risk that a plaintiff will "suffer an erroneous deprivation" of his or her rights through the procedure the government is using, the potential benefits of imposing additional procedural safeguards, and the government's interest in its procedural approach (*Mathews v. Eldridge*, 1976).

Public health laws that impose penalties, restrict movement, confiscate property, or otherwise interfere with personal liberties must be implemented in a way that meets procedural due process standards. Before taking a routine public health action like the suspension of a restaurant permit, the government must provide a written notice that sets out the reasons for the proposed action and notifies the restaurant or other affected party of a date and time for a hearing before the action is taken. Individuals cannot lose certain government benefits, or "entitlements," such as Medicaid without a hearing, though that rule may be modified by current federal regulatory proposals. The government must also offer a route to appeal the decision from a hearing, though it can generally carry out its plans while the appeal proceeds.

These procedural requirements may be more flexible when public health dangers call for immediate action. For example, in 1979, the Supreme Court upheld a Massachusetts law that immediately suspended the driver's license of anyone who declined a breath-analysis test when arrested for a DUI. Although the Court assumed that drivers' licenses are "property," to which due process protections apply, it rejected the argument a pre-suspension hearing was required. Appling the four-factor test from *Mathews v. Eldridge*, the Supreme Court concluded that Massachusetts had a strong justification for "promptly removing such drivers from the road" and that "a presuspension hearing would substantially undermine the state interest in public safety." The dissenting justices, however, argued that because licenses were suspended for "noncooperation with the policy, not drunken driving," failure to provide a presuspension hearing violated "the most elemental principles of due process" (*Mackey v. Montrym*, 1979). Despite traditional procedural due process requirements, the public health interest in motor vehicle safety prevailed.

Substantive Due Process

Unlike procedural due process, which deals with legal procedures like hearings and appeals, *substantive due process* relates to claims that a "fundamental right" has been infringed. What counts as a "fundamental right" has changed over time, but well-established fundamental rights include (and are not limited to) the right to marry, the right to vote, the right to custody of one's children, the right to procreate, and the right to travel within the United States. Like all constitutional rights, these rights are not absolute; for example, parents can be deprived of custody in child abuse cases, and the right to marry does not extend to marrying a close relative. Since these rights are labeled as "fundamental," any law or policy limiting their exercise must clear a high bar.

Application of substantive due process involves determining whether or not the right at issue is fundamental, and then applying the corresponding "standard of review" (*U.S. v. Carolene Products Co.*, 1938). If a right claimed is deemed fundamental, the court will apply *strict scrutiny*, requiring the government to show that the law is necessary to advance a compelling state interest and is *narrowly tailored*, or precisely written, to infringe as little on individual rights as possible. If the right claimed is not fundamental, the court will apply a *rational basis test* that is far more deferential to the government's decision. Rational basis review requires that the government articulate a purpose that is legitimate and rationally related to its action, a far lower bar than strict scrutiny. The level of judicial scrutiny or review will often determine whether or not government actions are upheld; policies and laws generally survive under rational basis review but rarely under strict scrutiny.

The Supreme Court has struggled over the years to create a framework that can consistently define fundamental rights, and it has sometimes missed the mark badly. Most egregiously, the Fifth Amendment's Due Process Clause was cited in the pre-Civil War *Dred Scott* decision as a basis for upholding a "right" to own slaves (*Dred Scott v. Sandford*, 1857). Fifty years later, the 14th Amendment's Due Process Clause was used to invalidate a New York law setting the maximum number of hours bakers could work in a day, with the Supreme Court holding that the liberty of employers to freely contract with workers was a vital protected right (*Lochner v. New York*, 1905). The *Lochner* decision, which was later reversed, is now seen as a dangerous misstep that threatened to allow courts to "substitute their social and economic beliefs for the judgment of legislative bodies" (*Ferguson v. Skrupa*, 1963).

While it is useful for Supreme Court justices to have a doctrinal source for protecting the important rights that are not explicitly set out in the Constitution, it is also important to set limits on such an obviously expandable list by courts at their discretion, as we will see later. Accordingly, in recent decades, the Supreme Court has been very reluctant to recognize other rights or rights of certain groups as fundamental.

Reproductive Freedom: The Evolving Jurisprudence of a Fundamental Right

In the 1960s and 1970s, justices found in substantive due process a basis for rights of privacy in reproductive matters. The reproductive rights series of cases show the Supreme Court's gradual recognition of a new fundamental right and demonstrates how it can expand or contract the scope of previously recognized rights. It began in 1965 with a decision striking down Connecticut's prohibition of prescribing, selling, and using contraceptives and naming a "right to privacy" for reproductive health decisions among married couples (*Griswold v. Connecticut*, 1965). This right was extended seven years later to all adults, regardless of marital status (*Eisenstadt v. Baird*, 1972).

Building on these precedents, in 1970, a pregnant, single woman sued the state of Texas, which criminalized abortions unless necessary to save the mother's life. In her case, *Roe v. Wade* (1973), the Supreme Court decided that "the 14th Amendment's concept of personal liberty and restrictions upon state action" allows women the fundamental right to decide whether to terminate a pregnancy. The Supreme Court in *Roe* maintained that although the right to terminate a pregnancy was fundamental, it was not absolute. Recognizing the state's legitimate interests in both the health of the mother and in protecting "prenatal life," it set graduated rules for the government's regulation of abortion by trimester of pregnancy: minimal regulation as for other medical procedures during the first trimester; increased regulation as reasonably related to maternal health during the second trimester; and as much regulation, or prohibition, during the third trimester, except when necessary to preserve maternal health.

Later, however, the Supreme Court reduced the scope of protection for a woman's right to obtain an abortion. In *Planned Parenthood of Southeastern Pennsylvania v. Casey* (1992), it permitted restrictions on abortion—even in the first trimester—as long as they did not place an "undue burden" on access to an abortion. Under this ambiguous standard, states have been allowed to impose a wide variety of requirements on abortion procedures and providers, such as banning government employees or facilities from using public resources for performing abortions and requiring physicians to conduct an ultrasound procedure before an abortion. Other laws have been struck down as violating this standard. Most recently, the Supreme Court invalidated a Texas law mandating that abortion providers have admitting privileges at a nearby hospital and that abortion clinics meet medical standards for "ambulatory surgery centers" (*Whole Women's Health v. Hellerstedt*, 2016). In the majority opinion, Justice Breyer concluded that these measures significantly limited access to abortion services and did not—as Texas had claimed—further the state's interest in protecting women's health.

The scope of the right to reproductive privacy, including the right to obtain an abortion, remains contentious. Though it was recognized as a fundamental right more than 40 years ago, the exact contours of that right remain in flux. As advocates on both sides press the Supreme Court to move in their direction, public health evidence may become increasingly important. As seen in *Whole Women's Health*, public health research is critical to the legal analysis of whether a restriction on abortion is actually necessary to promote women's health and whether or not it constitutes an "undue burden."

Due Process in Action: Involuntary Sterilization

One of the most troubling due process cases in Supreme Court history, in which public health served as the purported justification for involuntary sterilization, concerns the concept of liberty. In the 1920s and 1930s, many Americans—including many influential figures and even scientists—subscribed to the bogus theory of "eugenics," a belief that societies could improve public health and welfare through the systematic prevention of reproduction of genetically-inferior humans. This notion, carried to its extreme by the Nazis in the 1930s and 1940s, depended upon racist ideas about the inferiority of people of African, Slavic, Jewish, Southern European, and Asian descent. Many believers took poverty as a proxy for, and result of, of genetic inferiority. By the end of the 1920s, Virginia and some 30 other states had laws allowing the eugenic sterilization of the mentally impaired, laws that resulted in an estimated 65,000 involuntary sterilizations. One of the victims was Carrie Buck, who was held with her infant daughter and her mother at an institution called the Virginia State Colony for Epileptics and Feebleminded. The stigma of unwed motherhood landed Carrie in the institution, but after a superficial examination determined that her eight-month-old daughter was "feeble-minded," the head of the Colony ordered Carrie to be sterilized. In the famous case of *Buck v. Bell* (1927), Carrie sued the state of Virginia to prevent the forced procedure.

Despite the horrifying facts of the case and the lack of remotely credible medical standards used to deem a patient fit for sterilization, the Supreme Court saw only good (eugenic) public health practice.

> It is better for all the world if, instead of waiting to execute degenerate offspring for crime or to let them starve for their imbecility, society can prevent those who are manifestly unfit from continuing their kind. The principle that sustains compulsory vaccination is broad enough to cover cutting the fallopian tubes [citing *Jacobson v. Massachusetts*]. Three generations of imbeciles are enough (*Buck v. Bell*, 1927).

Only one justice dissented from the opinion, showing the powerful influence of prevailing popular beliefs on judges' views of due process rights. Additionally, the case also reminds us that simply providing adequate procedures does not guarantee fair outcomes. The Supreme Court's decision relies heavily on the fact that Carrie Buck and her guardian were offered the right to a hearing before an impartial decision-maker, timely information about the decision and hearing, and the opportunity to appeal the decision to the Circuit Court of Amherst County and Supreme Court of Appeals in Virginia. Though *Buck v. Bell* has never been overturned, it is clear that the Supreme Court would recognize the right to procreate as a fundamental right today.

Due Process in Action: Ebola

Due process arises in dramatic form to this day in the control of communicable disease, albeit in rare and extreme circumstances. Faced with frightening diseases like Ebola and highly drug-resistant tuberculosis, health authorities on occasion resort to *quarantine* (confinement of a person exposed to a disease) and *isolation* (confinement of a person with a disease). These personal control measures implicate the fundamental right to liberty, which is specifically mentioned in both the Fifth and 14th Amendments, and therefore triggers strict scrutiny. They also raise issues of procedural due process; quarantine or isolation can only be imposed through fair procedures that allow the confined individual a chance to show that the government's assessment of their personal risk is wrong. Procedural due process may also require further safeguards like access to counsel and the opportunity to present and review evidence as at a trial, although these issues have not been fully litigated in recent decades (*Greene v. Edwards*, 1980).

At the height of the 2014–2016 Ebola epidemic in West Africa, nurse Kaci Hickox flew from serving in the outbreak response in Sierra Leone to Newark Liberty International Airport, where she was screened for symptoms of Ebola. New Jersey airport officials, implementing an executive order signed by Governor Chris Christie to conduct active screening and impose quarantine when appropriate, quarantined her for 80 hours based on the health department's assessment of her exposure to Ebola patients and an initial elevated temperature reading. Hickox, who contended she had never seen patients and was not at risk of infection, later challenged the grounds for her quarantine for failing to provide a hearing upon her confinement and failing to provide adequate notice of her rights.

The federal district court was sympathetic to Hickox's arguments that the state overreacted and also sympathetic to the dilemma the state faced. It wrote: "Bad science and irrational fear often amplify the public's reaction to reports of infectious disease. Ebola, although it has inspired great fear, is a virus, not a malevolent magic spell. The State is entitled to some latitude, however, in its prophylactic efforts to contain what is, at present, an incurable and often fatal disease" (*Hickox v. Christie*, 2016). The court found that procedural due process did not require a predetention hearing in an emergency and that Hickox's 80-hour confinement had not been so unreasonable under the circumstances as to constitute a substantive due process violation.

In *Hickox*, the court put its finger on a problem common to quarantine cases: They tend to arise at times of uncertainty, when the chance of a mistaken or prejudiced decision is pretty high; yet, if there really is an outbreak, a court will be leery of supplanting the judgment of health officials or of punishing them after the fact when their good-faith judgements turned out to be mistaken. Thus "strict scrutiny" is not always so strict in emergency situations. Had Hickox been held longer, in poorer conditions, or with even less evidence, the decision might have been different—but her case shows how difficult it is to win due process cases when there is an ongoing risk of an infectious disease outbreak. Notably, although Hickox did not prevail on her due process claims, her lawsuit prompted New Jersey's health department to issue new regulations on quarantine that include explicit procedures for notice and a hearing.

The Requirement of "State Action"

Like other constitutional rights, procedural and substantive due process protections apply only to governmental actions. This is referred to as the *state action doctrine*. Sometimes, what qualifies as a state action is clear: constitutional protections apply to government actions that are codified in law, expressed in policies, and implemented by government officials (*In re Civil Rights Cases*, 1883). State, tribal, local, and territorial health departments are clearly subject to due process requirements and limitations.

In other cases, it may be less clear whether or not there is "state action." For example, the state action doctrine can apply to organizations sanctioned by government to conduct official functions, such as corporations receiving government funding. Whether or not those entities can be held responsible for due process violations would depend on the specific facts and circumstances of the case. In some jurisdictions, private entities run governmental public health agencies and fulfill basic public health responsibilities written in enabling acts and authorities, from routine inspections of healthcare facilities to essential public health services during an emergency. When these actions adversely impact individual rights, courts may apply the state action doctrine to these nongovernmental entities.

Although government actors (or those acting on the government's behalf) can be held responsible for actions that violate due process rights, it is important to recognize that government's failure to protect individuals from harms inflicted by private companies or individuals does not violate due process, no matter how severe the injury (*DeShaney v. Winnebago County Dept. of Social Services*, 1989). This is because the Constitution espouses "negative rights" that outline what the government is prohibited from doing but not what it must proactively do. Although this is a long-standing principle of Constitutional law, numerous public health scholars have criticized the "action/inaction" dichotomy as deeply problematic. As they have noted, government inaction in the face of public health threats can also deprive one of life, liberty, and property (Parmet, 1992).

Conclusion

Beliefs about due process change with the times, and practitioners should know how to identify government actions and decisions that can trigger a due process issue. By recognizing that each new issue has similarities and differences to long-standing public health actions, practitioners will be able determine what kind of scrutiny or deference will likely be given to government on any particular topic. Courts frequently analyze due process concerns along with those of equal protection, the subject of the next chapter.

Further Reading

Bryson, B. (2013). *One Summer: America, 1927*. New York: Doubleday.

Guttmacher Institute (2017). State Laws and Policies. Retrieved May 17, 2018, from https://www.guttmacher.org/state-policy/laws-policies.

Price, P. (2016). Quarantine and Liability in the context of Ebola. *Public Health Reports, 131*(3), 500–503.

12 | Constitutional Limitations
EQUAL PROTECTION OF LAW

Learning Objectives

- Understand the origins of the 14th Amendment's Equal Protection Clause.
- Identify suspect and quasi-suspect classes and explain the levels of scrutiny courts apply in equal protection review.
- Recognize factors that have historically led to equal protection violations by public health officials.

Introduction

The concept of fairness resonates in American society. As we move through our daily lives, we want to be treated fairly, especially by the government that represents us. Unfair treatment based on a characteristic a person cannot change—race, gender, disability, sexual orientation—strikes us as particularly egregious. Yet it is easy to name historical instances of this kind of discrimination, from the protection of slavery in the US Constitution through the World War II internment of Japanese-Americans, to bans on gay marriage by officials at all levels. Unfairness can seem obvious in hindsight, but courts have struggled throughout our history with how to address it as it happens. It was the Civil War, not a lawsuit, that led to the abolition of slavery. The Supreme Court's 1944 decision upholding Japanese internment has never been overturned, although it has been "thoroughly repudiated by history" (Cole & Eskridge, 1994).

The Constitution speaks to the issue of fairness though the 14th Amendment, which requires that the actions of federal and state governments be grounded in principles of equal protection. The Equal Protection Clause, as we shall see, requires that the law treat similarly situated people in similar ways and that disparate treatment of individuals be grounded in some meaningful difference. This institutional fairness requires that everyone enjoy the "equal protection of the law," but there are times when all people are not in the same situation, and there are sound policy reasons for drawing lines that are not driven by prejudice. We have good public health reasons, for example, to prevent people less than 21 years old from buying alcohol and to bar unvaccinated children from school.

In public health law cases involving equal protection claims, the courts are faced with difficult questions: What constitutes fair treatment? How do we identify people who should be treated similarly? What kind of evidence is required for governments to justify treating individuals or groups of individuals differently? Can government go too far? This chapter examines the origins of the Equal Protection Clause, provides an overview of equal protection doctrine, and examines its application to issues of public health to answer these questions.

The Origins of Equal Protection

The Framers included a Due Process Clause in the Bill of Rights, reflecting the experience of arbitrary governance that helped fuel the Revolution. It took a war over slavery to give the concept of equal protection of law an explicit place in the Constitution. After the Civil War, Congress faced the challenge of preventing the reimposition of second-class status on freed slaves through "Black Codes," laws designed to deny black Americans many rights including voting, holding office, serving on juries, and testifying in certain types of court cases. In part as a response to these codes, Congress amended the US Constitution to secure the freed slaves' basic civil rights (Goldstone, 2011). The 13th Amendment prohibited slavery, and the 15th Amendment prohibited the denial of voting rights on the basis of race, color, or previous condition of slavery (though this protection did not yet apply to women of color). Central to these Reconstruction Era amendments, the 14th Amendment secured rights to due process and prohibited states from denying any person the equal protection of the laws. Shamefully, it took nearly a century of legal and political advocacy for these legal promises to be seriously enforced, and law has not yet wiped out the unequal protection of laws (Blackmon, 2008).

The 14th Amendment does not create a blanket prohibition against a law creating or recognizing different categories of people or treating different people differently. As interpreted by the Supreme Court, the core doctrines of the Equal Protection Clause are that similarly situated persons receive similar treatment under the law, and that different treatment be based on meaningful differences (*Johnson v. Robison*, 1974; *Ohio Bureau of Employment Servs. v. Hodory*, 1977). As with due process, the Constitution does not define "equal protection," and courts' interpretations have avoided a formulaic description of what equal protection means. Because the requirement has been left purposefully broad over the years since its creation, the application of the Equal Protection Clause to government actions remains nuanced and complex.

Equal Protection Overview

Laws create classifications and place requirements upon different groups of people and organizations, sometimes for important health-related reasons. State laws that address possessing, purchasing, and drinking alcohol create two groups: people over the age of 21 are regulated one way and people under the age of 21 another. These classifications arise solely from the text of laws, which also create significant penalties for the people who violate them. Yet, legislatures recognized these classifications as acceptable because there is evidence to support the premise that people younger than 21 years old are less able to consume alcohol in a mature and responsible manner and disproportionately impose adverse health and financial consequences on the rest of society (Centers for Disease Control and Prevention, 2016).

Other classifications in the history of public health law have not been accepted as legitimate. In the early 1970s, Oklahoma prohibited males under the age of 21 from buying "nonintoxicating" 3.2% alcohol-by-volume (ABV) beer, but it continued to allow 18- to 20-year old females to buy the same type of beer. A man between the ages of 18 and 20 and a commercial vendor of 3.2% beer filed suit, claiming Oklahoma violated the Equal Protection Clause because it did not treat men and women the same way (*Craig v. Boren*, 1976). The case provides a window into the kind of justification that may be required for a law that treats groups of people differently on the grounds of public health.

Oklahoma defended its law in the Supreme Court as serving the interests of traffic safety and produced statistical evidence showing that males aged 17 to 21 were more likely to be arrested for drunk driving, to be killed or injured in traffic accidents, and to drink beer and drive. It also cited evidence consistent with these statistics from other states. Although the Supreme Court recognized that traffic safety was an important interest for the state, it pointed out flaws in the statistics and research provided to support the law. The Court found that none of the evidence looked at the dangerousness of 3.2% beer or connected its consumption to gender differences; instead, Oklahoma put forth evidence of alcohol use generally. The Court also pointed out the irony that Oklahoma was pursuing a traffic safety law that addressed supposedly "non-intoxicating" beer. It concluded that the law violated the 14th Amendment and declared it unconstitutional.

The analysis of the evidence tells us that the judiciary, at least in some cases, will look closely for a consistent thread connecting: (a) the distinctions a law makes between different classes of people, (b) the interests the law purports to serve, and (c) the evidence produced to support the law. Two key considerations drive equal protection challenges: whether the text or application of the law is being challenged and the nature of the classification involved.

Challenging the Text or Application of the Law

The first consideration in equal protection claims to note is whether the text or the application of the law is at issue. An aggrieved party challenging the text of a law can argue that it creates categories or classifications and outlines different treatment for different populations. A party challenging the application of a law can argue that, while the law is neutral on its face, it is being implemented in a discriminatory manner. The distinction implicates the analysis a court will perform.

First, a party may bring an equal protection claim when a law categorizes two or more groups of people differently and has specific requirements or prohibitions attached to those classifications. A proposed law that treats two (or more) categories of people differently should always be carefully reviewed, but note that not all such classifications are invalid. The 14th Amendment prohibits "invidious discrimination" (*Williamson v. Lee Optical*, 1955), but it "does not take from the State the power to classify" in its exercise of the police power (*Lindsley v. Natural Carbonic Gas Co.*, 1911). For instance, a state can use its police powers to bar unvaccinated children from enrolling in school, even though such laws clearly create two classes of people (those with up-to-date vaccinations and those without).

Second, the text of a law may not create a classification, but the government could apply it differently to different groups. For example, state regulations govern drinking water that comes from wells. The texts of these laws do not create classifications but apply to whomever wants to operate a drinking water well, so that "facially" there is nothing constitutionally invalid about these laws. However, a religious group operating a camp with a community well could claim an equal protection violation if it believed the regulating agency was enforcing the law against it, while ignoring the violations of other similarly situated groups that were not religious. In this situation, the application of the law would run afoul of the Equal Protection Clause by discriminating on the basis of religious beliefs—an impermissible classification.

Proving an equal protection violation when the law is neutral on its face is, however, extremely difficult. The fact that a law has a "disproportionate impact" on a particular group is not enough to establish an equal protection violation. There must also be evidence that the law is being implemented with a discriminatory purpose, as when requiring recruitment procedures that unfairly disadvantage members of certain races (*Washington v. Davis*, 1976).

The Classification Involved and the Level of Judicial Scrutiny

The second consideration in equal protection cases is the nature of the classifications made by the law or its application. Different types of classifications trigger different types of judicial review. The two levels of judicial scrutiny discussed in Chapter 11 also apply to equal protection cases, with an additional intermediate level, and many claims involve both due process and equal protection issues. Under substantive due process, cases involving fundamental rights trigger strict scrutiny and cases involving nonfundamental rights trigger rational basis review. Under equal protection, laws involving *suspect classes* trigger strict scrutiny, whereas *quasi-suspect classes* trigger intermediate scrutiny, and all other classifications trigger rational basis review. These distinctions have huge implications for governmental actions.

First, laws that divide people into suspect classes and create different consequences for the one class over another receive strict scrutiny. Suspect classes include race and national origin, factors the Supreme Court has stated "are so seldom relevant to the achievement of any legitimate state interest that laws grounded in such considerations are deemed to reflect prejudice and antipathy—a view that those in the burdened class are not as worthy or deserving as others" (*City of Cleburne, Tex. v. Cleburne Living Center*, 1985). The Court further explained the need for judicial interpretation because discrimination against minority groups "is unlikely to be soon rectified by legislative means." Laws that impose differing burdens on fundamental rights—such as the right to marry, obtain contraception, and raise and bear children—have also been subject to strict scrutiny in equal protection cases, even when a suspect class is not involved.

Beginning with *Craig v. Boren*, the 3.2% ABV beer case discussed previously in this chapter, the Supreme Court also introduced a new level of scrutiny for equal protection cases: *intermediate scrutiny*. Laws that divide people into quasi-suspect classes, such as gender or illegitimacy, and create consequences for one class over another receive intermediate scrutiny. Under intermediate scrutiny, the government must show that the law furthers an important governmental interest through means that are substantially related to that interest. This is a less exacting standard that strict scrutiny but calls a more searching inquiry than rational basis review. In the context of laws addressing gender, the Court has said that although there may be valid reasons for gender-based distinctions, "if the statutory objective is to exclude or 'protect' members of one gender because they are presumed to suffer from an inherent handicap or to be innately inferior, the objective itself is illegitimate" (*Mississipi University for Women v. Hogan*, 1982).

Finally, laws that create any classification of people other than suspect or quasi-suspect classes fall under rational basis review, requiring only that the law be rationally related to a legitimate government interest. Note that although categories such as age and disability do not receive heighted scrutiny under the Court's Equal Protection Clause jurisprudence, there are separate civil rights laws prohibiting discrimination on these bases.

Equal Protection in the Context of Public Health

Public health laws and the agencies that carry them out are subject to the 14th Amendment's equal protection requirements. As noted, public health laws can create different classifications of people, and many, if not most, of the distinctions are proper exercises of legislative and executive authority. They do not rely on suspect or quasi-suspect classes and are not subject to strict or intermediate scrutiny. For example, governments may use clinical disease criteria to sort people into those who have been potentially exposed to an infectious disease and those who have not. Officials can create permitting schemes for health-related activities, such as for restaurants, and apply different tiers of regulatory requirements based on the risks posed. Licensing laws can require some healthcare professionals but not others to register with the state. These laws, and many others, typically survive rational basis scrutiny because they are reasonably related to legitimate government interests.

However, when similarly situated people are subject to disparate treatment, either directly in the text of a public health law or through the implementation of an otherwise neutral law, an equal protection analysis may show the treatment to be improperly discriminatory. Equal protection violations in the enforcement of public health laws can stem from two dynamics. First, many public health laws, particularly communicable disease control authorities, are broadly worded so that the laws do not have to be changed with each new disease that emerges as a threat to human health. Second, time is often of the essence with outbreaks and other public health emergencies. The faster that public health can take action, the faster the condition may be brought under control, and political and community pressures to act may be tremendous.

These dynamics can lead to government officials implementing laws in ways that may have discriminatory impact. Particularly in crises, it is all too common for prejudices—including those against race, class, religion, and sexual orientation—to drive policy. Public health agencies may identify and target marginalized populations as perceived sources of infection, as happened when a quarantine line was established around Chinatown in San Francisco during a suspected bubonic plague outbreak at the turn of the 20th century. The quarantine was explicitly designed to cover only Chinese-Americans and immigrants, who were believed to be the source of the disease. Lawyers for the Chinese-American residents went to federal court, which struck down the order (*Jew Ho v. Williamson*, 1900). The court held that the ordinance violated the Equal Protection Clause because (a) the quarantine was "underinclusive," in that other people who were potentially exposed to the disease were not similarly restricted, and (b) the quarantine was also wildly "overinclusive," in that there was no reason to believe that *all* people in Chinatown had potentially been exposed. Racial prejudice, rather than epidemiology, seemed to be behind the quarantine.

Nearly a century later, during the early days of the AIDS pandemic, New York City was sued after it sought and obtained an order to shut down a gay bathhouse in an effort to combat the spread of HIV. The evidence presented in court stated that the spread of HIV was associated with what was termed "high-risk sexual activities," and public health inspectors observed these activities taking place at the bathhouse (*City of New York v. New St. Mark's Baths*, 1986). However, it was also apparent that the actions of the health department targeted gay men, a minority community that had traditionally not been part of the political system and had suffered a long history of discrimination. Other groups that engaged in high-risk sexual activity were not similarly singled out. At the time, though, equal protection issues were not even discussed by the Supreme Court because discrimination on the basis of sexual orientation was not considered to implicate heightened scrutiny. Even today, multiple appellate courts have ruled that laws that make distinctions on the basis of sexual orientation are only subject to intermediate scrutiny. The Supreme Court—though it has now recognized a right to gay marriage—has not expressly said what level of scrutiny is appropriate in such cases.

Conclusion

Equal protection is a doctrine that demands fairness from our laws and the government agencies that enforce them. By attempting to regulate behaviors for the protection of the public's health, some laws will necessarily create different classes of people and call for differential treatment among them. Equal protection requires that these distinctions not be based on irrelevant stereotypes or prejudices and that they have a relationship to the goal that government is trying to achieve. How close the relationship between the government's interest and the distinctions it draws depends on whether or not there are suspect or quasi-suspect classifications involved.

Further Reading

Chase, M. (2003). *The Barbary Plague: The Black Death in Victorian San Francisco*. New York: Random House.

Rothstein, R. (2017). *The Color of Law: A Forgotten History of How Our Government Segregated America*. New York: Liveright.

13 | Constitutional Limitations

THE FIRST AND SECOND AMENDMENTS

Learning Objectives

- Understand how the courts have applied the First Amendment's Free Speech Clause to the regulation of commercial speech.
- Identify the standards courts use to assess whether public health laws unconstitutionally burden religious practice.
- Explain the limitations imposed on gun control measures by the Second Amendment and the interplay of law and politics in the regulation of firearms.

Introduction

The First Amendment to the US Constitution is short: "Congress shall make no law respecting an establishment of religion, or prohibiting the free exercise thereof; or abridging the freedom of speech, or of the press; or the right of the people peaceably to assemble, and to petition the Government for a redress of grievances." The words are simple, but that does not make the amendment easy to interpret: "no law," to take just the first clause, does not mean that Congress is not permitted to enact *any* legislation that deals with religion or speech. Congress cannot create an official religion—or ban one; it cannot shut down newspapers or outlaw demonstrations; but it can and *does* make rules that pertain to these activities. Congress even starts its sessions with prayer.

When people perceive that a law or other government action is too strongly favoring one religion over another religion or non-religion, or putting an excessive burden on religion, free speech, or assembly, they can sue. In court, judges decide how far legislators and law enforcers can go.

Public health agencies face these challenges most commonly over how courts have defined the extent of free speech protections for corporations, when law "burdens" religion, and what sort of evidence the government must produce to justify limits on speech or religious practice. Though these issues may seem unrelated to health, this chapter dives into their important consequences for agencies and their activities.

The Second Amendment is even shorter: "A well regulated Militia, being necessary to the security of a free State, the right of the people to keep and bear Arms, shall not be infringed." For most of the nation's history, these words were not read by courts to confer a personal right to have guns, but the Supreme Court changed that in 2008 with its decision in *District of Columbia v. Heller*. Since then, some forms of gun control have been eliminated, and for the large range of other gun control measures, the ongoing political debate has been reshaped by a new starting point. Both amendments provide excellent illustrations of how legal, political, and social contexts influence how courts reason and interpret evidence and the limits courts place on public health work.

The First Amendment: Freedom of Speech Meets Public Health

Since infectious disease lost its place as the leading cause of premature mortality, the most immediate threats to public health now come from the products we use and the things we do in everyday life. Fatty foods, sugary drinks, alcohol, contact sports, automobiles, ladders, and power tools are all causes of death, injury, and illness, but they are also things we need and enjoy. A world in which everything that can cause harm is banned would be a sad and inefficient world indeed. In a world where good or popular things also hurt people, public health law has several ways to make a difference. As in the case of cars, it can regulate the manufacture and use of the product to increase safety. It can limit who has access to a product, as it does when it puts age limits on the purchase of tobacco or the driving of cars. It can use taxes to discourage consumption, as it does with alcohol. And it can try to change our knowledge about and attitudes toward a product, as when law requires product information or warnings to be placed on packages, or limits the kind of advertising or promotion a seller may conduct. Whenever public health law undertakes to interfere with or require information, it enters into the realm of the First Amendment's protection of speech.

First Amendment Limits on the Regulation of "Commercial Speech"

It was not always so. In 1956, the Rhode Island legislature passed laws banning any advertising about the price of alcohol in the state, including newspaper ads. The legislature was acting on the belief that advertising about sales or cut-rate alcohol would encourage more consumption, which would lead to greater alcohol-related harm. These laws were consistent with initiatives across the country to suppress alcohol consumption by increasing taxes or limiting the number of alcohol sellers in many neighborhoods. No one questioned the police power of the state to restrict commercial advertising, and states regulated all sorts of professional and commercial promotion that was considered bad for the public or against guidance from professional standards. The First Amendment was not thought to apply in any important way to these nonpolitical matters, a view that was also consistent with prevailing theories about why a First Amendment protection of speech existed in the first place.

There were and remain three enduring ideas of the social "goods" the First Amendment promotes and what policies it furthers. In the *marketplace of ideas* rationale, free competition of ideas will, like an invisible hand, separate the brilliant from the stupid, the false from the true. In the *self-governance* model, free expression is necessary for citizens to participate in the democratic process. In the *individual liberty* model, the ability to express oneself is a critical element of individual autonomy. In all these theories, the function of the First Amendment is to protect of individual rights from government interference. These rationales do not necessarily conflict with each other and can even be seen as complementary, but they can lead to different views of what speech should be protected. The self-governance model focuses on political speech and the relationship of free speech to democratic processes. The other two, particularly the marketplace of ideas rationale, lend themselves to applications that have nothing to do with politics.

In 1975, the Supreme Court ruled on a newspaper editor's challenge to a Virginia law that banned ads for abortion services (*Bigelow v. Commonwealth of Virginia,* 1975). With this link to abortion, the case had a political cast, but the Court's holding that a state could not ban truthful ads for legal products served as precedent the next year in another Virginia case challenging a rule that advertising prescription drug prices was "unprofessional conduct" for pharmacists (*Virginia State*

Pharmacy Board v. Virginia Citizens Consumer Council, 1976). Justice Blackmun's opinion for the Court made clear that the First Amendment protected factually accurate commercial speech and dismissed as paternalistic the state's argument that it was protecting the public from advertiser manipulation. Consistent with the marketplace of ideas model, the Court thought it more sensible "to assume that this information is not in itself harmful, that people will perceive their own best interests if only they are well enough informed, and that the best means to that end is to open the channels of communication rather than to close them." The decision also explained that the free flow of commercial information was a right, not just of the commercial speaker but also of the consumer as recipient of the information. The idea that the marketplace of commerce was also a marketplace of First Amendment ideas started to take hold.

Also important around this time was a ruling that corporations, as associations of individuals, had their own First Amendment speech rights (*First National Bank of Boston v. Bellotti*, 1978). This has led in at least two important directions. The rule means that there is no question that a corporation can itself be a plaintiff seeking First Amendment protection in a challenge to a public health regulation. It was also a major step on the road to the Supreme Court's decision in *Citizen's United*, which held that the government could not restrict political contributions by corporations and other legal associations (*Citizens United v. Federal Election Commission*, 2010). This has the indirect but important effect of increasing the power of corporations in the health policymaking process.

Though commercial speech and speakers were covered by the First Amendment, for the next few decades, the Court generally held to the view the government had greater leeway in regulating commercial speech than other forms. It set out what was initially treated as a fairly lenient test in the 1980 *Central Hudson* case, which used a four-pronged test to decide whether a limitation on commercial speech should be allowed: whether (1) the speech is truthful and related to legal products, (2) government's interest in the restriction is substantial, (3) the regulation "directly advances" that interest, and (4) the regulation is no more extensive than necessary to serve that interest (*Central Hudson Gas & Electric Corp v. Public Service Commission*, 1980). If the speech was false or concerned an illegal product, the case was over: the First Amendment does not protect the advertising rights of heroin dealers or stock fraudsters. But if the speech was protected, it was up to the government to satisfy the next three prongs of the test.

Though the *Central Hudson* test seemed to respect the public interest in commercial regulation, it had teeth. In 1996, that old Rhode Island law on alcohol-price advertising failed the test (*44 Liquormart, Inc., et al. v. Rhode Island et al.*, 1996). The price information was accurate and factual, so it was clearly protected. The state's interest in promoting temperance was accepted by the Court as substantial, satisfying the second prong, but that was not enough. Because the information was accurate and factual, the state bore the burden of proving under the third prong that the restriction "significantly" advanced that interest and that there was no reasonable alternative that did not limit speech. Put to this more stringent standard of proof, the state could not produce sufficient evidence that the laws reduced consumption. The state conceded that it could have just banned or taxed cut-rate alcohol instead of limiting speech by banning the ads.

The case was interesting in a number of respects. One was the Court's suspicion of paternalistic regulation of the information environment and its faith in the ability of consumers to behave rationally in the face of advertising. Another was the rejection of the state's argument that its legislative common sense should be enough to establish that the law was effective; the Court now wanted scientific evidence. Would legislatures have to start commissioning studies to justify laws touching commercial speech?

Perhaps of greatest interest was the way the Court applied the fourth prong. The Court treated taxing or banning cheap alcohol as an alternative that eliminated the need to limit advertising. The Court ignored entirely the question of whether these theoretical alternatives were available in political reality. Warnings and other informational strategies are often used precisely because a ban is not politically possible—tobacco is the case in point. More broadly, as Justice Thomas noted in a separate opinion, bans and prohibitive taxes will almost always be an option in cases of informational regulation, leading to the paradox of the Court preferring to minimize restrictions on speech "even if the direct regulation is . . . more restrictive of conduct generally." The commercial speech doctrine was emerging as a major impediment to public health's use of "soft" informational regulations to reduce the harm of products that were far too popular or useful to ban outright.

The steadfast protection of commercial speech, the demand for scientific evidence of significant effects, and the paradox spotted by Justice Thomas have all been seen in cases since *Liquormart*. In 2001, the Court struck down regulations that aimed to protect children from tobacco advertising by banning outdoor and point-of-sale ads within 1,000 feet of a playground, elementary school, or secondary school on the grounds that the restrictions were broader than necessary (*Lorillard v. Reilly*, 2001). A decade later, it struck down a Vermont law prohibiting pharmaceutical companies from using physician prescription records for marketing purposes (*Sorrell v. IMS Health, Inc.*, 2011), reaffirming its view that government has no legitimate interest in "preventing the dissemination of truthful commercial information in order to prevent members of the public from making bad decisions with the information" (*Thompson v. Western States Medical Center*, 2002). Cases in the lower courts have called into question the Food and Drug Administration's (FDA) long-standing ban on companies marketing drugs for uses that the agency has not approved, even if the marketing is truthful (*U.S. v. Caronia*, 2012). In all these cases, what was once deemed routine consumer protection has been recast in a First Amendment light as an unjustified burden on corporate speech.

Limits on Compelled Commercial Speech

Protection of commercial speech does not just apply to advertising; it also applies to the venerable tradition of product labeling. From the classic skull-and-crossbones warning label on a poison bottle to the list of ingredients on a soup can, laws require manufacturers and sellers to disclose information about their products to consumers. Once thought of as beyond challenge, the idea that this can sometimes be unconstitutional, "compelled speech" has started to influence public health law practice.

Government, as a general rule, can compel accurate, nondeceptive disclosures aimed at helping consumers make more informed, healthier choices. The Court has, for example, upheld discipline of an attorney who failed to provide required information about his fee arrangement in an ad for his services (*Zauderer v. Office of Disc. Counsel*, 1985). The decision was understood to set out a relaxed standard of review for such rules, as long as the required message was "factual and uncontroversial." This fits the marketplace of ideas premise that more speech is good.

Regulation requiring disclosures, such as food labels or drug warnings, have been regularly upheld. Tobacco supplied the initial model for special warnings on dangerous products, with the Surgeon General's warnings that have appeared in various forms on tobacco products for decades. A national advocacy campaign on fetal alcohol syndrome led Congress to require similar warnings on alcohol products. But, as the effort against tobacco continued and as continued reductions in smoking became more difficult to achieve, tobacco control advocates pushed for more dramatic warnings. The issue of warnings also became a feature of the politics of obesity control, with some calling for health warnings on sugary products.

In the 2009 Family Smoking Prevention and Tobacco Control Act, Congress gave the FDA authority to regulate the manufacturing, marketing, and sale of tobacco products. As part of the law, Congress instructed the FDA to issue regulations creating a new warning label system that included not only more forceful textual warnings of risk but also arresting graphics (see Figure 13.1), all of which would take up a larger portion of the package.

Tobacco companies challenged the warning provision in two different cases. Although one federal appeals court upheld the warning require-ment, the Court of Appeals for the D.C. Circuit rejected the new labels in a manner that sent chills down many a public health law spine (*R.J. Reynolds Tobacco Co. v. U.S. Food & Drug Administration*, 2012). The court suggested that the graphic warnings could not be considered "fac-tual and uncontroversial" because of their emotional impact, and therefore tobacco companies were being unconstitutionally forced to express nega-tive views on their own product. From the public health perspective, that was the whole point: decorous, neutral warnings were not very effective anymore. On the question of effectiveness, the court set an impossible standard of evidence, essentially requiring the most rigorous scientific proof that labels alone would have an independent and substantial impact

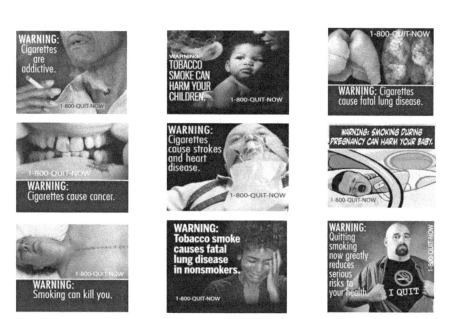

FIGURE 13.1. Proposed FDA graphic tobacco warning images.
US Department of Health and Human Services

on smoking. People in public health knew that the labels were not a panacea but part of a web of efforts to change attitudes and behavior. No place in the world had relied solely on labeling for this, so there was no evidence that could meet the court's standard of proof. Perhaps the scariest part for the public health community was the court's repeated suggestion that health warnings were not factual but merely "ideological" opinions trying to influence smokers to adopt a particular point of view. Indeed, the court wrote, "we are skeptical that the government can assert a substantial interest in discouraging consumers from purchasing a lawful product, even one that has been conclusively linked to adverse health consequences" (*R.J. Reynolds Tobacco Co. v. U.S. Food & Drug Administration*, 2012). Improving public health, it seemed, was not the government's job, at least not if it got in the way of business.

The decision was later partially overruled, but by then the FDA had decided to withdraw its rule and start over. As a result, it will be a long time before the United States has the kind of labels called for in the World Health Organization's Framework Convention on Tobacco Control and now used effectively in dozens of countries around the world (Noar et al., 2016). The defeat was another blow to public health efforts to use soft means to change behavior around a dangerous product and yet another example of the courts continuing to ratchet up the evidentiary standard used in deciding commercial speech cases.

Overall, the Speech Clause of the First Amendment has become a major limit on public health legal action, but the story is still unfolding. The trend could continue, or the pendulum could swing back. As some commentators have noted, the Court's exacting scrutiny of any law that seems to touch a broadly defined concept of free speech is now running up against other important constitutional values: the police power to protect health, the separation of powers, and our system of federalism, all of which have traditionally given legislatures and state governments considerable leeway to decide how best to protect the public and regulate the marketplace (Parmet & Jacobson, 2014).

Religious Freedom and Public Health

Another feature of the First Amendment is its guarantee of religious freedom. Its Free Exercise Clause protects the right to exercise religion without unreasonable governmental interference. Its Establishment Clause prohibits the government from giving official status or sanction to a religion or favoring one religion over another or religion over non-religion. Limits on public health actions have come mainly from the Free Exercise side.

Government regulations using the police power to protect health, safety, and welfare typically apply to everyone involved in a regulated activity. It would actually be an Equal Protection problem to pick out particular groups, like Catholics or atheists, to cover or exclude (see Chapter 12). Occasionally, though, religious people have perceived laws and policies as preventing the free exercise of their religion. Amish plaintiffs, for example, persuaded the Supreme Court in a 1972 case that the state's interest in requiring children to complete two years of high school was not sufficiently important to justify the burden it placed on Amish practice, which directed children into vocational training meant to support their maintenance of the traditional way of religiously-governed life in the community (*Wisconsin v. Yoder*, 1972). Free Exercise claims come up periodically in public health. Amish people have resisted traffic safety laws requiring reflective signs on their buggies. Other religious people have sought religious belief exemptions from vaccine requirements. In a 1990 case, the Court rejected the claim by two Native American drug-abuse counselors that the Free Exercise Clause protected them from being fired for the sacramental use of peyote (*Employment Division v. Smith*, 1990).

So far, the Supreme Court has hewed to the rule that laws that are neutral and have a secular purpose do not violate the Free Exercise Clause even if they have no exception for religious practices. In contrast to the free speech cases, the Court has not required states to make strong scientific showings that the rule is necessary, and it has not pressed them on less restrictive alternatives. At the same time, however, a state can generally provide exceptions if it wants to—for example, exempting the Amish from some road safety laws—without violating the Establishment Clause. Many states allow people to forego required vaccinations for religious reasons.

This story got a little more complicated, though, after the peyote case, when Congress passed the Religious Freedom Restoration Act (RFRA; 1993). The law requires that any statute or regulation that substantially limits religion be narrowly tailored to serve a compelling government interest. Congress was, in essence, attempting to force courts to apply strict scrutiny to Free Exercise cases arising from general laws. The Court found RFRA unconstitutional as applied to state and local law, and limited its application to federal laws (*City of Boerne v. Flores*, 1997).

RFRA has accordingly figured in important cases of federal health policy. The Court has ruled that the closely held corporations whose owners objected on religious grounds to a federal law requiring employee insurance plans to cover contraceptives were entitled to an exemption because the federal government could find ways to ensure employees were covered that did not burden religious beliefs (*Burwell v. Hobby Lobby*, 2014). *Hobby Lobby* did not extend this protection to all corporations, nor did it suggest that this kind of protection was also available under the First Amendment. Only time will tell if the expansion of regulatory immunity that the Court has found in the Free Speech Clause will spread to the Free Exercise Clause as well.

The Second Amendment and Gun Violence

Firearms cause more than 30,000 deaths a year in the United States, including both homicide and suicide. This is a major source of preventable and early mortality, about the same as motor vehicle deaths. As with cars, then, we can see guns as legal products with legitimate uses whose harms can potentially be significantly reduced by regulations that make the product safer (e.g., trigger locks), restrict access to people at high risk of misuse, and warn users of the risks. There is, however, no auto-safety equivalent of the National Rifle Association, which lobbies and organizes aggressively against virtually any form of serious gun regulation (and, indeed, any form of government-funded gun safety research). Nor does the gun issue have an equivalent of the National Highway Transportation Safety Board, a government agency that focuses on public safety. Even setting aside any constitutional issues, the regulation of guns has long been politically fraught.

For most of US history, it was settled law that the Second Amendment did not confer an individual right to bear arms, meaning that it placed no limitations on the regulation of firearms and their use, including complete bans on certain kinds of weapons or their possession in particular settings. The primary limit on gun regulations was political. States and cities whose voters favored gun control had strong regulations, and states and cities whose voters opposed gun regulation had more relaxed gun laws. In Congress, there was a relatively restrained federal role in regulation, interrupted by moments of stronger action (the Brady law after President Reagan was shot) and reaction (a ban on gun research at the Centers for Disease Control and Prevention; the preemption of gun-related tort suits). In 2008, *District of Columbia v. Heller* changed the law; it did not change the politics that much at all.

In *Heller*, the Supreme Court ruled for the first time that the Second Amendment provided an *individual* right, unconnected from service in a militia, to possess a gun for self-defense (*District of Columbia v. Heller*, 2008). However, as with other constitutional rights, this right is not absolute. The Court was clear that the Second Amendment does not confer a right "to keep and carry any weapon whatsoever in any manner whatsoever and for whatever purpose." The justices indicated that guns can be denied to certain groups of people, such as felons and the mentally ill, and banned in "sensitive places" like schools and government buildings. Moreover, the Court suggested that "dangerous and unusual" firearms—apparently those not in "common use" for traditionally lawful purposes—can be banned entirely, as can certain forms of arms-bearing, like concealed carrying.

Under *Heller*, gun regulations that focus on these categories of people, arms, and activity are generally regarded as consistent with the Second Amendment's protection of individual gun rights. Regulations that go beyond these "long-standing" and "presumptively lawful" categories may also be constitutional, but they will have to pass a stricter test. In those cases, courts typically ask whether the burden imposed on the Second Amendment is justifiable in light of the governmental interest being asserted (usually public safety or crime control) and the degree to which the regulation furthers it (*Hollis v. Lynch*, 2016). The weight of that burden varies depending on the extent of the intrusion and the evidence supporting the law.

The Court's majority in *Heller* struck down Washington, D.C.'s blanket prohibition on handgun possession in the home, concluding that "the enshrinement of constitutional rights necessarily takes certain policy choices off the table," including D.C.'s citywide handgun ban and safe storage requirement. This matters for federalism and localism, because some strict forms of gun control at the state and city level are now unconstitutional. But D.C.'s law was an outlier to begin with—among major cities, only Chicago had anything similar, and it, too, was struck down shortly after *Heller* (*McDonald v. City of Chicago*, 2010). Most of the measures that poll well with Americans appear still to be legal—subject as always to political limitations. Even after *Heller*, courts have upheld a wide range of gun control laws, including assault weapon bans, restrictions on high capacity magazines, bans on concealed carrying, permit requirements for public carrying, and the background check provisions of the federal Brady law.

The continued room for regulation and the continued importance of politics were both displayed in California in 2016. Its legislature passed a dozen separate gun controls that included requiring an ID and a background check to purchase ammunition, creating a new state database of ammunition owners, banning ammunition magazines that hold more than 10 bullets, and restricting the loaning of guns without background checks to close family members. Governor Brown signed these, but he vetoed other bills authorizing judges to issue "gun violence restraining orders," which authorize seizure of guns from people at high risk of violence, and limiting purchases of rifles or shotguns to one per month. All the laws would likely have passed muster under *Heller*.

Conclusion

The rights protected by the US Constitution have a powerful status in law and culture. None of them are absolute; all of them are subject to necessary limitations for important purposes. What is protected and what restrictions are reasonable changes over time. In the early 21st century, the First Amendment has become a powerful tool for challenging limitations on corporate speech, and there have been more aggressive efforts to use the Free Exercise Clause and the Second Amendment to overturn public health laws.

Further Reading

Parmet, W., & Smith, J. (2006). Free Speech and Public Health: A Population-Based Approach to the First Amendment. *Loyola of Los Angeles Law Review, 39*, 363–446.

Sharfstein, J. M. (2015). Public Health and the First Amendment. *The Milbank Quarterly, 93*(3), 459–462.

Webster, D. W., & Vernick, J. S. (Eds.). *Reducing Gun Violence in America: Informing Policy with Evidence and Analysis*. Baltimore: Johns Hopkins University Press.

14 | Administrative Challenges

Learning Objectives

- Understand the law governing how administrative agencies make and enforce rules.
- Explain how the public can participate in the rulemaking process and how individuals can directly challenge public health agency actions and decisions.
- Describe the legal standards that courts apply to determine the validity of agency regulations.
- Recognize the role of the writ of habeas corpus as a mechanism for challenging administrative actions that result in confinement.

Introduction

Enactment of a statute or an ordinance by an elected body of legislators is the most familiar form of lawmaking in the United States and its states, territories, and cities and counties. Agencies inside the executive branch of government also make rules, usually referred to as "regulations." For public health agencies, these rules can cover a range of topics, from food safety to immunizations. These agencies also make a variety of other legal decisions that must conform to existing law or follow specified procedures (such as issuing or denying permits, or defining eligibility for certain programs). The area of law that captures all of these functions is called *administrative law*.

This chapter introduces the basic elements of administrative law and some key related legal doctrines. It starts with how agencies make or promulgate regulations and the rights of the public to have input. It then addresses the law governing legal challenges to the validity of the rules that agencies succeed in issuing. Finally, the chapter discusses how people can challenge enforcement actions, both through administrative channels and via the writ of habeas corpus, a venerable form of challenge to government action that plays an occasional, dramatic role in public health cases.

How Agencies Make Regulations and the Public Participates

The process for creating and adopting new regulations is determined by legislatures in statutes. Because legislatures do not typically have the expertise to determine the details for how to improve transportation, housing, and public health, they create and delegate authority to agencies to implement programs and promulgate regulations. This relationship holds true at the federal, state, and local levels. As noted in chapter 10, states have *administrative procedures acts* (APAs) that outline this process. They are generally modeled after the federal APA and look similar across states, though there may be variation in the details. APAs provide a structured and transparent process for agencies to make regulations. Once they go through this process and are finalized, regulations have the binding force of law, just like statutes.

Under most APAs, agencies must first publish a notice of their intent to draft a new regulation. These notices will include basic information about the proposed regulation, including the underlying statutory authority and a description of what it will cover. The agency then publishes draft language of the new regulation. This publication allows interested parties to review the specifics of the regulation the agency is proposing. The agency may also have to publish details about the potential impacts of the proposed regulation, including assessments of the fiscal impacts to government budgets and economic impacts to the jurisdiction.

After publishing draft regulations, APAs generally require administrative agencies to allow the public to submit written comments to the proposed rules within a certain time period. Many APAs also require agencies to respond to comments as part of the process, either by incorporating the ideas into the proposed language or by stating why a change is not needed. Some states even require agencies to hold public hearings about proposed regulations to allow people to voice their thoughts and concerns. For example, in response to a proposed regulation on tattoo parlors, a health department might receive comments about individuals who suffered skin infections from unregulated, unqualified tattoo providers and from trained professionals who want regulations to make the field safer.

Once the time period for review and comment has passed and the agency has reviewed and addressed all the comments received, the agency—if it decides to move ahead with the regulation—publishes it in final form. Some states then require legislative approval of the final regulation, either through an affirmative vote to approve (or reject) or by the lapsing of a specified amount of time without legislative action. At this point, the regulation is ready to be implemented and enforced by the applicable agency.

Legal Challenges to Regulations

A person or a business that wants to prevent a regulation from taking effect can challenge it in court. Though participation in the review and comment period is not a prerequisite for challenging a regulation, the person or business must have an individual stake in the outcome of the grievance. A party that raises a challenge must have *standing* to raise the dispute and pursue it through the process. "Standing" means that the party is affected by the regulation and will suffer (or has suffered) some form of injury as a result of it being enforced.

Standing is a fundamental legal requirement in instituting a challenge (*Lujan v. Defenders of Wildlife*, 1992). Generally, there is three-pronged test to determine if a challenger has standing. The first part of the test requires that the challenger, or plaintiff, suffer from an actual or imminent injury that is not conjectural or hypothetical. Second, the injury must be fairly traceable to the alleged action taken by the administrative agency. Third, it must be likely, and not just speculative, that the plaintiff's injury could be adequately redressed by a favorable decision.

Once standing to challenge a regulation is established, a common challenge to regulations is that the agency exceeded its statutory authority when drafting and adopting it. An aggrieved party can challenge the interpretation of the underlying statutes and argue that the agency has exceeded the authority expressed in them. This challenge is known as *ultra vires* (meaning "beyond the powers"). If a court determines that an agency has acted ultra vires, the regulation could be overturned. For example, businesses could argue a health department exceeded its authority to conduct disease investigations when writing a new regulation that allows it to access healthcare facilities' businesses records, including credit card receipts.

In the seminal case of *Chevron USA Inc. v. National Resources Defense Council* (1984), the Supreme Court suggested that federal administrative agencies should be given discretion to interpret the statutes they administer if those statutes are unclear. *Chevron* outlined a two-step process: (a) If Congress has "directly spoken to the precise question at issue," the agency must "give effect to the unambiguously expressed intent of Congress." (b) However, if "the statute is silent or ambiguous with respect to the specific issue," the Supreme Court should defer to the agency's interpretation so long as it is "a reasonable interpretation"—even if the Court might have come a different conclusion on its own. This doctrine—known as the *Chevron deference*—was intended to give administrative agencies wide latitude in interpreting the statutes they administer.

Even with broad delegations, there can be questions about when agencies are overstepping their bounds. These issues come up, almost by definition, when agencies try to regulate products or activities that have previously gone unregulated. In the 1990s, the Food and Drug Administration (FDA), based on its broad authority to regulate "drugs" and "drug-delivery devices," tried to regulate tobacco products for the first time. It concluded that, despite the tobacco industry's denials, nicotine was an addictive drug, and therefore cigarettes and other tobacco products were "drug-delivery devices." The text of its authorizing statute, the Food, Drug, and Cosmetic Act, said nothing specific about the regulation of tobacco (indeed, it had been passed before the health hazards of tobacco use were widely recognized), but it provided the FDA with broad authority to regulate "drugs" and "devices" that were "intended to affect the structure or any function of the body."

The FDA's assertion of jurisdiction over tobacco products was challenged in court and ultimately worked its way up to the Supreme Court in *FDA v. Brown and Williamson* (2000). In a 5–4 decision, the Supreme Court ruled that the FDA had not been delegated the authority to regulate tobacco. Sidestepping the question of whether the FDA's interpretation of the statute was "reasonable," the majority collapsed the two steps of the Chevron analysis into one and conducted its own investigation into the meaning of the act's language, ultimately concluding that Congress would not have wanted the FDA to regulate tobacco without more explicit authorization.

Just as disputes occur at the federal level about whether agencies are acting within the scope of their delegated authority, similar dynamics play out at the state and local level. For example, the legal dispute involving the widely publicized attempt by New York City's Board of Health and then-Mayor Michael Bloomberg to restrict the serving size of sugar-sweetened beverages revolved around the issue of delegation. Despite broad authorizing language giving the Board of Health authority to "control . . . communicable and chronic diseases," the New York State Court of Appeals (the state's highest court) concluded that the board had exceeded the scope of its delegated powers. In the majority's view, the board had engaged in setting "new policy, rather than carrying out preexisting legislative policy" (*Matter of N.Y. Statewide Coal. of Hispanic Chambers of Commerce v. N.Y.C. Dept. of Health & Mental Hygiene*, App. Div. 2013). The dissent cautioned that the court's narrow interpretation of the board's delegated authorities—implicitly requiring very specific instructions from the legislature to address the issue—would leave the board stuck in the past and unable to adequately address contemporary public health challenges.

People can also challenge the constitutionality of regulations. A main function of the judicial branch is to determine whether statutes and regulations are constitutional. For example, a party could raise an argument that a public health regulation is unconstitutionally vague for failing to set a clear standard of what constitutes a violation. Other constitutional rights could be infringed by regulations as well, including all of those discussed in the proceeding chapters: the rights to free speech, to free exercise of religion, to bear arms, to due process, or to equal protection of the laws.

Challenges to Agency Decisions

Administrative agencies make decisions every day that affect individuals and businesses. Implementing and enforcing public health programs involves interpreting statutes and regulations and translating those interpretations into decisions and actions. Much like aggrieved parties can challenge the regulations themselves, they can also challenge these interpretations and decisions. Challenges to discrete agency decisions are initially heard by a single person, often called a hearing officer or administrative judge. These tribunals are different than traditional courts in that they are not part of the judiciary; they are part of the executive branch of government. Sometimes these tribunals sit within the agencies themselves and hear only cases related to the agency, but other tribunals are a completely separate agency and can hear challenges from multiple agencies.

The nature of these administrative tribunals may affect the arguments that they can rule upon. Executive and judicial branch courts can hear similar challenges, such as arguments that the agency violated a party's due process or equal protection rights. For example, if a health department seeks to revoke a food service permit based on a series of poor inspections scores, a party could argue that the officials' inspection reports leading up to the revocation order did not provide sufficient details about the violations and therefore did not provide constitutionally adequate notice under due process requirements. A religious camp cited and fined for numerous food preparation, drinking water, and solid waste violations could argue that the health department violated its First Amendment or equal protection rights by failing to treat other similarly situated camps in a like fashion.

Following through with these administrative challenges is a critical step for individuals or businesses aggrieved by health department actions and decisions, because parties who fail to pursue remedies in these administrative tribunals are generally legally barred from taking the same issue to state or federal court. In a recent case, two parents challenged a decision by a state health department to deny their request for a religious exemption from childhood immunization requirements. They claimed the denial of the exemption violated their right to the free exercise of religion (*Phillips v. City of New York*, 2.d. 2015). As described in the court opinion, the parents first filed their grievance with the health department, not a judicial branch court. Only upon an adverse decision from their appeal to the health department did the parents file suit in a judicial court. If they had not followed the proper administrative procedure, a judicial lawsuit would have probably been dismissed. This is referred to as the *exhaustion requirement*, and it serves an important public policy interest. Because administrative tribunals generally use simpler procedures and take less time than court cases, dispute resolution becomes more efficient. As in the *Phillips* case, people who are unhappy with this result can seek further review in court. However, as mentioned, courts are generally deferential to the decisions of agency tribunals.

Habeas Corpus

The *writ of habeas corpus*, which means, "produce the body," is another way decisions by administrative agencies can be challenged. It asks a court to order someone to be released from confinement if there is no adequate legal justification for holding him or her. Habeas is typically associated with challenges to criminal confinements, but it has a long history of being used to challenge detentions that occur in the civil context as well, including in public health cases. For example, habeas has been used to challenge confinement on grounds of refusal to undergo HIV/AIDS testing, suspicion of sexually transmitted disease infection, and likelihood of engaging in sexual violence (Ogolla, 2011).

Habeas can be also used to challenge isolation and quarantine orders, especially where the procedures laid out in the applicable laws are not sufficient to provide due process. In 1980, the West Virginia Supreme Court struck down a court order to have a tuberculosis patient isolated for treatment and to protect others from infection (*Greene v. Edwards,* 1980). When a petition was filed with the circuit court to have Mr. Greene isolated (presumably by the health department, although the decision does not say), it scheduled a hearing within a week but did not inform him that he was entitled to legal counsel at the hearing. At the hearing, the court learned that Mr. Greene did not have an attorney and appointed one for him, but it continued taking evidence without allowing time for him and his attorney time to confer. The court issued an order involuntarily isolating Mr. Greene in a hospital for treatment, and he filed a writ of habeas corpus with the West Virginia Supreme Court. The court accepted the writ, found that Greene had been denied his constitutional rights to due process, and struck down the court order of isolation.

Conclusion

Public health agencies take actions and make decisions at two different levels: the community level and the individual level. When a health department proposes a new regulation, the public can submit comments, and when it takes action in an individual case, the affected individual can directly challenge the decision. Commenting and challenging are both governed by administrative law. Because of the central role played by administrative agencies in public health, understanding administrative law is critical for anyone engaged in public health practice or research.

Further Reading

Asimow, M., & Levin, R. (2009). *State and Federal Administrative Law*, 3rd ed. St. Paul, MN: West Academic.

Barnett, K., & Walker, C. (2017). *Chevron* in the Circuit Courts. *Michigan Law Review, 116*(1), 1–73.

IV | From Policy Idea to Law on the Books

ADVOCACY AND LEGAL STRATEGY

15 | Strategic Considerations in Creating a Legal Proposal

Learning Objectives

- Identify the steps used to create a strategy for enacting a new legal proposal.
- Understand that stakeholder views on a legal intervention may be based on values or practical concerns.
- Learn the importance of opposition and support research and anticipating challenges.

Introduction

So far in this book, you have learned about how ideas for using law in health are developed, the broad authority of governments to enact health laws, and the various legal limits on that authority. Once a public health lawyer has a plausible policy idea that is not in conflict with other laws or the Constitution, he or she still faces the task of putting that idea into sound legal text. Whether a statute, a regulation, or an executive order, enactment will require the lawyer to work closely with others. Later chapters in this section examine the process of drafting a law and engaging in advocacy. In this chapter, we discuss the development of a legal-political strategy to guide drafting and support enactment. We focus on the strategic process of identifying stakeholders and figuring out who is likely to support or oppose a proposal. Stakeholder analysis is an essential starting point for any advocacy effort.

The Four Steps to Assessing Stakeholders

New laws and changes to existing public health laws will trigger reactions from individuals, businesses, and advocacy groups. Assessing the stakeholders who support and oppose a proposal is crucial to successfully navigating the policy process from beginning to end. Doing so in a meaningful and useful way is not as simple as identifying the usual suspects, such as listing the National Rifle Association as likely to oppose a gun control law and the Brady Foundation Campaign to Prevent Gun Violence as likely to support the same law. Rather, it requires a careful strategic planning process to

- Understand your own position and proposal and why others would care about it;
- Identify groups of people who will care about the aims of the proposal or the burdens it may impose;
- Research the history and positions of these groups; and
- Anticipate challenges that opponents may bring.

Figure 15.1 depicts the elements that make up a strategic approach to assessing the relevant stakeholders.

These steps should be taken in a generally linear fashion: you must identify stakeholders before you can analyze their support or opposition. However, the process is iterative, in that a detailed analysis of opposition could lead to modifications to an initial proposal to convert opponents into supporters or passive bystanders. These analyses should begin at the earliest stages of proposal development and drafting into sound legal form, rather

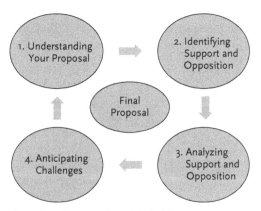

FIGURE 15.1. The four steps to assessing stakeholders.

than once it is finalized and rolled out for formal enactment. Understanding the stakeholders to a proposal should begin even before drafting specific language because that understanding could directly influence its details. Undertaking this process can also help you anticipate challenges and construct a better proposal that can survive the enactment battles.

Understanding Your Own Proposal and Why Anyone Would Care

It may seem counterintuitive to begin an exploration of how stakeholders think by examining one's own ideas, but successful proposals depend on it. It is critically important to understand the details of what you may or may not be asking of your community before you can confidently assess who may support or oppose new requirements or prohibitions. Many groups support the higher-level goals that lie behind public health laws and policies, but the legal intervention proposed to reach those goals, however laudable in theory, may inspire ardent support or vocal and organized opposition. For example, it may be difficult to find people who oppose a proposal to lower morbidity or mortality for a disease in a state, but proposing a new tax on sugary drinks to address that goal may divide important stakeholders. The details of the proposal can fundamentally change the positions of potential stakeholders from support (or silence) to opposition.

You cannot rest on the fact that your goals are valid. The legal means you choose may touch upon deeper, more immediate interests or cross abstract, but important, ideological lines. Consider proposing a policy calculated to reduce tobacco smoking rates. Through research, you learn about two proven ways to reduce smoking rates: raising cigarette taxes and prohibiting smoking in public places. As a group, a majority of restaurant and bar owners would probably recognize smoking as an unhealthy behavior and support a reduction in smoking rates in their community. They might support, or at least remain silent, about a proposal for an increase in cigarette taxes. However, they may oppose a law that prohibits smoking in restaurants and bars because they view smokers as a valuable customer base and would be concerned about an impact to their businesses. By contrast, and for similar reasons, corner store operators and other tobacco retailers are unlikely to actively oppose restrictions on smoking in public places but may be more strongly opposed to increases in cigarette taxes. Then again, there may be important voices in the community that oppose taxes on ideological grounds, regardless of the goals for the taxes or who has to pay them. Identifying the values and interests that inform a proposal can help identify what may motivate support or opposition.

Framing—how you describe your proposal and its rationale to stakeholders—can help, but it is not a panacea, and you should not let yourself be fooled by the appeal of your own arguments. For example, a state health department may propose a new statute that requires healthcare facilities to report preventable healthcare-associated infections (HAIs) so that it can track the incidence of HAIs over time and promote safer patient care. The proposal is a sensible surveillance activity from a public health point of view: reporting can set a baseline rate, and problem facilities that do not meet that standard can be identified and assisted. Like other forms of surveillance, HAI reporting can help deliver quality healthcare, increase consumer awareness, reduce adverse outcomes, and improve confidence in healthcare facilities. Politically, one might think of framing this proposal as enhancing personal or organizational responsibility and accountability, rather than another rule requiring people to send information to the government. The fact is, though, that people and groups whose values and interests are threatened by the proposal can and will use framing themselves. Patient groups may raise objections in terms of privacy. Others may see it as violating a political ideology of small or limited government. Healthcare providers may see a reporting law as an attack on their professional autonomy. Framing is important, but stakeholder analysis comes first.

It is crucial for your stakeholder analysis to figure out the extent to which potential opposition is primarily practical or values based. This can be difficult, because people use the arguments they have at hand, regardless of the roots of their opposition (Haidt, 2012): A person who objects to HAI reporting in principle may, in all sincerity, argue that it costs too much, while a person who resents the additional time required may argue her case in privacy terms. Sometimes, values and practicalities may even go in opposite directions: Healthcare facilities and professional organizations may support the primary goal of a new HAI reporting law—reducing the occurrence of HAIs. However, they may be opposed to the intervention of reporting on purely practical grounds—reporting would be an additional, burdensome requirement that takes time and providers' attention away from patients. Laws that require or prohibit activities can affect several different responsible parties on a range of grounds. Sometimes practical objections will raise issues you never thought of, or even convince you that your proposal will not work.

Revising or even abandoning a flawed idea may feel painful, but it will be a lot less painful than investing significant resources in promoting an idea that is set for failure.

Identifying the types of parties and activities that may be affected, and trying to anticipate the real roots of their concern, can help you get an initial list of people who could oppose a change to the public health law landscape and help you get ideas of how you might win them over or neutralize them through your legal work. Facilities may oppose HAI reporting based on the belief that collecting the required information and filing a report to the health department is burdensome and makes them look bad. As an alternative, state laws now require that facilities simply provide the health department with access to the information they already report for reimbursement purposes to the Centers for Disease Control and Prevention's (CDC) National Healthcare Safety Network. Hospitals may still oppose this requirement, but it at least obviates the need to submit separate reports to the state and CDC on the same topic. There may not always be an easy alternative to complex interventions addressing social determinants of health, but understanding the details of the intervention helps you analyze why someone may care and how a proposal may or may not trigger support or opposition.

Identifying and Engaging Opposition, Support, and Community Stakeholders

Once a new proposal is clearly understood and potential value interests and practical concerns are mapped out, lists of actual stakeholders can be made. Start with generic categories and then try to identify specific individuals in leadership positions within affected communities and organizations that represent those groups. It is important to engage with the stakeholder community early in the process. Internet research will be necessary but will not be sufficient. There are bound to be individuals and organizations that you are not familiar with, and only by talking to people will you be able to generate a complete list of stakeholders and their positions. In the case of an HAI reporting law, if physicians are a stakeholder group with possible opposing views, engagement might begin with physicians who serve as medical directors at large hospitals and leaders of the state medical association. Meetings and conversations may begin to reveal reasons they would support or oppose the proposal, including those based on values and interests or purely practical concerns. This matching allows a more detailed look at stakeholders who could potentially oppose change and on what grounds.

When viewed on its own without direct engagement, opposition could look powerful and overwhelming. It is beneficial to also identify and interact with a law or a policy's actual or potential supporters for two main reasons. First, an analysis of support can provide a list of allies that can be drawn upon when the strategy shifts to pursuing new or amended laws and policies, as described in Chapter 17. As with opposition research, it is important to engage with potential supporters. They may be able to provide more information than just their position on your proposal. They may have worked on similar proposals before and be able to provide suggestions to improve, pitfalls to avoid, and potential opposition to add to your research. Engaging with potential supporters can also provide a scale against which to measure the opposition. A reporting law aimed at reducing HAI incidence benefits patients primarily, and patient advocacy groups in the jurisdiction may support it. Healthcare facilities that have excelled at reducing HAIs could also welcome the chance to support a law that would highlight their efforts, and this might lead to physician and nurse champions who have publicly supported interventions and programs to reduce HAIs. When viewed in contrast to known and potential support, opposition could begin to look surmountable.

Stakeholder research can focus on the split between opposition and support, but community groups who are not the direct subject of a new legal intervention may also have significant interests in a proposal. They may provide background information or unique perspectives on a proposal and its goals, such as former HAI patients or family members who know about the problem but do not have formal position statements developed. For many proposals, engaging community members and groups becomes an issue of inclusion and health equity and is a critical component of developing a sound proposal. For example, individuals who live in a community where a proposal envisions zoning restrictions on fast-food restaurants as a way to combat obesity may have very different ideas on the relationships between the restaurants and the community and may offer other ways to encourage the consumption of healthy foods. Upon learning about the proposal, they may not support it because it does not fit within their community development ideas. Rather, they may support laws that address the food desert in which they live. A key to community engagement is not just to communicate about your proposal but to learn about the priorities a community has about its local health burdens and integrate community concerns and goals in your own policy agenda. Without engaging with the community, proposals could be reasonably criticized as top-down, tone-deaf approaches that do not address the conditions that people face every day.

Complete engagement and outreach with opposition, supporters, and community stakeholders facilitates mapping the stakeholder landscape for a proposal. This map can show the backdrop for mounting a campaign to advocate, and potentially lobby, for the passage or adoption of a new law or policy. Once a support and opposition identity-and-interests analysis is completed, research into the history and positions of stakeholders can begin.

Deeper Research on Support and Opposition

Many individuals and groups will have a history of advocacy or documented positions on public health law issues that can be found through research. Relationships, public positions, and legal actions are all sources of information that can help create a picture of the opposition and support for your proposal. In-depth, detailed stakeholder research is critical as a proposal develops, because potential supporting and opposing positions may shift as you learn more about their histories. In the case of HAI prevention, a state's hospital association may oppose public reporting laws based on the experiences of facilities in other states with similar laws. The same association may have been an ally on other proposals in the past and may support its members' facilities addressing the problem of HAIs through facility-based infection control plans and increased budget support for infection control practitioners—or perhaps it has not taken a position on reporting and access through the National Healthcare Safety Network. These details could lead to your relying on this relationship and discussing the proposal with them in the hopes of finding a compromise.

Another reason that detailed research can be useful at this stage is that you can study analogous individuals and groups to learn about their histories of support or opposition to similar proposals. If a proposal is new or novel, individuals and groups in the community may not have an established position, but those from other jurisdictions where the issue has been raised may have taken positions, for or against. Just as the language of public health laws and policies can be replicable across jurisdictions, positions of support or opposition may resonate widely and become adopted by groups who have not been faced with a particular public health law or policy.

Existing professional networks can help to understand stakeholder positions. Friends and allies who work in the policy field can be especially helpful in learning about positions that may have not been made public enough to appear online or in other resources. Your jurisdiction may have not addressed HAI prevention through law, but other jurisdictions may have. Reaching out to public health practitioners and attorneys in other areas of the country could reveal positions that healthcare facilities or hospital associations have taken for or against proposals similar to yours. Sometimes you will be able to draw key support from respected individuals and organizations outside your state or city to help you win over their local colleagues or affiliates.

Research into stakeholders can reveal if they have public positions on the type of law or policy proposed. They may have issued formal position statements on certain laws that you could find on their websites. However, thorough research is critical, as they could have expressed their points of view through the media in the form of interviews and op-eds or engagement in public fora. These public statements can be mined for details on how and why they may oppose or support your proposal.

Legal background research can be conducted from the perspective of researching potential opposition. Two areas of legal background that you should cover are prior legislative and regulatory activities and court cases. Bills from previous legislative sessions that did not pass can provide abundant research on potential supporters and opponents as they wound their way through legislatures, gained sponsors, and passed through committees. Depending on the jurisdiction, it may be possible to track the legislative opposition through the record of the previous legislative sessions. It may also be possible to identify individuals and groups who testified against a previous bill. Through board minutes, state registers, and agency records, failed attempts to promulgate a new regulation can also be researched. If time and resources allow, stakeholders connected with these legislative and regulatory histories can be a great source of information to understand opposition that may materialize against a new proposal.

Records from court cases can also contain opposition information. Opinions can be a one-stop shop for learning about why stakeholders have opposed a proposal. For example, those who opposed mandatory childhood vaccination in *Phillips v. City of New York* argued that the requirements and their associated exclusion rules violated their substantive due process, freedom of religion, and equal protection rights—claims that were all unsuccessful but still popular in the media (*Phillips v. City of New York,* 2015). Courts sometimes allow groups that are sympathetic to one side of the litigation or another to file *amicus curiae*, or "friends of the court," briefs that set out their views on the issues in the case. Amicus briefs, which can often be obtained through public court access systems, can be a font of detailed information about a stakeholder's views and their "evidence base."

Research into past positions of specific individuals and groups within stakeholder communities is necessary but not sufficient. Thorough research must also look for the interests of previous support and opposition, both value-based and practical. These interests become important as support and opposition analysis becomes more detailed. Positions on a previous public health law or policy based on one set of interests may not translate to new proposals or from one region or state of the country to another. Practical considerations for a new proposal may be even more difficult to gauge based on previous positions. Using a detailed version of the proposal, current potential practical interests may have to be reexamined and mapped out. Table 15.1 depicts part of a stakeholder analysis for a hypothetical HAI reporting bill.

It is important to develop a comparative analysis of what a proposal asks of the affected community, the potential practical considerations, and previous statements supporting or opposing similar proposals. This analysis could show potential disconnects between the details of previous practical opposition and the details of a new proposal, which can in turn be addressed as the campaign strategy is developed and plans are made to interact with the various supporting and opposing individuals and groups.

Anticipating the Challenges

Anticipating the most likely challenges is the end game of understanding the opposition. The steps in the process up to this point all focus attention on realistic challenges that opposition could raise as the proposal comes to life or after it is passed and implementation begins.

The distinction between enactment and implementation becomes a good way to organize potential challenges to a proposal. Opponents can certainly lobby policymakers to block or heavily amend a legislative proposal. However, opposition and challenges do not necessarily end when a law is passed. Many opponents to new public health laws will continue opposition into the implementation phase: they will challenge the promulgation of regulations or the appropriation of funding, and they may file challenges in the courts. Understanding the nature and depth of this

TABLE 15.1. Sample HAI Comparative Stakeholder Analysis

PROPOSAL—ESTABLISH STATEWIDE HAI COMMITTEE, REQUIRE REPORTING OF HAIS TO HEALTH DEPARTMENT, REQUIRE HEALTH DEPARTMENT TO PUBLISH REPORT AND INFECTION RATES, PROVIDE FUNDING TO HEALTHCARE FACILITIES FOR INFECTION CONTROL ACTIVITIES, MANDATE HAI CONTINUING EDUCATION CREDITS.

STAKEHOLDER	ROLE	CONTACTED?	POSITION ON PROPOSAL	NETWORK OR RELATIONSHIP INFORMATION	NOTES
Representative Charles Strong	Member of Health Labor Education Committee in house.	No	Opposed to previous reporting proposal	No	MD—former physician. Lead opposition to previous, reporting-only proposal
Dr. Sam Superman	Medical director, Suburban Hospital Inc.	Yes, phone introduction and meeting	Not opposed to HAI reporting in concept but concerned about methods and burden of double posting information	Suggested speaking with Dr. Wendy Wonder Woman	Would consider working on proposal with health department
Dr. Wendy Wonder Woman	Chief medical officer, Healthy Intown Hospital	Yes, quick phone call	Not known for sure but said she had thoughts, need to reschedule	Not yet	Very new in position, less than one year. State where she previously worked had an HAI reporting law
Patient Protection Union	Statewide patient advocacy group Sarah Goodheart, CEO	Yes, frequent contact. Contacted about reporting proposal	History of fully supporting proposal	Suggested contacting their national organization as they may have legal language that could be used	Goodheart is contacting patient advocates to inquire if they would like to actively support
State Medical Association	State association for physicians John Brown, chief lobbyist	Yes, frequent contact Contacted about reporting proposal	History of supporting infection control measures, including HAI focused CMEs John thinks board will support reporting, but devil is in the details, more to follow	Suggested waiting to contact other physicians until he can run issue internally with association	John retiring after next legislative session, may change dynamic within association

HAI = healthcare-associated infection.

opposition can help shape the advocacy campaign launched in support and the drafting of the proposal itself.

Challenges to enactment can certainly be associated with individuals or groups that have grounding in interest-based or practical concerns and be based on the history of stakeholders in a jurisdiction or in other similar ones. These challenges do not have to have a solid grounding in legal theory or doctrine, though they may form around the specific aspects of a proposed law or policy. Opposition can be based on, or expressed through, generalized economic, freedom, or other concerns. For example, motorcycle riders could object to passage of a new helmet law based on the argument that such a law would impinge the freedom of feeling the wind in their hair as they ride. This argument has little to no legal basis—there is no constitutional right to feel wind in your hair—but such a position could connect with powerful ideas of personal choice, freedom, and autonomy and has been sufficient to block passage of the law. The argument that a helmet law impinges a legal "right" to ride helmet-free would almost certainly not succeed in litigation after passage, but challenges before enactment can be raised even if they are based on misconceptions about the law. Challenges to enactment can also take a more concrete form. Stakeholders may seek amendments that weaken the requirements or enforcement provisions in your proposal. For example, in a hypothetical HAI reporting bill, opponents may offer amendments that create a statewide HAI committee, authorize the health department to investigate HAI outbreaks, and publish information about HAIs but eliminate the requirement for hospitals to report HAIs to the health department. The amendments could also delete a provision that sets monetary penalties for hospitals that do not comply with the law. With their proposed amendments, the opponents may shift to supporters, but your proposal has lost all of its regulatory "teeth." Even if opponents do not seek amendments to weaken the heart of your proposal, they may lobby appropriations committees to make sure the annual governmental funding bill does not contain any money devoted to implementing your new proposal.

Legal issues can also be raised to block passage, and if they are discovered during the opposition research process, these challenges should be anticipated and noted at this stage. For example, background research may have turned up a challenge to an HAI reporting regulation in another jurisdiction as being *ultra vires*, or beyond the authority of a health department. This argument could be raised in litigation against your HAI proposal after promulgation, but it has a legal grounding and could be used to block final passage of the new rule. Opposition could argue that the proposal should not be passed because it is *ultra vires* and vulnerable to litigation after passage. A threat of litigation can evolve into a basis of opposition if these arguments accumulate and gain traction.

Challenges to a new law can continue after passage. Opponents can file lawsuits or mount a public relations campaign against a new law. Opponents to your new HAI reporting law could file a lawsuit after passage and continue the argument that the regulations creating the requirements are *ultra vires* or that they violate procedural due process by not allowing sufficient validation of the submitted HAI data. They could forego litigation and mount an advertising campaign to influence a future legislative battle on eliminating your new regulation or the funding for implementation. The important lesson is to research, anticipate, and plan ahead. It is vital to consider these potential challenges and not only formulate responses but examine the proposal critically, revise it if need be, or even question the wisdom of moving forward at this stage.

Conclusion

Understanding opposition and support is a critical part of the public health law process. Pursuing new or amended public health laws and policies will not be met with universal support. Opposition and support groups will form, or will already be in place. Following a process of understanding your own proposal, exploring why anyone would care about your proposal, identifying groups of people who sympathize with or oppose the interests or burdens underlying all aspects of your proposal, researching the history and positions of these groups, and anticipating challenges allows you to develop a well-informed sense of where you stand. A realistic and organized view of the potential opposition and support can make proponents critically examine their own proposals before they are launched and serve as an effective first step in designing an advocacy campaign.

Further Reading

Brugha, R., & Varvasovszky, Z. (2000). Stakeholder Analysis: A Review. *Health Policy and Planning, 15*(3), 239–246.

Weible, C. (2006). An Advocacy Coalition Framework Approach to Stakeholder Analysis: Understanding the Political Context of California Marine Protected Area Policy. *Journal of Public Administration Research and Theory, 17*(1), 95–117.

16 | How to Write a Law

Learning Objectives

- Learn the basic anatomy of a law.
- Explain the steps in the process of writing a law ("drafting"), including understanding the goal of the law, incorporating the existing science and law, capturing the goal and intervention in organized language and structure, and soliciting expert and stakeholder feedback.
- Understand how definitions, cross-references, consistent terminology, and the use and placement of modifiers can affect drafting.

Introduction

Once the strategic considerations for a new or updated law are addressed, the details of the proposal must be drafted into legal or policy text. Clearly writing laws and policies ensures that they can be followed and enforced: providing individuals and businesses notice for how they must act, requirements to achieve compliance, and the processes necessary to take enforcement action. Laws must be captured in a form that can be read and understood by its targets, enforcement entities, and the courts. In writing a "law," drafters must add or amend the text of statutes, regulations, and even agency policies implemented with the force of law that impact public health activities.

So how do you write a law?

This is a simple question with a complex answer. Writing a law is much more than just putting pen to paper. It is a process that spans from the conceptual to the mundane, from the understanding of social goals to the proper placement of commas. Public health laws must balance the changing dynamics of science, the specific authority of agencies, the enormous diversity of populations, and the pre-existing rights of individuals.

Public health law is a transdisciplinary profession, and the task of writing laws is not an exception (Burris, Ashe, Levin, Penn, & Larkin, 2016). Although lawyers should be central to the drafting process, a well-crafted law or policy draws upon the expertise and experience of a wide range of professionals to achieve its goal. This chapter walks through the process of writing a law: understanding the goal of the law, incorporating the existing science and law, capturing the goal and intervention in organized language and structure, and soliciting expert and stakeholder feedback.

Understanding the Goal

The initial, and possibly most important, phase of writing a law or policy is to articulate the goal. What are you trying to achieve? A well-drafted law will name its intended public health goal and memorialize its intent through language (often in the law's preamble). Clarifying—and explicitly stating—the goal is critical. When the judiciary reviews a law during litigation and finds the language unclear, the first issue examined is often the intent of the legislative body that considered and passed the law. The overall goals of a law can be worded broadly, such as to "improve public health" or "increase health equity," or can be identified more specifically, as in "reducing racial disparities in heart disease."

As an individual who may be asked to assist with writing a law, you may be presented with a clear public health goal as the foundation for seeking change. If not, thoughtful discussion with the law's proponents and other public health professionals can be used to discern the public health problem they are trying to address. This transdisciplinary dynamic requires a team approach to identify the goals and incorporate them into the writing process.

Incorporating the Existing Science and Law

Once you understand the goal of the law, the next step is to understand and incorporate relevant legal and scientific principles. This step is critical to achieving the goals the law seeks to achieve. Understanding the science and law related to a proposal has two primary purposes.

First, science can provide the ingredients for the legal text. If you work within a government entity, you may have access to subject-matter experts in your own agency who may provide the content of your new law or the amendments you want to make to an existing law. An example is a New York law passed in 2013 requiring hospitals to follow protocols for the early identification and treatment of sepsis that had been developed through lessons from clinical research (Nguyen et al., 2007). Even when scientist colleagues are helping to draft the new law, it is important for attorneys involved to be conversant in the relevant scientific issues. Otherwise, key issues may be overlooked or the language may not be technically accurate.

Second, legal research can illuminate the context in which the law will operate. This context may help capture the subject matter, identify any existing laws or legal models in this area, and highlight independent legal doctrines, such as freedom of speech or preemption, that may influence how a law needs to be drafted to survive any future judicial scrutiny. If you are not an attorney, consultation with lawyers is critical to understanding this context; for attorneys who do not specialize in public health law or in the area of law at issue, it will be important to consult with other lawyers who work in the particular field.

For example, background research into the legal context for reducing access to highly addictive opioid prescriptions drugs will reveal prescription drug monitoring programs (PDMPs) as a potential intervention. Some jurisdictions have passed PDMP laws that require certain opioid prescriptions to be reported to a database and may also require healthcare professionals to consult the database prior to issuing a prescription. Among other purposes, such databases can help identify patients who are receiving opioid prescriptions from many different providers. Drafting a PDMP law (or any law) requires examining similar laws that have been passed by other jurisdictions, though they may not necessarily provide models to follow. (See www.pdaps.org for current and past PDMP laws.) Those laws may have been modified for political (as opposed to public health) reasons during the lawmaking process, and jurisdictions may have already identified problems with them. Contacting people familiar with the drafting and implementation of these laws can provide important context, as can entities that have created "model laws." One such entity, the Prescription Drug Monitoring Program Training and Technical Assistance Center at Brandies University, published the Prescription Monitoring Program Model Act that requires dispensers to submit certain prescription information to the PDMP and outlines other aspects of a system (Prescription Drug Monitoring Program Training and Technical Assistance Center, 2010). Although model laws may provide good ideas and language, they should also be approached with caution: the entity publishing the model may have a political agenda, the model may be out of date, or the model may be designed for a different state. In short, you should gather as much as you can from available sources, but be careful about "cutting and pasting" without knowing the full story behind a model or enacted law and how it has worked in practice.

Other constitutional provisions, judicial opinions, and legal scholarship may all be relevant to the construction of your law. Background legal research may reveal that your proposed legal text implicates First Amendment protections on speech or religion or that it is potentially preempted by a state or federal law. For example, in 2016 the City of Philadelphia passed a tax on sugary beverages including sodas (*Williams v. City of Philadelphia*, 2016). Pennsylvania had a state law that preempts a soda tax at the point of retail sales, so the drafters in Philadelphia drafted the tax to fall on distributors, to be paid regardless of whether the soda was ever sold at the retail level. Having an understanding of the larger legal context in which their tax would operate allowed them to draft an intervention that survived multiple challenges.

Capturing the Goal and Mechanism in Language

Finally! Now comes the time to blend everything you have learned into the language of a new law. Laws are rules created and enforced by legislatures and government agencies that have been granted the authority to do so. Laws have an "anatomy" and are made up of parts that play different roles in how they operate. At a minimum, a law will specify *rules of conduct*— activities people must do or not do—and who is subject to them. For rules that apply to ongoing activities, such as healthcare and business operations, many laws also contain an approval process, such as a permitting requirement, and monitoring mechanisms, such as inspections or reporting mandates. Penalties and enforcement procedures are critical elements of laws that outline the consequences for not complying and provide authority and direction for agencies that must implement them. Finally, because language is inherently vague, a law can have a definitions section to help guide the reading and interpretation of terms used in the other provisions. All of these elements are organized into sections with "provisions" that help people make sense of what the law is about, what behaviors need to be modified, and how the law will be implemented and enforced.

One key issue to consider is whether the law will be a *statute* or a *regulation*. The scope of statutes and regulations usually differ, and this contrast can significantly affect the drafting process. Statutes may grant authority to an agency to engage in an activity, such as conducting disease investigations and compiling data, and regulations can provide the details to make activities laid out by those authorities actionable. Statutes are often written broadly, with a provision that enables an administrative agency to promulgate regulations that describe how the law will be implemented and enforced. Regulations, on the other hand, are drafted as detailed statements that allow the regulated community to understand specifically how to comply with the rules and provide an administrative agency with guidance on how to implement and enforce the law.

With these initial considerations in mind, drafting a basic rule of conduct is a good place to start. Take aim at your goal, armed with the information obtained from experts on the background science and the legal context, and write down a simple statement of what the law will do. Within this statement, describe whether the law should be mandatory or discretionary. For example, the law could require a health department to modify its disease and injury reporting system to include information about opioid overdoses: "The health department *must* establish a mandatory reporting system for opioid overdoses to include information designated by the department." The same law could also be framed as a grant of discretionary authority to the health department: "The health department *may* establish a mandatory reporting system for opioid overdoses to include information designated by the department." Likewise, filing reports with the system could be mandatory, or it could be voluntary for health professionals. The exercise of starting with the simplest expression of the authority granted, or the behavior required or prohibited, will focus the text on the goals and provide a touchstone to revisit as the law becomes more complex. As a law develops through the drafting process, many elements can and will be added to flesh out the details, and the language can be cleaned up and made more precise.

Part of developing a simple statement of what the law will do includes identifying the people and entities to whom the law will apply. A law could require healthcare providers to consult the state's PDMP before prescriptions are written: "Healthcare providers who have the authority to prescribe drugs shall check the patient's prescription history in the prescription drug monitoring program prior to writing a prescription." The identity of these people and entities can be clarified as the law takes shape, or the law could simply require supervising physicians to check the system before writing a prescription. When identifying this potential variation, it is important to consider the possible effects (both positive and negative) of each option. For example, given the realities and burdens of running a medical practice, physicians may want to delegate checking the PDMP to affiliated professionals, such as registered or licensed practical nurses. A modification to delegate checking the PDMP could further the law's goals: "Healthcare providers who have the authority to prescribe drugs, *or their designees*, must check the patient's prescription history in the prescription drug monitoring program prior to writing a prescription." If physicians are permitted to delegate certain activities under this new PDMP law, the appropriate delegates must also be identified.

Additionally, a PDMP law would also need to identify the agency responsible for implementing and enforcing the law or multiple agencies with different roles. For example, the state health department may be responsible for maintaining the PDMP database and processing applications, and the boards of physicians and pharmacists may be responsible for enforcing the requirements the laws places on their respective licensees. To the extent the PDMP laws provide any criminal enforcement provisions, the law would also need to identify which law enforcement agency would be responsible for receiving criminal referrals and investigating alleged violations.

A law or policy must also specify exactly how it will work, such as articulating the enforcement and other consequences if a mandatory provision is not followed. A new law requiring doctors and pharmacists to check a PDMP prior to writing and filling a prescription may establish several possible consequences for violations. These could include civil fines, revocation of a system user's access, or suspension or revocation of the healthcare provider's license: "A prescriber or a dispenser who fails to comply with any of the provisions in this chapter may be fined not more than $2,000 per violation; may have his or her system access revoked; and may be reported to his or her respective board for disciplinary action." Many laws that require people or organizations to take certain actions must also tell them how to comply. If the crux of a statute requires a person to obtain a license before engaging in a particular behavior, a subsequent regulation would need to contain procedures on how to apply for the license.

Technical Drafting Issues

As a law is refined and becomes more complex, technical drafting issues arise, including definitions, cross-references, consistent terminology, and the use and placement of modifiers. If these issues go unaddressed, the law may be poorly written. Bad drafting has consequences: the law is difficult to interpret and implement, or it is challenged in court and overturned because the language is overly broad, ambiguous, or vague.

Consider the issue of access to care. Some jurisdictions have been looking to telemedicine as a way to increase access to health services in underserved areas of the country. One limitation to telemedicine has been that healthcare providers are traditionally prohibited from prescribing medicines without first conducting an in-person medical exam of the patient. A new law could address this problem by permitting prescribing solely through telemedicine, while limiting the practice in certain circumstances. Incorporating all of your objectives in one provision can be difficult and confusing. A hypothetical provision can highlight several problematic issues:

> A healthcare provider who has the authority to prescribe under law, physicians and nurse practitioners, has the authority the write a prescription notwithstanding physical examination requirements other than painkillers and muscle relaxers without conducting an in-person exam and documenting said examination in the patient's medical record through remote telemedicine means and mechanisms.

To say the least, this provision suffers from many problems. (Before reading further, see how many you can identify.)

The first issue is that the provision tries to define the individuals to whom the law applies at the same time it says what they can do. Trying to include these details in the middle of a law can make a substantive provision confusing and hard to interpret. The hypothetical telemedicine law is not clear about which healthcare providers it covers. The language also refers to the authority to prescribe "under law," but it is not clear under what law it is referring to. Additionally, the provision names specific professions, "physicians and nurse practitioners," but it is not clear if these are the only professions to whom the law applies or if they are included only as examples. This is made all the more confusing because there are other healthcare professionals who can prescribe, such as dentists, physician assistants, and veterinarians.

In our hypothetical telemedicine law, "healthcare provider" could be defined with more precision. That definition could be included in a section that covers only definitions or could be linked to other parts of the state's code or both. Terms can have "default" definitions that span across an entire code or chapter or definitions that apply to only a limited number of sections. Definitions can clarify many aspects of a law, including to whom the law applies, the scope of application, and the triggers for when a law becomes active or enforceable. Otherwise, the law could use a completely different term. In a similar law from Indiana, the term "prescriber" is used in the substantive provisions and is paired with a definition that lays out who qualifies as a prescriber under specific laws.

As used in this chapter, "prescriber" means any of the following:

1. A physician licensed under IC 25-22.5.
2. A physician assistant licensed under IC 25-27.5 and granted the authority to prescribe by the physician assistant's supervisory physician in accordance with IC 25-27.5-5-4.
3. An advanced practice nurse licensed and granted the authority to prescribe drugs under IC 25-23.
4. An optometrist licensed under IC 25-24.
5. A podiatrist licensed under IC 25-29 ("Provider," 2016).

This definition provides a more precise term—*prescriber*, rather than *healthcare provider*—and links the term to the specific legal authorities that grant each profession the ability to prescribe under Indiana law.

The hypothetical telemedicine law is also vague in several instances and lacks technical specificity and consistency. What is meant by "telemedicine means and mechanisms?" Without specific language or definitions, this phrase would be difficult to interpret and apply after the law is passed. *Cross-references* to other parts of a state's statutory code can be a way to tie different provisions together and provide more specificity. In the Indiana telemedicine law, a cross-reference ties the prescribing provision to a definition of telemedicine elsewhere in the code: "As used in this section, 'telemedicine services' has the meaning set forth for 'telemedicine' in IND. Code 25-1-9.5-6." ("Reimbursement for Telehealth Services and Telemedicine Services for Certain Providers," 2013). Also, the hypothetical language appears to create an exception for certain types of drugs. However, the descriptions of these drugs—"painkillers" and "muscle relaxers"—are everyday terms, rather than medical or legal terms that may be more precise. Consulting subject matter experts or finding terminology that is used in other parts of the code are ways to make sure you are using the right words in the right places. With this provision, the goal may be to exclude Schedule II drugs or a class of drugs that could be more precisely described or defined. Without such precision, laws may be vulnerable to attack on the grounds that they are "void for vagueness."

The provision also suffers from inconsistent use of terms. The language shifts from referring to a "physical exam" to an "in-person exam" and changes from "exam" to "examination." Though these variations may seem minor, shifting terminology can lead to questions about the scope of a law. Is the "physical examination requirement" the same thing as an "in-person exam?" Importantly, do they apply the same way to physicians and nurses as they do to different professionals who may have direct interactions with patients prior to prescriptions being written? The solution to the dangers of inconsistent terminology is to look for technically precise terms in other areas of legal code. If the law must create a new term of art, legal research may reveal how other jurisdictions have defined it (but again, be wary of uncritically importing language from other laws). If not, work out a term, define it, and use it consistently. The hypothetical law would probably include a phrase describing the examination that a physician must do to establish a physician-patient relationship, which would add specificity to its application.

Drafters also have to be careful with the placement of punctuation, modifiers, and subordinate clauses. In this draft provision, it is not clear whether the clause "without conducting an in-person exam" applies to prescribing generally or to prescribing painkillers and muscle relaxers. The choices drafters make about clauses can have significant consequences. In *United States v. Hayes* (2009) Supreme Court justices differed in reading a modifying clause in a criminal firearms statute. In 2005, Hayes was convicted under a law requiring the offender to have a predicate misdemeanor crime of domestic violence, defined as follows: "[T]he term 'misdemeanor crime of domestic violence' means an offense that—(i) is a misdemeanor under Federal, State, or Tribal law; and (ii) has, as an element, the use or attempted use of physical force, or the threatened use of a deadly weapon, committed by a current or former spouse, parent, or guardian of the victim" ("Unlawful Acts," 1994). The issue in the case was whether the phrase beginning "committed by" modified the word "element" or the word "offense." Hayes had a 1994 conviction under a generic battery statute against his wife. The majority found the phrase modified the word "offense" and upheld Hayes' conviction; the minority found the phrase modified the word "element" and would have overturned his conviction. The Hayes opinion is not a significant public health case, but it does show that poor placement of modifiers can have significant impacts, especially when criminal convictions are on the line.

Soliciting Expert and Stakeholder Feedback

No one writes a law or policy alone. By their very nature, laws affect a population of people, agencies, and businesses. The individuals within these affected populations can help craft the substance of a law, either through providing their subject matter expertise on the science or law at issue or by bringing to bear their practical experiences with the activities or communities the law will impact. As discussed in Chapter 15, you can identify potential stakeholders and analyze their positions and beliefs on your proposal. These stakeholders can play a significant role during the background research phase by providing input on the substance of your law or perspectives on their experiences with similar proposals. Once a draft law has been written, this engagement changes because stakeholders and experts now have detailed provisions they can read and evaluate. This step in the process serves two purposes. Soliciting review and feedback of your language can help you write a better law, and it can provide a preview of stakeholders' views on your proposal, an issue that feeds into advocacy considerations covered in Chapter 17.

If you are in a governmental or non-profit organization, it is likely that internal colleagues who are experts in the topic of the law can serve as consultants throughout the drafting process, not only to help set or clarify the law's goals. Attorneys who are tasked with drafting a law do not always have enough technical expertise to capture the nuances necessary to make a law comprehensive and meaningful. For example, in drafting new standards for drinking water systems, it would be critical for an attorney to consult with experts who know construction standards for drinking water wells and safe maximum contaminant levels of certain pollutants. Internal experts can be a credible and objective source of details that will make a new law or a proposed amendment come to life. External experts can also be a good source of feedback on the details of a proposed law. When a law is being drafted from one state's perspective, external experts may be able to provide a national perspective on issues faced by other states in the drafting or implementation process. This may be a way to learn valuable lessons from other jurisdictions.

Sharing proposals and soliciting feedback from external stakeholders may also be a politically wise and, in some cases, legally necessary step in creating a change in law. Before promulgating a new regulation, notice and comment may be required by a state Administrative Procedures Act (as discussed in Chapter 14). The first stop in this process may be sharing the draft proposal with parties who will be subject to the law and involve stakeholders to recommend how to make the requirements and procedures of the law better. These parties also may request changes be made as a condition of support for the law or regulation during the legislative or regulatory approval process. For the PDMP law discussed earlier in this chapter, physicians who run medical practices may suggest ways to make the processes more efficient or might suggest exceptions to the requirements of the draft law as a condition of supporting the law. Although input from the regulated community is often necessary, remember to use caution when assessing the value of suggestions. Particularly when dealing with industries that fundamentally conflict with public health, such as tobacco, alcohol, and firearms industries, the feedback may be designed to weaken the impact of the law. Accordingly, keeping focused on the overall goal of your proposal is critical.

Conclusion

Writing a law is a complex undertaking. From setting a goal to finalizing specific language, the process involves many steps that should be taken into account. By breaking down the process into discernable steps, an individual or a drafting committee can assure that the complex dynamics of law and public health science can be balanced to produce the best language to improve the public's health. Once a law is drafted, the next step (and the focus of Chapter 17) is to get it passed.

Further Reading

Hart, H. L. A. (1958). Positivism and the Separation of Law and Morals. *Harvard Law Review, 71*, 593–629.
LeClercq, T. (1996). Doctrine of the Last Antecedent: The Mystifying Morass of Ambiguous Modifiers. *The Journal of the Legal Writing Initiative, 2*, 81–112.

17 | Public Health Advocacy

Learning Objectives

- Identify the basic components of successful advocacy efforts.
- Describe the tension between expert-led advocacy and community-empowered advocacy.
- Understand the main legal limits on lobbying by tax-exempt entities and organizations that receive federal funding.

Introduction

We define advocacy broadly as the many ways that individuals and organizations introduce their policy preferences into law and practice. Advocacy encompasses everything from speaking up on social media to whispering in legislative lobbies, from participating in marches and sit-ins to testifying before congressional committees. Because public health goals, values, and priorities are expressed in policy, understanding the basics of advocacy—and its legal limits—is necessary for anyone engaged in public health practice.

Advocacy requires many skills beyond law and public health expertise. The literature is replete with checklists, toolkits, and models to help advocates achieve impact, but there are no secret formulas. In this chapter, we cover three important pieces of the public health advocacy picture. First, we describe the basic steps in developing and implementing a program of advocacy: articulating goals, recruiting allies, and identifying strategies for success. Then we invite you into the fundamental debate about the public health advocacy process: whether it should be focused on winning the best policy through institutional action or aimed first at empowering communities to set their own priorities and pursue their goals as they think best. Finally, we review legal limitations on political advocacy by public employees and tax-exempt organizations, limitations that have important effects on how advocacy works in public health practice.

The Anatomy of Advocacy

Those engaged in advocacy come to the process with a wide range of resources. Some bring little more than their bodies, voices, and brains, while others are part of well-funded organizations staffed with lobbyists and communications specialists. Resources help, but we can all point to political instances of David beating Goliath. In either case, there are some basic steps that make up virtually any advocacy campaign.

Advocacy begins with trying to understand the problem you want to solve and finding others who care. Learning about an issue or problem involves diving into the data and stories that illuminate the nature and scope of the issue and studying the relevant policies already in place. Advocacy also includes finding other people and organizations that are experiencing the problem or are sympathetic to those who are. Consider the example of a parent who has lost a child to opioid overdose and wants to do something to address the issue. Others who have suffered the same loss, or who have children at risk, are natural allies, but supporters may also come from law enforcement, healthcare, harm reduction, and public health. There is no magic to forming advocacy relationships. Like other settings in life, it takes reaching out, listening, and finding common ground.

The next step is to set goals. Once advocates understand an issue and assemble a network of people and organizations willing to take action, they must work with the most engaged actors or the group as a whole to define their objectives in the short and perhaps long term. Coalition partners rarely agree on everything, so they may most effectively work by consensus or rely on leaders respected by the group to provide direction and keep things moving. Because advocacy coalitions are voluntary, members or leaders who do not listen or work from consensus usually cannot accomplish much.

Coalitions coalesce around a formal or informal core agreement that includes at least the specific goals of the advocacy effort and, often, a broader set of values. Initial steps, like advocacy for a specific bill or a lawsuit, can feed into longer-term goals to change public attitudes. For example, an opioid response coalition might agree on the immediate goal of getting a law passed to fund more treatment programs, but a broader vision, such as decreasing incarceration of drug users, could strengthen bonds within the coalition and enhance its influence over time. With goals and values clarified, coalitions can deliberate about how best to achieve their immediate goals and promote long-term change.

Finally, an agreed-upon destination helps advocates define the path, or strategy, for their work. When public attitudes are still a major barrier to action, an advocacy campaign might begin with broad efforts to change hearts and minds about an issue instead of directly calling for changes to law. Early advocacy on opioid overdose simply sought to make more people aware of the problem as a significant public health issue, rather than a criminal matter.

A strategy usually has these key components:

- An *explicit plan*: A strategic advocacy plan includes a realistic timeline with a roadmap for what needs to be done, when it needs to happen, who is responsible for certain tasks, and who will provide the funding. A plan should be realistic and identify barriers, determining how they will be addressed before, during, and after the adoption of the policy goal.
- An identified *target audience*: Advocacy is always aimed at other people, such as policymakers with powerful interests, whose action or support is indispensable, and the broader public, whose attitudes can influence policymakers and powerbrokers. Learning about the current political dynamics in the city council or legislature, and the biographies of key policymakers, can help. At a minimum, advocates gain a better sense of who will oppose the proposal and why. Nothing beats presenting ideas to and finding support among elected officials or their staff, meetings that any person in a jurisdiction can request.
- A set of *key messages to influence the target audience:* At some point, a coalition must frame its goals in a way that will most resonate with the community and policymakers. This process may also involve developing responses to potential arguments against the proposal. Messaging and framing is crucial but difficult. The cardinal rule is to never assume that arguments that persuade you and your allies will persuade others (Matthews, Burris, Ledford, & Baker, 2016; Matthews, Burris, Ledford, Gunderson, & Baker, 2017). In public health advocacy, there are often well-funded opponents with carefully crafted, catchy messages (think "nanny state"). Key messages must anticipate opposition and respond to it.
- A *communication plan:* Developing a roadmap to deliver key messages to the audience(s) in light of the context and history of an

issue is essential. Reaching out directly to the leaders you want to persuade should always be part of the plan. Other methods for publicizing and disseminating your messages can include press conferences, direct outreach to reporters who cover relevant issues, public events, demonstrations, social media campaigns, petition drives, and paid advertisements. Particularly when meeting with policymakers, coalition members should carry *concise* versions of their key messages to deliver, both as "elevator speeches" and written materials.

In the movies, an advocacy story that changes history can be told in two hours. In real life, legal change is often measured in years and decades. Patience, and a long-term perspective, is crucial for advocates. Collaboratively designing measurements for the advocacy process, as well as its outcomes and downstream effects, helps coalitions communicate internally, keeping members on the same course and celebrating small victories along the way. Monitoring and evaluating progress, including successes and setbacks, can help advocates be as responsive as possible to changing conditions and to seize opportunities as they arise.

Critically, advocacy does not end when a law is passed. Coalitions need to stay engaged through the implementation process, monitoring how a law is being applied, ensuring that the necessary resources are available to implement it properly, and identifying problems with current practices that need to change. Advocacy campaigns may be required to defend the goals of the law, secure more funds for implementation, or keep public attention on long-term impact.

Advocacy By, With, and Beyond Professionals

Professionals working in advocacy quickly internalize these best practices and become accustomed to conducting advocacy *for* a cause or a group. The "for" in this usage captures the idea that professionals are working on behalf of a cause or a person but also that professionals are doing the advocacy, making strategic and tactical decisions a part of their job. Experts try, based on evidence and experience, to identify the "right" goals for the populations and communities they care about. In some cases, the people they work for will be perfectly happy for them to deploy their expertise to put new policy in place.

There are pitfalls in this approach: policy requires judgments about values and priorities that top-down, expert-led decision-making does not allow. Everyone, not just professionals, values having a say about things that affect them, even if they do not disagree with the experts. As Chapter 5 explores, experts and evidence also have their own biases and limitations, which can lead to policy mistakes. Advocacy *with* others—as opposed to *for* others—means that professionals share, or even forego, the power to decide on goals, priorities, and methods. They pursue equity not simply in results but in the advocacy process itself.

The Collective Impact Model

The tension between a professionalized approach to public health advocacy and one more rooted in values of community voice and participation can be seen in the story of the Collective Impact Model, an advocacy approach introduced in the *Stanford Social Innovation Review* in 2011. The model posited five conditions necessary for advocacy campaigns to build true alignment within a coalition and have a strong impact in the world: "a common agenda, shared measurement systems, mutually reinforcing activities, continuous communication, and backbone support organizations" (Kania & Kramer, 2011). National public health proponents, including the Centers for Disease Control and Prevention (CDC), recognized and adopted these principles into funding requirements and other tools. We discuss some of the powerful insights in the paper and then examine the controversy.

The Collective Impact Model was aimed at major advocacy organizations and, particularly, the philanthropies and other funders who pay to spread good ideas and practices. It rested on a simple, but compelling, problem statement: too much advocacy is designed to have "isolated impact" rather than to "change the world." Organizations often focus on a particular battle in a particular place, hoping that their success will be adopted by others, but without a plan to make that happen. Among competitive funding applications, the authors argued, grants should be awarded to applicants with effective organizations and coalitions that prioritize strategically and systematically spreading best practices, rather than to advocates focused only on the here and now.

The paper highlighted successes from complex projects with many partners and ambitious, but clear, goals. For example:

[C]onsider Shape up Somerville, a citywide effort to reduce and prevent childhood obesity in elementary school children in Somerville, Mass. Led by Christina Economos, an associate professor at Tufts University's Gerald

J. and Dorothy R. Friedman School of Nutrition Science and Policy, and funded by the Centers for Disease Control and Prevention, the Robert Wood Johnson Foundation, Blue Cross Blue Shield of Massachusetts, and United Way of Massachusetts Bay and Merrimack Valley, the program engaged government officials, educators, businesses, nonprofits, and citizens in collectively defining wellness and weight gain prevention practices. Schools agreed to offer healthier foods, teach nutrition, and promote physical activity. Local restaurants received a certification if they served low-fat, high nutritional food. The city organized a farmers' market and provided healthy lifestyle incentives such as reduced-price gym memberships for city employees. Even sidewalks were modified and crosswalks repainted to encourage more children to walk to school. The result was a statistically significant decrease in body mass index among the community's young children between 2002 and 2005 (Kania & Kramer, 2011).

You will recognize some of the elements of success from our earlier discussion of advocacy basics. A *common agenda* means that groups of diverse stakeholders have made the effort to reach and articulate a "common understanding of the problem and a joint approach to solving it through agreed upon actions" (Kania & Kramer, 2011). Though basic, coalitions all too often skip this step or reach only a very abstract agreement, and their efforts are uncoordinated or break down in conflict. *Shared measurement tools* help diverse, busy groups stay on task because "agreement on a common agenda is illusory without agreement on the ways success will be measured and reported" (Kania & Kramer, 2011). The model promotes data and measurement to align efforts, share lessons learned, and hold partners accountable to each other.

Mutually reinforcing activities and *continuous communication* further support coordination in networks and coalitions, recognizing that an individual or group can rarely campaign for change alone. Coalitions of diverse stakeholders work "not by requiring that all participants do the same thing, but by encouraging each participant to undertake the specific set of activities at which it excels in a way that supports and is coordinated with the actions of others" (Kania & Kramer, 2011). Without this coordinated independence, coalitions can easily devolve into debating societies, renegotiating their work and roles without accountability. By agreeing on goals, tracking agreed measures of progress, and contributing to a regular flow of information, coalition partners independently calibrate their activities and adapt to changing circumstances.

Finally, the Collective Impact Model took a practical view on how to run a volunteer coalition. It recognized that effective coordination, mobilization, and occasional peace-making require time, money, and people—a *backbone support organization* with "dedicated staff separate from the participating organizations who can plan, manage, and support the initiative through ongoing facilitations, technology and communications support, data collection and reporting, and handling the myriad logistical and administrative details needed for the initiative to function smoothly" (Kania & Kramer, 2011). Particularly in this feature of the model, it is clear what won the support of large organizations that fund and participate in coalitions. The resources used in a backbone support organization keep advocacy campaigns moving forward and provide structure to make broad-based coalitions sustainable over time.

The Collective Impact Model emphasized getting stuff done, and it was based on sound attention to management realities, as one would expect from an approach laid out in a Stanford University business journal. Yet not all advocates signed on.

The Collaborating for Equity and Justice Framework

In 2017, a group of social change advocates published a counter-framework called Collaborating for Equity and Justice (CEJ; Wolff et al., 2017). The authors' critique of the Collective Impact Model was comprehensive: it fails to address the basic need to engage the communities most affected by the problems to be solved, it ignores underlying conditions and drivers of racism and inequality in the United States and avoids the need for structural changes, it misses the commitment to social justice that drives many coalitions, it seems to assume that most coalitions can get the resources for backbone support organizations, and it ignores the need to invest in building the leadership capacity of people to assume that role. Drawing equally from their expertise and a commitment to social justice as the most direct path to better population health, the authors offered a framework that directed advocates to:

- Explicitly address issues of social and economic injustice and structural racism.
- Employ a community development approach in which residents have equal power in determining the coalition's or collaborative's agenda and resource allocation.
- Employ community organizing as part of the process.

- Build resident leadership and power.
- Focus on policy, systems, and structural change.
- Construct core functions for the collaborative based on equity and justice.

The CEJ principles offer two key insights for advocacy in public health law. The first addresses the fundamental question of what advocates are trying to accomplish. The authors quote Thomas Frieden's reminder (see Chapter 1) that laws and policies are the factors with greatest impact on health. Taking social determinants of health seriously means taking seriously the need to change the "upstream" laws, policies, and practices that produce disparities, yet the impetus for advocacy is usually an immediate change to deal with a current downstream problem. Parents who have lost a child to opioid overdose may want to see more naloxone or more methadone treatment available in the community and work with others to remove legal barriers. But 70,000 deaths a year from opioid overdose is a symptom of deeper problems, reaching back to lack of treatment capacity, a failed national "war on drugs" approach, and economic and social factors that drive drug abuse and dependency (Scutchfield & Keck, 2017). CEJ insists that advocates try to go up that stream of causes, in this example, addressing opioid overdose with better jobs, education, and access to healthcare.

The second insight of the CEJ approach is that participation in advocacy by regular people is critical and will rarely happen robustly on its own. The framework suggests that addressing social injustice is not only ethically right and epidemiologically effective but often essential to getting people and communities who have traditionally been excluded to join in collaborative advocacy. The paper uses this illustration:

> When the Boston Public Health Commission's REACH (Racial and Ethnic Approaches to Community Health) Coalition was launched to address breast and cervical cancer health disparities, it circulated a brochure in the community that stated, "If you're a black woman living in Boston, you have a greater chance of dying from breast or cervical cancer than a white woman. Why? Racism may play a key role in determining your health status. It may affect your access to health services, the kind of treatment you receive, and how much stress your body endures." Black women in the community came to the coalition drawn by the honesty and resonance of that statement (Wolff et al., 2017).

It is imperative to put people experiencing the issues at the forefront of advocacy coalitions. This focus requires investment in the capacity and resources of hard-working people in a community. Public health professionals and advocates may have learned advocacy skills during their education or on the job and have been part of complicated organizations and networks with good access to information, advantages many people in the community have not enjoyed. Bringing communities into self-directed, adaptive participation in coalitions requires the professionals who instigate or fund advocacy efforts to share resources and affirmatively invest in organizational infrastructure—something most organizations are not used to doing.

The lesson of this chapter is that advocacy depends on organization and relationships, efficiency and measurement, and recognition of different values, paths, and capacities. All advocacy projects are different. They range from the localized, bottom-up social change contemplated in the CEJ framework, such as efforts to get a single school board to require healthy food options in school vending machines, to federally funded health or environmental programs managed according to the Collective Impact Model. There is no single, correct way to think about or engage in advocacy, but there are important legal limitations to understand.

Legal Limitations on Advocacy

When any proposed solution is promoted by an initiative or program that receives governmental support, laws may limit or prohibit certain kinds of advocacy. This is complex but impactful material: many public health organizations incorrectly assume that they are completely prohibited from advocacy activities, which makes their work less effective than it would otherwise be. This section describes the rules that coalitions and practitioners receiving tax benefits or funding from government must know before undertaking advocacy activities.

Federal Tax Prohibitions

The federal tax system provides important incentives to public health organizations: they can avoid paying taxes if they comply with section 501(c) of the federal Internal Revenue Code and its implementing regulations ("Exemption from Tax on Corporations, Certain Trusts, Etc.," 2015). However, organizations that qualify for this "tax-exempt" status, including

501(c)(3) public charities and private foundations, may not engage in partisan political activities, including endorsing or contributing to candidate campaigns, and may not "lobby" as a substantial part of their activities.

In this context, *lobbying* is defined as seeking to influence pending legislation or public referenda in either federal or state government. This can be *direct lobbying* accomplished by directly sending staff members or hiring paid lobbyists to meet with lawmakers and ask them to support or oppose a specific bill, or it can be done more indirectly through *grassroots lobbying*, in which organizations ask their members or the general public to communicate with their representatives in the legislature about pending legislation. Under the Internal Revenue Service (IRS) rules, lobbying does *not* include nonpartisan educational activities aimed at informing policymakers and the public about public health problems and solutions.

Tax-exempt organizations can do some lobbying; it just cannot be a "substantial part" of an organization's activities. Because this standard is open to interpretation, the IRS has developed tests to determine whether organizations are exceeding the allowed amount of lobbying. The default "insubstantial part" test considers factors such the amount of time spent on lobbying by employees and volunteers, expenditures on advocacy, and facts and circumstances specific to each case (IRS, 2017b). Typically lobbying is deemed "insubstantial" if it is less than 5% of an organization's overall activities, but because this standard is still vague, entities concerned about their compliance may elect to have their lobbying reviewed under an alternative test.

The "501(h) expenditure" test generally limits lobbying to 20% of an organization's annual expenditures, capped at $1 million overall (IRS, 2017b). For many organizations, this means that more money can be legally devoted to lobbying under this test than under the insubstantial part test. Unlike under the insubstantial part test, activities that do not require expenditures—such as activities by volunteers—do not count against an organization's lobbying limit. The expenditure test also provides clear definitions of what counts as lobbying, and activities that do not meet the exact definitions are not counted against an organization's limits. For example, an issue-focused communication to an organization's members that does not include an explicit call to action would not count as lobbying, even if it mentions a specific, pending piece of legislation.

"Too much" lobbying activity subjects a section 501(c)(3) organization to the risk of losing its tax-exempt status and disqualifies new organizations from seeking that status (IRS, 2017a). However, groups interested in engaging in more advocacy can organize themselves under different sections of the tax code. Although they have less preferential tax status, 501(c)(4) social welfare organizations, 501(c)(5) labor unions, 501(c)(6) trade associations, and 527 political organizations have much more flexibility to lobby and engage in partisan political activities (Schadler, 2012).

Anti-Lobbying Rules Related to Funding

Federal and state authorities support governmental, non-profit, and academic institutions in every aspect of public health through funding. This support promotes prevention strategies, data collection and analysis, dissemination of research results, and capacity building and leadership training and even provides services and outreach to vulnerable populations, but both federal and state funding mechanisms impose restrictions on lobbying.

At the federal level, grantees that accept federal funds face restrictions on using those funds for direct lobbying, grassroots lobbying, and legislative liaison activity (meeting with legislative staff to share information about specific legislation). The federal Office of Management and Budget (OMB; 2011) has stated that these restrictions limit the ability of grantees to lobby at both the federal and state levels. However, grantees and their employees can still lobby if using nongovernmental, unrestricted funds.

In 2012, Congress passed the Consolidated Appropriations Act (CAA), which imposed new restrictions on federal grantees related to lobbying. This provision extended OMB's lobbying restrictions by applying them to advocacy relating to administrative actions and executive orders at both the federal and state level. For the first time, it also applied lobbying restrictions to local-level advocacy before city councils and county commissions. The CAA added a prohibition on using federal grant funds for "any activity to advocate or promote any proposed, pending or future Federal, State or local tax increase, or any proposed, pending, or future requirement or restriction on any legal consumer product, including its sale or marketing, including but not limited to the advocacy or promotion of gun control" (Pub L. No. 112-74, Div. F, § 503(c), 2012).

As the last clause suggests, this provision was inserted after advocacy by the National Rifle Association, which complained that "[t]oo often, community action groups are utilizing federal money to lobby for increased regulation of firearms including trigger locks, bans on semi-automatic rifles, regulated magazine capacity, etc." (National Rifle Association Institute for Legislative Action, 2011). The language reaches much more than gun control, however, and has already had a "chilling effect on local public health agencies and nonprofit organizations" (Gostin & Wiley, 2015).

Though grantees must be careful to comply with these limitations, guidance issued after CAA lobbying rules came into effect continues to allow CDC's grant funds to be used for policy research, education and sharing of lessons learned, collaboration on institutional or system-based policies, and health communications about evidence-based policy (CDC, 2012). Additionally, grantees that are part of a state or local executive branch can lobby other parts of that same executive branch without running afoul of the CAA (e.g., a state health department can lobby the state governor's office). As before, grantees concerned about lobbying restrictions can segregate their accounting so that nonfederal funds can be used for lobbying. However, because tax-exempt organizations may also receive federal grants, they face two potential restrictions: IRS restrictions related to lobbying on all activities and grant-related lobbying restrictions on the portion of their activities funded by federal dollars (Mehta, 2009).

Lobbying Disclosures

Apart from direct restrictions on lobbying, some laws also require disclosures of lobbying activities so that the public can understand the players and resources that influence legislation at all levels of government. The federal Lobbying Disclosure Act requires organizations that spend over a certain threshold of money or time on federal lobbying to disclose their efforts ("Lobbying Disclosure Act of 1995," 2017). State and local laws impose disclosure requirements on all kinds of organizations, regardless of federal tax or funding status. Governmental ethics boards and committees may also license and impose requirements on professional lobbyists. Understanding the disclosures required, as well as researching the lobbying activities of opposition groups, is an essential part of public health advocacy.

Organizational Roles in Coalitions

When diverse organizations work in coalitions to coordinate and communicate regarding their advocacy activities, including lobbying on legislation, they must also consider IRS requirements and funding-related restrictions. A coalition may conduct advocacy activities such as research, education, or even non-partisan voter registration without issue, but organizations that participate in lobbying through a coalition must still individually comply with legal and policy requirements. For example, a 501(c)(3) organization may not support individual candidates or participate in other partisan political activities, and it must tailor its expenditures on any lobbying it does to fall within legal limits. Coalitions can be structured to exclude organizations from activities they are prohibited from undertaking while still fulfilling responsibilities toward the larger goals of an advocacy strategy. For example, 501(c)(3) organizations can focus on broad, issue-related public education (without an explicit call to action), while entities that are not subject to the same lobbying restrictions can directly ask lawmakers to support specific legislation.

Conclusion

There is a pressing need for public health advocacy. Building support for public health law through an advocacy framework strengthens the message, improves education, builds capacity, measures progress, and allows organizations to promote evidence-based policy while still taking advantage of governmental tax benefits and funding mechanisms to support their work. Although policy change can take years to achieve, we must remember that every public health strategy we have depends on our routinely demonstrating the need for, and effectiveness of, public health laws. The next chapter describes the continuous cycle of creating, enforcing, and challenging laws to improve how we address public health problems going forward.

Further Reading

Bolder Advocacy. (n.d.). State Lobbying Registration Thresholds. Available from https://www.bolderadvocacy.org/wp-content/uploads/2015/09/NEW-State-Lobbying-Registration-Thresholds.pdf

Chapman, S. (2001). Advocacy in Public Health: Roles and Challenges. *International Journal of Epidemiology, 30*(6), 1226–1232.

Christoffel, K. K. (2000). Public Health Advocacy: Process and Product. *American Journal of Public Health, 90*(5), 722–726.

County Health Rankings. (n.d.). http://www.countyhealthrankings.org/roadmaps/action-center

World Health Organization. (2006). Stop the Global Epidemic of Chronic Disease: A Practical Guide to Successful Advocacy. http://www.who.int/chp/advocacy/chp.manual.EN-webfinal.pdf?ua=1

V | Putting Law into Practice

ENFORCEMENT AND

IMPLEMENTATION

18 | Models of Regulation

Learning Objectives

- Define *regulation* and identify its three generic elements.
- Recognize that the elements of regulation can be practiced by many different actors within and outside of government.
- Understand the theory of responsive regulation.
- Grasp the practical challenges to effective regulation.

Introduction

Regulation is the art and science of getting individuals and organizations to adhere to stipulated standards of conduct. The term *regulation* "refers to sustained and focused control exercised by a public agency over activities that are socially valued" (Majone, 1994). It is built on the assumption that the regulated activity has social benefits as well as risks, so regulation is about modifying behavior over time, rather than just preventing or punishing it. This means "regulation is not achieved simply by passing a law, but requires detailed knowledge of, and intimate involvement with, the regulated activity" (Majone, 1994).

Public health regulations, from requiring safety belts and vaccinations to limiting air and water pollution, have had huge positive effects on our health and well-being. They set rules that regulated parties, the people and companies subject to regulations, must follow. Ideally, regulations act almost invisibly so that these parties voluntarily comply and pay related costs, as for mandatory safety belts and auto airbags (although the industry fiercely opposed both requirements when they were first proposed). Other regulations make good public health sense but are not popular with their targets—think motorcycle helmet laws—so reaching compliance is difficult, and political fights about government interference with individual rights or the free market ensue. Some regulations are ill-conceived or seem to cost more to enforce than the benefits they produce, like requiring people to get tested for HIV before marriage (which, in the case of a brief Illinois program, cost $312,000 per case identified [Turnock & Kelly, 1989]). These tend to give regulation a bad name.

Typically, regulation is carried out through law and government enforcement processes, but that is just the most familiar model. In the most generic terms, regulation consists of three elements: (a) a standard of behavior, (b) means of monitoring whether the standard is being practiced, and (c) means of incentivizing those who have not adopted the behavior to do so (Scott, 2001). The abstraction of this definition reflects the fact that modern regulation is a sophisticated practice in which every element can take many forms and be carried out by many different actors, even within a single agency. Statutes, agency regulations, executive orders, and other legal instruments are frequently used to set a standard of behavior, confer enforcement powers on agencies, define procedures for observing compliance, and set the penalties for noncompliance. Each of the generic elements of regulation also can be conducted outside of government, and a mix of regulatory entities both internal and external to government can work together. In medical malpractice, for example, the standard of care is set by doctors themselves, infractions are identified by private citizens (the victims), and the compliance determination and punishment are carried out by courts.

Regulation is essential to economic efficiency and public health in the modern world. Anyone who thinks that 350 million people can live, play, and do business without sensible rules is living in a dream world. But the scale and complexity of rules required for such a large population demands that they be well designed to do important things and that they be enforced fairly and efficiently. These are daily responsibilities of regulators in public health. These workers are often not lawyers, and though they need to understand the laws they are enforcing, the key to their success is how they use regulatory authority to get the most compliance at the lowest cost. We start this chapter with a brief discussion of standard setting and then focus on good practices for monitoring and enforcement, concluding with a review of common challenges to regulation.

Standard Setting

In this book and throughout your life, you have encountered innumerable standards set by law. Behind phenomena as diverse as the lunches you ate in the grade school cafeteria and the sexual harassment policies of your university, there were regulatory standards guiding institutional and individual behavior. Standards can take various forms. They may specify procedures that the regulated parties must follow or outcomes (e.g., emission levels for particular pollutants) that must be attained or avoided. The regulations may go into great detail as to exactly how an activity is to be conducted, or set outcome goals while leaving it to the regulated parties to figure out how to achieve them. We may agree that the goal is to create "good" standards, but what is "good" in regulation? The Organisation for Economic Co-operation and Development (OECD), an international organization of major democratic countries, has offered this list of desirable qualities. For the OECD, good regulations should

1. Serve clearly identified policy goals, and be effective in achieving those goals;
2. Have a sound legal and empirical basis;
3. Produce benefits that justify costs, considering the distribution of effects across society and taking economic, environmental and social effects into account;
4. Minimi[z]e costs and market distortions;
5. Promote innovation through market incentives and goal-based approaches;
6. Be clear, simple and practical for users;
7. Be consistent with other regulations and policies;
8. Be compatible as far as possible with competition, trade and investment-facilitating principles at domestic and international levels (OECD, 2014).

These regulatory virtues should be seen as a lot easier listed than done. Standard-setters need to learn about the businesses or activities that are being regulated, so that the standard is practical and the cost reasonable; this in turn often requires technical or scientific knowledge about industrial processes and hazardous outcomes. Uncertainty is a given, as is disagreement over any cost-benefit calculations based on predicted risks or benefits. Writing good standards requires a process that can balance value judgments with scientific data, draw on the expertise of the people to be regulated while avoiding undue influence, and combine specialized regulatory expertise with an understanding of the broader regulatory picture— all without making the process so slow and onerous that standard setting becomes impossible.

In the United States, we generally take two approaches to making rules. Legislators can write statutes, and regulatory agencies can promulgate regulations. In the former case, the necessary expertise and input comes from staff research and interest groups interacting with legislators and their staffs. Input from (and debate among) interested parties can happen in hearings. Often, input is more informal and not so transparent, but overall this process, at least in theory, can lead to rules that reflect and balance all sorts of interests. The regulatory process used by administrative agencies is more formalized and transparent: a proposed rule is opened for comment by the public and affected parties, and agencies are supposed to respond to the comments and explain how they have or have not addressed concerns in a final rule. This process creates a voluminous administrative record documenting the evidence used and decisions made. After a final rule is issued, affected parties can sue the agency on the ground that it exceeded its mandate or acted in an arbitrary and capricious manner.

Although not heavily used in the United States, there are other models for developing rules that use different mechanisms for combining a regulated entity's concerns with the public's interests. Here is a description of how "environmental improvement plans" (EIPs) have been developed in the Australian state of Victoria:

> The collaborative approach under an EIP involves the participation of the polluting enterprise, the environmental regulator, local government, local non-governmental stakeholders, and interested local citizens . . . [T]he stakeholders collectively participate in and are given responsibility for defining and assessing the aspects of the enterprise's environmental performance that are to be regulated. . . . The resulting plan stands as a form of agreement between stakeholders for a settled period of time. At the end of that period there is a complete review and reauthorization of a new plan (Gunningham, 2009).

The EIP model is based on the idea that standards can be more effective, at least sometimes, if the regulated parties have input in shaping them. This logic extends in some instances to the concept of "self-regulation," the development of standards from *within* an industry that then may be adopted as binding or voluntary. There are real risks of capture and strategic behavior (discussed later), but we should not dismiss self-regulation out of hand. There may be powerful incentives to set meaty standards and to comply with them. For an industry, standards can solve collective action problems and discourage free-riders and laggards. If everyone in the industry adopts the same standards, no company has an advantage and the new practices are, at least in theory, competitively neutral. Companies may embrace and obey voluntary standards in the hope of forestalling government regulations that might be less congenial or because they hope that their corporate social responsibility will improve the public image of the company or its products.

An example of the self-regulatory process is the food industry's Healthy Weight Commitment Foundation (HWCF) Pledge. In the face of growing public concern about obesity, 16 large food companies constituting the HWCF promised to cut the total calories they sold by 1.5 trillion between 2007 and 2012. This is an example of an *outcome standard*, since each company agreed to the target but could decide for itself how it would modify its products to achieve its share of the target calorie reduction. An independent evaluation showed that the pledge companies cut calories in products they sold significantly more than other companies (Ng & Popkin, 2014; Ng, Slining, & Popkin, 2014), and some health groups called this a victory in the fight against obesity. In other cases, such as voluntary standards for marketing soda in schools, results have been more ambiguous, and skeptics have suggested the whole exercise was mainly driven by a desire for publicity and to forestall more effective government regulations (Mello, Pomeranz, & Moran, 2008).

Standards may also be set by nongovernmental organizations. Standard-setting is an essential function in the global economy, as exemplified by organizations like the International Organization for Standardization, an independent nongovernmental organization that has developed and maintains more than 21,000 distinct manufacturing and technology standards. Industry participates with representatives of governments, consumers, and research in the development of standards. The organization does not certify compliance or otherwise enforce its standards. Rather, standards are adopted voluntarily or enacted into law at the national or state level or enforced by courts (International Organization for Standardization, 2017). Another well-known model is the variety of private accreditation or certification programs, such as entities that certify products as complying with "fair trade" standards. These set out criteria and processes for companies to get a brand label for this positive attribute.

Monitoring

Enforcement is the process of ensuring that the standard set in a regulation is being met and moving the noncompliant back to compliance or out of the activity. A prerequisite to enforcement is monitoring compliance and noncompliance. Government officials have a range of traditional tools for monitoring whether regulated actors are obeying. Some behaviors are apparent and can be monitored simply by observing behavior in public. Police can see if drivers run red lights, or government personnel can see if cigarette billboards are too close to schools. New technology—like red-light cameras—can enhance the efficiency or extent of this direct observation, but officials are still using the same mechanism.

Some standards are enforced through "inspection," by which we mean a process of investigating a property, process, or product that could not simply be observed in public. Monitoring housing conditions, restaurant sanitation, or fire code compliance requires public health officials to access private property, triggering laws protecting that property and the right against unreasonable search and seizure (see Chapter 19). We can think of inspection more broadly to encompass things like breath or blood tests of drivers (a search or inspection of the body) or chemical analysis of a product (e.g., to ensure purity). Because of the sometimes more elaborate processes and required legal procedures for these observations, regulatory requirements can be expensive and time-consuming. To the extent deterrence is an issue, greater cost produces less frequent inspection, all things being equal, which in turn lessens the deterrent effect. Other forms of monitoring include

- *Audit*, a form of inspection that focuses on the adequacy of records, such as for disposal of hazardous waste. Regulated entities are required to maintain records documenting compliance or compliance processes. On a regular basis, or randomly, the regulators review these documents or processes to determine the extent they meet the regulatory standard.
- *Self-report*, in which regulated entities are required to report certain events when they occur or file reports of activities or outcomes on a periodic basis, such as for surveillance of serious infections. Reporting can be voluntary or mandatory and can be supplemented by audits or inspections. Reporting can be integrated into agency information systems or rely on paper reports.
- *Permitting*, which requires an entity to get advance permission to engage in an activity. Like licensure, which requires people or entities to demonstrate qualifications before they can engage in an activity or profession, permitting requires a regulated actor to show the competency or other conditions necessary to conduct the activity to

the prevailing standard. It can be linked to inspection and periodic requalification processes or tests, as for lead testing of landlords' rental units prior to their licensure for rental housing businesses.

- *Technology-based systems*, which can integrate record-keeping or other actual steps for compliance within a mechanized process. For instance, Facebook and other Internet providers can use search algorithms to detect improper content and flag it for action.

Perhaps the most common form of monitoring is to enlist citizens—in other words, to rely on complaints—to identify actors who are not meeting the required standard. When a restaurant sells a tainted meal, doctors or family members may report the illness to the health authorities, which triggers further investigation. Using technology like cell phone cameras, anyone can easily report dangerous or unsanitary conditions. Some laws also provide legal protections (and occasional monetary compensation) for whistleblowers to encourage employees to report violations by their organizations. Consumer complaints can be effective even when they are not officially logged or investigated: When a customer criticizes a restaurant's hygiene in a website review, he or she is "reporting" noncompliance with an implicit standard of quality for the product or service and, through bad publicity, even inflicting a punishment to encourage compliance.

Enforcement and Responsive Regulation

Enforcing regulations serves at least two functions: changing the behavior of the individual or entity that is directly subject to the regulation (also known as specific deterrence) and influencing or deterring others (also known as general deterrence). We might think of this as the simple part of regulation—imposing a punishment on a known violator—but it is not. Having a range of sanctioning options is crucial to regulatory effectiveness and efficiency.

Responsive regulation is an approach to enforcement that aims to calibrate the resources invested and punishments assigned to the motives of the regulated party and the severity of the violation. The responsive regulation approach is typically depicted in the form of a pyramid (see Figure 18.1). The starting assumption is that most regulated individuals and organizations—those at the base of the pyramid—are willing to comply. A failure to do so is usually the result of mistake, lack of information, or lack of capacity, so the most efficient and effective response is to provide

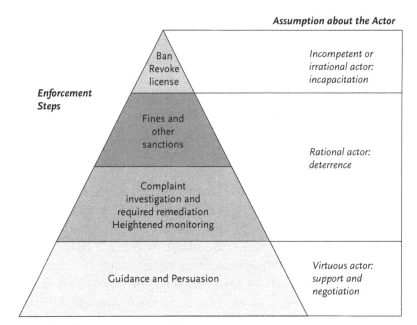

Assumption about the Actor

Enforcement
Steps

Ban
Revoke
license

Incompetent or
irrational actor:
incapacitation

Fines and
other
sanctions

Rational actor:
deterrence

Complaint
investigation and
required remediation
Heightened monitoring

Guidance and Persuasion

Virtuous actor:
support and
negotiation

FIGURE 18.1. The regulatory pyramid.

assistance. Punishment will not increase and may reduce willingness or ability to comply. Punishment also takes more resources because of formal procedures used for fact-finding and adjudication. In the middle of the pyramid, another large group of regulated parties are "rational actors" in the economist's sense: they will do whatever gives them the best return on their investments. If they think the rules do not hurt the bottom line, or help them against their competition, they will comply without any enforcement. Even if they see a way to benefit from cutting corners, they will follow the rules if they think violators will get caught and the penalties will be greater than the savings that come from disobedience. For these actors, the most efficient enforcement strategy is to let them know that regulators are watching and are reasonably likely to detect and punish disobedience. The punishment does not necessarily need to be large, just enough to outweigh the benefits of cheating. The greater the "temptation" or value of noncompliance, the higher a penalty the regulator will want to assess. At the top of the pyramid are the bad or incompetent actors who will not or cannot follow the rules. These are often the worst or most persistent offenders, but persuasion and punishment will have limited effects on them. If the regulator decides a party is in this group, the most efficient step is to remove them from the market by taking away licenses, denying permits, or imposing heavy fines.

Responsive regulation reflects traditional ideas of culpability. In many legal domains, we recognize a difference in the "blameworthiness" of intentional, reckless, careless, and mistaken behaviors. Someone who deliberately throws a rock off a building to harm another person deserves a worse punishment than someone who was playfully tossing the rock off the roof, who in turn is more culpable than someone who accidentally kicked a stone off the roof while walking across it to repair a hole. The pyramid ties differing perceptions of wrongdoing to the range of punishments available for any given infraction and to a predictive model of future behavior.

Having a range of sanctioning options is crucial to regulatory effectiveness and efficiency. It is both unfair and inefficient to overpunish. In fact, the prospect of overpunishment can actually weaken regulation. When, for example, the only sanction available is to charge the actor with a crime, regulators who might impose a civil fine may decide not to punish. They might be aware, for example, that a company that is convicted of a crime may be barred from seeking government contracts or an individual may lose a license, so that what seems to be a minor punishment becomes a business death penalty. Regulators may also consider punishments inflicted by others. Imagine a restaurant chain found to have violated proper sanitary procedures. The regulator can be pretty sure that whatever punishment she imposes will be less painful to the company than the consumer backlash that will result from the failure. This is why some cities have adopted a public grading system for restaurants: A prominent grade of "C" in a restaurant window will usually be incentive enough for a restaurant to clean up its kitchen. Responsive regulation also fits well with the research that demonstrates the strong relationship between compliance with rules and the actor's sense that he or she has been treated fairly by the authorities (Tyler, 1990).

Common Challenges for Regulation

Regulators face challenges of all kinds as they go about the business of setting standards, monitoring compliance, and dealing with those who break the rules. To start with, they face a public that has been bombarded for the last several decades with the message that government is bumbling and inefficient, and regulation is bumbling inefficiency on stilts (Shapiro, 2012). The "war on regulation" hurts morale and recruitment, contributes to cutting budgets and staffing, and weakens public and policymaker support for regulations and those who enforce them.

The negative view of regulation has been one factor contributing to the steady ratcheting up of the requirements for issuing a regulation. Paperwork reduction rules, regulatory impact studies, and extensive notice and comment processes have come into use that can take months or years, followed by lengthy court challenges. These are all part of the regulatory landscape for federal agencies and in many states. In 2017, President Trump issued an executive order requiring that each new regulation issued accompany at least two prior regulations identified by the same issuing agency for elimination. Such requirements throw sand into the regulatory process, making it much more difficult for agencies to finalize any new regulations. They also assume that reducing the number of regulations, regardless of their content or intended impact, should be a goal in and of itself.

Another challenge is *regulatory capture*, which can impair both strong standards and effective enforcement. Capture arises when the agencies that are supposed to be driven by the public interest become so aligned with the industry being regulated that they cease to be effective. This can arise from regulators taking jobs in the industries they used to regulate and vice versa, or it can be a side effect of responsiveness when regulators come to overly sympathize with the people they regulate. To some public choice economists, capture is an almost inevitable byproduct of the fact that regulated industries often have the most to gain or lose from regulation and so will invest in showing up, building relationships, and lobbying for the standards and enforcement levels that work best for them.

The enforcement of regulations unfolds over time. The enforcers, ideally, learn how to be more efficient in monitoring compliance, assessing the motives of the noncompliant, and picking the right sanctions to get them back on track. Research suggests that none of those tasks is easy and that resources and training make a difference (Braithwaite, Walker, & Grabosky, 1987; Mascini & Wijk, 2009). Meanwhile, the regulated are also learning and adapting, finding ways to better hide noncompliance or avoid punishment.

Conclusion

Regulation is a vital public health function. Many members of the public health workforce—lawyers and non-lawyers—are engaged in setting and enforcing health and safety standards many important services, such as food, housing, and healthcare. Public health laws require compliance from individuals and businesses, which in turn depends on clear, enforceable standards that make realistic demands of those who are regulated. These regulations require responsive enforcement, in which enforcers calibrate their efforts to the intentions of the actors and the risks of their activities. They also require regulators to overcome some chronic challenges, including organized political opposition to regulation and the ability of regulated industries to adapt to or even capture regulatory agencies.

Further Reading

Drahos, P. (Ed.). (2017). *Regulatory Theory: Foundations and Applications.* Canberra, Australia: ANU Press. Available from https://press.anu.edu.au/publications/regulatory-theory/download

19 | Enforcement

Learning Objectives

- Understand that enforcement is critical to the success of public health laws.
- Identify the scope of activities that comprise a comprehensive enforcement system.
- Explain the variety of enforcement approaches and recognize some examples of enforcement in action.

Introduction

Chapter 18 described three essential components of regulation: the standard of behavior, the means of observing compliance or noncompliance, and enforcement mechanisms to ensure that people comply with the standards. Without some form of enforcement, otherwise well-designed public health laws typically fail to accomplish their public health purpose. Although the common image of enforcement is a police officer writing a speeding ticket or arresting a suspect, this is rarely the mechanism used to enforce public health laws. Indeed, these blunt tools can be counterproductive.

Effective enforcement begins with the drafting of the law, when the penalties and enforcement mechanisms are devised. In the enactment process, the law's potential must be protected against compromises that adopt the rule but soften it by reducing sanctions or failing to assign or fund regulatory responsibility. Once a law is passed and implementation is delegated to an administrative agency, the agency needs appropriations to fund the activities necessary to make the law come alive, and the agency must set a budget for enforcement. With a budget and staff, an administrative agency can begin community outreach and education about the substantive requirements of the law. Much of the enforcement of a law can be achieved with "persuasion by education," helping most people to comply with legal requirements without direct governmental oversight. Once community members know about public health requirements, they also can act as force extenders and report violations through complaint mechanisms.

Enforcement also involves regulatory tools. Many activities that affect the public's health require licensure, allowing agencies to ensure these activities start off with health and safety in mind. Inspections and investigations allow health department staff to go into the field, check for compliance with applicable requirements, and conduct investigations of possible violations. If violations are found, health departments can assist parties with compliance and potentially avoid the cumbersome process of enforcing the requirements through formal legal action. Of course, if people and organizations cannot come into compliance with public health laws, the requirements can be enforced through administrative notices and orders, and health departments have various sanctions available, including penalties and permit or license suspension or revocations. This chapter discusses each of these concepts in the context of public health law.

Design and Drafting of the Law

One of the most important, and sometimes most overlooked, parts of enforcement is the design and drafting of the law. A legislator or administrative agency may create a fantastic, new, common-sense legal requirement that will protect and save lives. The standard is clear, unambiguous, and popular, and the proposal passes and becomes law. But when the law hits the streets, people realize the law did not delegate authority to an agency for implementation and oversight and did not properly address what happens if someone does not comply with the law. In this hypothetical, we have a new public health law, but one that is not operational or effective.

Enforcement mechanisms exist to bring legal requirements to life, and the requirements and mechanisms must be created and put into actionable language. It is imperative that drafters pay as much attention to the enforcement language as they do to the language of regulatory standards. Enforcement mechanisms should be drafted to achieve the law's purpose, while still being realistic and attainable. If compliance with a requirement is impossible, the nature and variety of its enforcement mechanisms will be irrelevant. If compliance is difficult or expensive, discussions about compliance can sometimes dominate the creation and passage of a law because people who would be subject to the law are afraid of unreasonable enforcement. Lawmakers, regulators, and public health advocates must learn enough about the industry being regulated to tell the difference between political posturing and bona fide concerns that a law's requirements are unworkable or will have unintended consequences.

Appropriations and Budgeting

Appropriations and budgets are important foundations of public health law that can be overlooked, but they are essential to securing the staff and systems to undertake implementation and enforcement. In addition to the laws that create requirements for people and entities, legislatures also pass appropriations bills that provide money to administrative agencies. Without funds, it does not matter how well standards and enforcement mechanisms are drafted—they will not be effective because there are no people to do the work.

Opponents of a new law can use the requirement for appropriations as a strategic leverage point during its drafting and passage. If they cannot muster enough support to defeat a bill as a whole, they can have language added that says the law will have no effect until money is appropriated for its implementation. They can also alert legislators who unsuccessfully opposed a new law to effectively prevent its implementation through an appropriations bill.

Budgeting within administrative agencies—the process though which agencies ask for and use appropriations—can also be used to strategically support or negate enforcement. New standards and enforcement mechanisms can be built on existing systems that already have resources, lessening the fiscal impact of a new law. Conversely, administrations uninterested in enforcing a legal requirement can overstate its future budgetary impact or allocate insufficient funds for its enforcement. The bottom line is that without funding, enforcement is stifled, even if a law is artfully drawn and passed with support in the community: people who care about effective public health law care about strong and properly funded regulatory agencies.

Community Outreach and Education

Community outreach and education concerning legal requirements is an ongoing process and a critical aspect of enforcement. Outreach and education begin during the design and drafting process. As noted in

Chapter 16, one way to improve upon a draft law is to share it with subject-matter experts and the people who will be affected by its requirements. This stakeholder engagement can result in a law that is more realistic and enforcement mechanisms that the regulated community agrees are fair and workable. This outreach should not be limited to explanations of the requirements and the enforcement mechanisms; it should also include a description of the underlying problem the law is meant to solve.

Often, people will comply once they appreciate that the law is a reasonable response to a serious public health problem, irrespective of the threat of penalties. For instance, many people comply with laws that prohibit driving while impaired because they understand the devastating consequences that impaired driving can have on the victims of resulting accidents, not simply because the behavior is illegal. Likewise, many hospitals comply with laws requiring the tracking and reporting of health-care associated infections because they understand that having surveillance in place for these conditions can improve their healthcare operations and reduce morbidly and mortality at their facilities. Voluntary compliance does not eliminate the need for enforcement but rather allows regulators to put resources where they are needed most.

Outreach and communication do not stop once the law is passed. Some public health measures take a community to implement and enforce. Childhood immunization requirements are a perfect example. All 50 states have designed childhood immunization laws that require up-to-date vaccinations as a condition of attendance at public and private schools and day care centers. School and day care administrators check compliance with these requirements before allowing children to enroll in their programs, and health departments (typically) ensure that they do so. However, many people and organizations play a role in ensuring that kids receive timely vaccinations. The federal government runs the Vaccines for Children program that provides the United States with a stable, low-cost inventory of vaccines. Pediatricians regularly educate parents about the importance of immunizations in protecting children against vaccine preventable diseases and make the vaccines available at childhood wellness checkups. Insurance companies cover the costs of administration and the vaccines themselves. Health departments and other safety net providers administer low-cost or no-cost immunizations to children not covered by health insurance. As we can see, health departments are not always solely responsible for, or even at the front lines of, enforcement of our public health laws, and many of these efforts begin with effective community outreach and education.

Licensing and Compliance Assistance

Licensing can be the basis of a comprehensive system for enforcing behaviors and practices that can protect public health. First, licensing acts as an enforcement mechanism through the application process. When an application is submitted, the agency responsible for the license can begin to determine if the applicant is in compliance with regulatory requirements. Depending on the activity and the regulation, the agency can look at where the activity will be located, how any physical structures or facilities will be constructed, what technologies will be used, and how the activity will be managed. Before the activity even begins, issuance of the license can be used as leverage to gain compliance with the requirements. In fact, in many regulatory schemes, the agency is expressly prohibited from issuing a license until there is full compliance with all requirements. For example, with retail food establishment licenses, the applicant must meet construction, plumbing, and equipment standards before being allowed to operate.

To have licensees is to know licensees, and health department personnel cannot help but get to know the people and businesses that apply for and obtain licenses. Licensing can be an involved process and can take days, weeks, and even months for complex activities. All the while, people at the agency and the licensee are getting to know each other, the nuances of the proposed activity, the details of the standards, and the policy reasons behind their implementation and enforcement. As this relationship unfolds over time, many questions of how to comply with the standards are answered, and many possible violations are avoided or quickly resolved through compliance assistance.

Compliance assistance is a formal or informal tool for regulating agencies to provide people and businesses with advice, guidance, and tools to help them meet regulatory standards. Informal assistance can be talking a customer through the application process, onsite suggestions during an inspection, or on-the-spot corrections of cited violations. Formal assistance can be anything from printed guidance documents to requested inspections and audits. Whatever their form, compliance assistance programs are a pervasive part of enforcing public health laws across the country.

Investigations and Inspections

Investigations and inspections are another way that public health laws are enforced, and they are what many people think of as traditional enforcement activities. For purposes of our discussion, investigations are when a health department exercises its authority to learn the facts about a situation that may be a violation of law or a threat to the public's health. Inspections are visits to regulated facilities and operations, for which there may be a permit or a license, to determine if the operations are in compliance with regulatory standards. Like any administrative agency action, investigations and inspections are subject to Constitutional requirements. These activities may constitute searches that are subject to the warrant requirements under the Fourth Amendment. Two stories—of Joe and Martha—will help us see how Fourth Amendment constraints apply in the public health context.

> *Joe, a residential home builder, owns a large tract of land in a rural part of Covered Bridge County, where he maintains a hunting camp for occasional visits and grows trees for harvesting. A neighbor calls the local health department to report her suspicion that Joe is dumping and burning construction waste on his tract of land. She says the smoke is hazardous to her respiratory health and that the population of rats, flies, mosquitos, and other vermin has recently increased dramatically. The health department sanitarian who took the call knows that open dumping and burning are under the authority of the health department; he reads through the law and sees that the health department is authorized to investigate complaints. Without contacting Joe, the sanitarian enters the property, finds the pile of construction debris, takes GPS readings, and photographs the area. He returns to the health department, checks the general sanitation and open dumping laws, and drafts an order for the health director to sign. The order requires Joe to clean up the site and to pay hefty fines.*
>
> *Joe, through his attorney, files an action against the order and objects that it is based on an unconstitutional search of Joe's property and should be vacated. The lawyer argues that Joe had a reasonable expectation of privacy on his property, especially with the presence of his hunting camp, complete with no trespassing signs, a cabin, mobile homes, and bathroom facilities, and that the government must obtain a warrant to search his property according to the Fourth Amendment. He argues that the open dumping and burning laws are old and vague, do not grant the health department the authority to inspect property, and do not provide enough notice to landowners that the agency might make unannounced visits to property*

where dumping and burning are suspected. He says the information the neighbor provided may have given the health department probable cause to obtain a warrant, but a warrant was not obtained, and as a result the search was unconstitutional. The county judge dismisses the claims about the laws being old and vague but agrees that the search violated the Fourth Amendment. He vacates (i.e., removes) the health department's order.

Martha is an excellent cook and decides to open a restaurant. She does business research, lines up financing, and contacts the local health department to find out about licensing. Because of her limited funds, she buys used cooking equipment. The health department inspector warns Martha about the importance of temperature control and how old, used equipment can be unreliable and unable to maintain the required temperatures. Martha feels she has little choice and proceeds with used equipment. Martha obtains her license and schedules her grand opening to coincide with a local festival event that will bring lots of customers. The food inspector has remaining concerns about the used equipment and decides to conduct Martha's first routine inspection on the third day of the festival. The inspection team arrives, conducts a quick inspection, and finds many violations, including malfunctioning equipment and many temperatures out of safe range. The food inspector provides Martha with a notice of the violations and an order to remain closed until all violations and equipment are corrected and repaired.

Martha files an action in court to dispute the notice of violations and the order to remain closed. Through her attorney, she argues that she had no expectation she would be inspected on her third day of operation, that she did not consent to the inspection, and that, without a warrant, the inspection violated her Fourth Amendment rights to be free of unreasonable searches and seizures. The judge agrees that the Constitution applies to the analysis of her case but disagrees that a warrant was required. The judge informs Martha that she is engaged in a heavily regulated industry and that by seeking and obtaining a license, she subjected herself to unannounced inspections and gave up any reasonable expectation of privacy in the restaurant.

Why did the judges treat these two cases differently? The U.S. Supreme Court has found that public health investigations and inspections are subject to the Fourth Amendment warrant requirements (*Camara v. Municipal Court of City and County of San Francisco*, 1965) but also that administrative agencies, like health departments, do not always need a warrant before engaging in administrative searches (*Colonnade*

Catering Corp. v. United States, 1970). Whether or not a warrant is required to conduct a particular public health inspection depends on the nature of the regulatory scheme being enforced. The Court has established that in situations similar to Martha's, administrative searches do not require a search warrant if (a) they are related to heavily regulated industries where the government has a substantial interest in oversight, (b) the underlying laws provide adequate notice of warrantless searches and adequate parameters outlining the proper scope of such searches, and (c) the searches are necessary to achieve the oversight. If any of these elements are missing, an administrative search may be declared unreasonable and unconstitutional. Joe was not engaged in a heavily regulated industry, and the law at issue did not provide adequate warnings that unannounced inspections might occur. Therefore, the health department should have obtained a warrant before entering and searching Joe's property, and the judge was correct to dismiss the health department's order against him. Figure 19.1 is a guide to Fourth Amendment analysis of an administrative search.

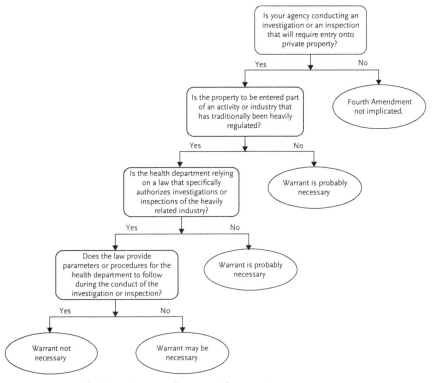

FIGURE 19.1. Administrative search warrant decision tree.

Examining the scope and language of the laws used to enforce requirements is critical to applying the 4th Amendment. In 2007, two commercial fishermen were driving along a public road in Washington State when fish and wildlife agents stopped their truck and searched the contents of a tote in the bed (*Tarabochia v. Adkins*, 2014). The agents found recently-caught salmon in the tote but failed to find any violations of state game and fish laws. The fishermen sued the agents for violating their constitutional rights by conducting an illegal search. The agents relied on two laws, one that gave them the authority to stop people engaged in fishing to inspect licenses, equipment, and fish and wildlife and another that gave them the authority to inspect the premises, containers, fishing equipment, fish and wildlife, and records of commercial fishermen. Although the Ninth Circuit Court of Appeals found that the government has an important interest in preventing illegal fishing and that commercial fishing has been a heavily regulated industry, it held the statutes the fish and wildlife agents relied upon did not support a warrantless search of the truck or its contents. The fishermen were not engaged in fishing at the time of the stop, and the stop was too far from their boat and commercial fishing activities. Similar to Joe's hypothetical case, the laws relied upon did not provide sufficient notice to fishermen that their cars or trucks could be subjected to searches on public roads, and they did not provide the agents with sufficient standards to govern such searches. As a result, the court found that the searches strayed beyond the scope of the laws and were unconstitutional in the absence of a warrant.

Investigations and inspections clearly have an important role to play in the enforcement of public health laws. Investigations can allow health department employees to follow up on complaints and discover violations of public health laws that may be endangering people. Inspections are particularly valuable for monitoring compliance in heavily regulated industries with complex facilities and ongoing operations that could endanger health if not maintained or conducted in compliance with legal standards. In either case, the Fourth Amendment and its search warrant requirements must be followed when using these regulatory tools.

Sanctions for Violations

Sometimes punishment or the threat of punishment is the leverage needed to enforce public health laws. Well-crafted laws, healthy budgets, outreach and education, licenses, compliance assistance, investigations, and inspections will address the vast majority of enforcement issues that we face in public health. Just as most disputes between people and businesses do not end up embroiled in litigation and in front of the court system, most enforcement disputes in public health do not end up with any kind of legally binding sanctions. But, behind all of the efforts to bring regulated communities into compliance with public health law standards, a well-designed enforcement system will have sanctions at its disposal. As Chapter 18 points out, agencies should adopt a "responsive regulation" perspective that carefully allocates enforcement resources and penalizes violators in a carefully calibrated manner.

The first step is to clearly define what a violation is and to connect it with a consequence. This relates back directly to the design and drafting stage discussed earlier. The language of the law must set standards, clearly explain what would be considered a violation, and tie a punitive consequence to the violation. The statements of violation and consequence do not necessarily have to be located right next to each other in a statute or regulation, but they must exist and they must be connected. Laws can include express language. For example, "it is a violation of this law to dispose of construction debris in an area that is not a licensed construction debris landfill." Violations also can be implied: "potentially hazardous foods must be kept at or below 41 degrees at all times except immediately prior to and after cooking." However they are stated, they must be clear enough to let people know that if they do or do not do something, they will be in violation of the law and that there will be consequences.

The consequences that follow from violations can come in many different forms. The most recognized is the fine: comply with the standards or pay money to the government. We experience this model every day in motor vehicle laws that impose fines for speeding and running stop signs. For some of us, the motivation to comply with speeding and stop sign laws comes from a desire to contribute to safe roads or simply a desire to abide by the laws. For others, the motivation is economic: a violation will cost money, and paying a fine is expensive and painful.

Sanctions can also take nonmonetary forms, requiring the violator to take action or to stop a behavior or activity. During inspections, many laws authorize the health department to require immediate correction of violations—corrections on the spot—and to conduct follow-up inspections to ensure there is no ongoing risk to the public's health. If violations are not corrected or if an establishment has a series of poor inspections, the health department may be authorized to implement stronger measures, such as license suspensions or revocations. Sometimes more immediate action is required. Many food codes have immediate health hazard provisions that allow immediate closure of a facility to address high-risk situations, such as loss of water service or refrigeration. In other situations, the immediate threat may be narrower, such as food out of temperature, and the agency may be authorized to immediately hold or destroy the specific product that may be a risk.

Some laws may provide public health agencies with a more general authority to require people and businesses take action or to stop engaging in certain activities. Forms of legal action include imminent direct health hazard, or cease and desist orders issued by the agency, and *injunctions* issued by a judge; these include temporary restraining orders, preliminary injunctions, and permanent injunctions. Health laws can be broadly worded and provide flexible authority to pursue an enforcement strategy that will meet the exact situation confronting the agency (e.g., "The Department of Health may seek injunctive relief to enforce the provisions of this chapter").

Injunctions are one of the oldest and most powerful remedies in the legal system. At their core, they are flexible orders that judges can issue to protect or restore the rights of the party seeking the injunction. In most civil cases, the typical remedy available is the exchange of money. However, money is often not sufficient to right the wrong at hand. For example, a federal judge issued an injunction to enforce the desegregation of Little Rock, Arkansas, schools after the *Brown v. Board of Education* decision. Shifting money from the State of Arkansas to the children denied entry into the schools would not have solved the problems of the separate but unequal school system.

Injunctions are generally divided into three categories, depending on the effect they have and how long they last: temporary restraining orders, preliminary injunctions, and permanent injunctions. *Temporary restraining orders* (TROs) are used to preserve the "status quo." In many jurisdictions, TROs can be obtained ex parte, meaning the judge will grant a TRO to a party without the other party present to submit evidence or his or her argument. As a result, most jurisdictions require the party seeking the TRO to attempt to give notice to the opposing side and will place strict time limits on the duration of a TRO, usually two to three days. These guidelines are designed to preserve the status of the situation at the time the order is issued and until there is an opportunity for further investigation and argument. TROs are used in emergency situations where the alleged injury is imminent and will have lasting and potentially irreversible effects.

Preliminary injunctions, sometimes referred to as *temporary injunctions*, are similar to TROs in their effect, but they will not be issued ex parte. A judge will issue a preliminary injunction to preserve the status quo and provide time for a full hearing or trial on the merits of the case. The judge will schedule and hold a hearing on the facts and arguments for and against the injunction. They will generally last longer than TROs, sometimes for months, pending the outcome of the underlying lawsuit.

Permanent injunctions are just that—they are injunctions that are permanent. The defendant will be permanently required to do something or stopped from doing something. They are issued as final rulings and judgments at the conclusion of a lawsuit. They may continue the terms and conditions established in a preliminary injunction issued at the outset of the litigation or be modified depending on the evidence presented or any changes in the circumstances of the parties.

Injunctive relief is useful when enforcing public health laws because many situations that confront health departments are complex and unique, requiring actions that fall outside the specific sanctions outlined in governing rules. Importantly, though, issuance or enforcement of injunctive relief often requires a court order. Accordingly, the use of this remedy may be limited to emergency or other risky circumstances.

Conclusion

Enforcement of our public health laws includes a wide and complex scope of activities. Beginning with the design and creation of the laws themselves, enforcement touches every point on the lifecycle of a law. Appropriations, budgets, outreach, education, licensing, compliance assistance, investigations, inspections, and sanctions all play a role in the enforcement of the laws we pass. Importantly, effective enforcement is tailored to match the industry or activity that is being regulated and may involve multiple parties working through a comprehensive enforcement system to make sure our laws are having their intended effect of protecting the public's health.

Further Reading

Center for Community Progress. (2015). Building a Strategic, Data-Driven Code Enforcement Program for Gary, Indiana. Technical Assistance Report. Retrieved from http://www.communityprogress.net/filebin/150928_TASP_Gary_Report__FINAL.pdf

Primus, E. (2011). Disentangling Administrative Searches. *Columbia Law Review*, *111*(2), 254–312.

20 | Defending Lawsuits

Learning Objectives

- Understand the strategic reasons why entities may challenge public health laws and the typical steps involved in such litigation.
- Identify the attorneys involved in defending public health laws on behalf of local, state, and federal government entities and explain how "legal technical assistance" from public health organizations can support their efforts.
- Understand what an *amicus curiae* brief is and how it can most effectively contribute to the defense of public health laws and regulations.

Introduction

Public health laws and regulations are regularly challenged in court. This should come as no surprise. As we have seen, public health laws implicate fundamental issues of ethics and personal autonomy and, in many cases, place significant restraints on business practices. Those opposed to these laws try to prevent them from being enacted in the first place, but, if they are unsuccessful, they may resort to a legal challenge after they come into effect. The overarching goal of such lawsuits is usually to obtain a legal decision overturning the law or regulation at issue. There may be other strategic goals at play as well: delaying a law from taking effect, dissuading other jurisdictions from enacting similar laws, or using the financial pressure of litigation to get a jurisdiction to repeal its law.

The goal of careful policy development, legal drafting, public health advocacy, and enforcement is *not* to avoid all legal challenges; the defense of lawsuits should be viewed as simply another step in the process of promoting the effective use of law for public health. It is critical to be as well prepared for them as you would for any other step in the process.

Dealing with a lawsuit can be very frustrating after you have gone through the hard work of getting a new law passed, but if you have not prepared for defending it against a potential lawsuit, all of your work could be undone.

Much of the work crucial to successfully defending against lawsuits must be done *before* the law is passed or the regulation is finalized. This involves developing the evidentiary basis for the regulatory approach; putting the evidence into the public record, such as by providing testimony or submitting public comments; and working with legal counsel to ensure that the wording of the law avoids constitutional or other legal issues. In lawsuits involving administrative rules, for example, courts typically look only at evidence that was available to the agency at the time the rule was issued. All of the relevant evidence needs to be in the administrative record before the rule is finalized, as new evidence, however relevant to the potential effectiveness of the regulation at issue, cannot be introduced for the first time in litigation.

Using the example of the legal challenge to the Food and Drug Administration's (FDA) proposed health warnings for cigarettes, this chapter first provides an abbreviated overview of the typical steps involved in litigation challenging a public health law or regulation. After outlining the steps of a lawsuit, it discusses the role of governmental attorneys and the ability of interested groups to participate in litigation by filing *amicus curiae* ("friend of the court") briefs.

The Litigation Process: The FDA's Graphic Warning Labels

In Chapter 13, we discussed the litigation relating to the FDA's proposed graphic warning labels for cigarettes. In 2009, Congress instructed the FDA to develop nine graphic images to be paired with nine new textual warnings. These warning labels (the graphic images plus the text) were to cover the top 50% of both the front and back panels of cigarette packs, as well as the top 20% of cigarette advertisements. The FDA went through the notice and comment process required by the Administrative Procedure Act (APA), reviewed more than 1,700 comments, and finalized a rule mandating the use of graphic warning labels in 2011. (The images selected by the FDA, paired with the required text, are shown in Figure 13.1.) As soon as the FDA finalized its rule, it was challenged in court by a number of tobacco manufacturers.

We use the resulting case—*R.J. Reynolds Tobacco Company v. FDA*—to walk through the steps of a legal challenge to a public health law. (Since the lead plaintiff was R.J. Reynolds, we refer to that company as the plaintiff, even though other companies were also involved.) Although you already know how this story ends—a federal appeals court ultimately concluded that the graphic warning requirement was a form of unconstitutional "compelled speech" and could not be implemented—let us examine the process that led up to that point.

Step 1: The Complaint

R.J. Reynolds initiated the lawsuit by filing a complaint in the U.S. District Court for the District of Columbia, which has jurisdiction over federal agency actions. A *complaint* is a document that seeks some sort of order from the court and sets forth the legal basis for the request. When public health regulations are involved, the plaintiff is typically seeking a *declaratory judgment* (an order from the court declaring the law or regulation be invalid and unenforceable) and an *injunction* (an order barring the law or regulation from going into effect). The plaintiff may also seek monetary compensation, though this is less common.

In its complaint, R.J. Reynolds asked the court for both declaratory judgment, to invalidate the rule, and an injunction, to bar it from taking effect during the course of litigation. It did not request monetary damages, though it did ask the court to order the FDA to pay its attorneys' fees and litigation costs. Plaintiffs in public health cases often request attorneys' fees and other litigation-related costs, but those requests are rarely granted unless the government's action was clearly in violation of the law.

A complaint must set forth a legal objection to the law being challenged. A company may have a strongly held belief that a law or regulation is unduly burdensome and unnecessary, but this objection must be framed as a *legal* objection—for example, that the law violates the First Amendment—before a court will consider it. How the legal claims are set forth in the complaint determines what the plaintiff must prove in order to prevail. The nature of the legal claim may also determine whether the lawsuit should be filed in state court or federal court. In this case the plaintiff asserted two claims: (a) that the regulation was unconstitutional because it violated the company's First Amendment rights and (b) that the regulation was unlawful because the FDA did not properly comply with the requirements of the APA.

Notably, the lawsuit challenged only the FDA's regulation—the rule imposing specific images selected by the FDA. It did not challenge the underlying law that instructed the FDA to require graphic warning labels on cigarettes, because R.J. Reynolds was concurrently challenging that in a separate lawsuit. In that other suit, the Sixth Circuit Court of Appeals ultimately found that the graphic warning requirement did not violate the First Amendment, concluding that "[b]ecause graphics *can* present factual information regarding the health risks of using tobacco . . . the Act's graphic-warning requirement is constitutional" (*Discount Tobacco City and Lottery, Inc. v. United States*, 2012; emphasis added). The Sixth Circuit left open the possibility, however, that any specific set of images required by the FDA in regulations could be legally problematic.

It is possible that R.J. Reynolds thought it had a winning legal argument against the regulation (which, it turns out, it did). At the very least, it was probably hoping to delay the rule from taking effect, even if it ultimately lost the lawsuit. Seeking to put off compliance with a costly new require-ment is a common reason for filling a complaint, even when the legal theory is untested or of questionable strength. Other strategic reasons for filing a lawsuit challenging a public health law or regulation may include imposing costs on the government defending the lawsuit, in hopes it will withdraw the law; deterring other communities from passing similar laws; creating leverage for negotiation, in hopes of obtaining changes to the law; and "chilling" future regulatory action by signaling a willingness to sue.

Litigation, even by deep-pocketed tobacco companies, is unlikely to alarm a federal agency like the FDA, which is used to having its actions challenged in courts. State and local government entities, particularly those that are cash-strapped and do not have much money set aside for lit-igation expenses, may be much more unsettled by the prospect of facing a costly legal challenge. The chilling effect of a threat of expensive litigation is thought by many public health experts to be a significant barrier to the effective use of public health law at the local level.

Step 2: Preliminary Injunction Hearing

After the complaint is filed, the next step is often a hearing on a prelim-inary injunction, a request to stop the law from going into effect while the case proceeds. This is often dealt with quickly, especially if the law is scheduled to go into effect soon. In considering whether or not to grant an injunction, courts typically consider the following four factors (*Winter v. Natural Resources Defense Council, Inc.*, 2008):

- Whether the plaintiff is likely to succeed on the merits of the legal claim, if the case is fully litigated;
- Whether the plaintiff will suffer "irreparable harm" if an injunction is not granted;
- The "balance of equities" between the parties; and
- Whether an injunction is in the public interest.

In the *R.J. Reynolds* case, District Court Judge Richard Leon, after reviewing the relevant First Amendment case law, concluded that the plaintiffs were likely to succeed on the merits. Judge Leon ruled that the public's interest in reducing tobacco use had to give way to "the public's interest in preserving its constitutional protections," and he issued a preliminary injunction barring the FDA's graphic warning requirement from going into effect (*R.J. Reynolds Tobacco Co. v. U.S. FDA*, 2011). Because he concluded that the FDA's regulation likely violated the First Amendment, he did not analyze R.J. Reynolds' APA claim in the preliminary injunction ruling.

If the court had refused to grant the preliminary injunction (and if that ruling had been upheld on appeal), the plaintiffs might well have dropped the case. Once a law goes into effect and the affected individuals or industries adjust to it, the plaintiffs may no longer desire to keep investing in the legal fight. For instance, restaurants may strongly oppose a local law prohibiting the use of trans-fats in prepared foods, anticipating that compliance with the law will entail significant costs. But once they have already spent the time and money to reformulate their products and remove trans-fats, their incentive to keep fighting the law in court is significantly diminished.

Step 3: Discovery and a Ruling on the Merits

The next step in the process is *discovery*, the fact-finding process in which the parties use *depositions* (recorded out-of-court testimony), *interrogatories* (written questions and answers), *requests for documents*, and other legal tools to obtain relevant information from the other side or from third parties. This process can be extremely lengthy; in complex litigation, it can take years. Often, challenges to public health laws center on legal, as opposed to factual issues. For instance, in the *R.J. Reynolds* case, the central question was a legal one: Did the FDA's required graphic health warnings violate the First Amendment? The parties agreed on what the regulation said and did; they just disagreed on whether it was constitutional. In such cases, there is often little need for discovery and the case can move along more quickly. The judge can grant a *motion for summary judgment* if he or she decides that there are no major factual issues in dispute and one side's legal argument should prevail. If a judge grants a motion for summary judgment on all of the plaintiff's claims (in favor of either the plaintiff or the defendant), the case is over unless one of the parties appeals. The judge can also grant summary judgment on only some of the claims, narrowing the issues remaining in the case.

In the *R.J. Reynolds* case, the judge had already strongly signaled in his ruling on the preliminary injunction that he thought the FDA's graphic warning requirement was unconstitutional. Thus it was no surprise when, less than three months later, he granted R.J. Reynolds' motion for summary judgment. In that decision, Judge Leon wrote that the FDA's images were "more about shocking and repelling than warning" and that accordingly they were not the sort of "purely factual and uncontroversial information" that the government could require on cigarette labels (*R.J. Reynolds Tobacco Co. v. U.S. FDA,* 2012).

In cases where there are disputed issues of fact—whether or not a certain pollutant causes cancer, for example—summary judgment cannot be used to resolve the case, and it may be necessary to have a full trial before a judge or a jury. Trials are rare in challenges to public health laws because the issues are usually legal in nature, and there are rarely major factual disputes. Additionally, because trials can be costly and risky for both sides, many cases settle, or come to agreement outside of court, before reaching a trial.

Step 4: Appeal

After the motion for summary judgment was granted, the FDA promptly filed an appeal, hoping that the appellate court—in this case, the U.S. Court of Appeals for the District of Columbia Circuit—would reverse Judge Leon's decision striking down the required warnings. Appeals do not involve new evidence or new witnesses; rather, a three-judge panel reviews the lower court's rulings and considers the parties' arguments regarding whether or not the judge (or jury, if there was one) committed errors in applying the law. Appellate courts will not revisit a trial court's factual determinations unless they were clearly wrong, but they are more willing to second-guess legal conclusions.

On appeal, the FDA argued that Judge Leon's First Amendment analysis was "seriously mistaken" and he "plainly erred in concluding that the warnings are made less accurate by inclusion of images along with the text"

(*R.J. Reynolds Tobacco Company et al. v. Food and Drug Administration et al.*, Brief of Defendants-Appellants, 2011). By contrast, the tobacco companies asserted that "the district court correctly held that the Rule's graphic 'warnings' cross the line that separates factual and dispassionate disclosures from policy-laden and controversial advocacy" and violated the companies' First Amendment rights (*R.J. Reynolds Tobacco Company et al. v. Food and Drug Administration et al.*, Brief of Plaintiffs-Appellees, 2012). Ultimately, by a 2–1 margin, the D.C. Circuit Court of Appeals agreed with the tobacco companies and upheld the lower court's ruling (*R.J. Reynolds Tobacco Co. v. U.S. FDA*, 2012).

In both state courts and federal courts, at least one level of appellate review is guaranteed if one of the parties requests it. Further review by the full set of Circuit judges (known as a *rehearing en banc*) or the U.S. Supreme Court is usually discretionary. The U.S. Supreme Court, on average, reviews fewer than 3% of the cases it is asked to hear in a given year. The FDA might have been able to convince the Supreme Court to hear its appeal, given that the D.C. Circuit and the Sixth Circuit had reached somewhat conflicting conclusions about the graphic warnings requirement. Resolving a *circuit split*—where two appeals courts have reached different outcomes—is one of the primary reasons the Supreme Court agrees to hear a case. In the *R.J. Reynolds* case, however, the FDA decided not to appeal to Supreme Court, likely because it was not confident the Court would rule in its favor. Instead, it stated that it would go back to the drawing board and develop new graphic warnings that would pass constitutional muster. As of this writing, however, it has not done so.

The Role of Government Attorneys

As a case challenging a public health law or regulation moves through the litigation process outlined here, the primary individuals tasked with defending the case are government attorneys. Various types of attorneys represent the array of government entities that exist at the local, state, and federal level. At the local level, it is typically the city attorney's (or district attorney's) office that is responsible for representing the local government. Major cities will have large city attorneys' office, sometimes with hundreds of full-time lawyers. These offices essentially serve as the city's full-service law firm and have the capacity to represent the city in nearly any legal matter, though their budgets are often stressed. Smaller communities, on the other hand, may only have one or two attorneys in the city attorney's office, or they may contract with a private firm to act as the city's attorney. These smaller communities may not have the capacity to defend their own laws in court without hiring outside assistance (which can be expensive—partners at private law firms typically charge hundreds of dollars an hour).

At the state level, it is usually the state attorney general's office that defends state laws and regulations in court. State agencies and state legislatures usually have their own in-house attorneys as well, who provide legal guidance as laws and regulations are developed, but the attorney general's office often takes over once a lawsuit is filed. At the federal level, the U.S. Department of Justice, which is led by the Attorney General, is tasked with defending federal laws and regulations when they are challenged. When agency regulations—such as the FDA's proposed cigarette warnings—are involved, attorneys at the relevant agency provide support and assistance, but the Department of Justice leads the legal team. If a case goes all the way to the Supreme Court, government attorneys in the Office of the Solicitor General (a part of the U.S. Department of Justice) represent the United States.

At all levels of government, the attorneys who defend public health laws in court are almost always legal generalists, *not* experts in public health. Therefore, it is important, when possible, to incorporate these attorneys into the policymaking process as early as possible. That provides them with an opportunity to become more familiar with the importance of the public health issues involved and the evidence supporting the policy approach. At the local level, city councils are often unwilling to vote in favor of a public health law unless the city attorney has signed off on it. Thus, in addition to defending a law when challenged, the city attorney is a critical player in a law's adoption and should be viewed as an important stakeholder in the advocacy process. If there is a legal challenge, city councils usually seek the city attorney's advice on whether it is a wise decision to allocate money for a legal defense (or, instead, whether it would make more sense to just rescind the law). In this way as well, the city attorney's perspective on the law can be pivotal.

One difficulty encountered at the state and federal levels is that—as was the case with the R.J. Reynolds litigation—the attorney general's office or the Department of Justice is not brought into the matter until there is active litigation. Thus it is impossible to involve those attorneys in the lawmaking or rulemaking process at an earlier stage. However, attorneys within government agencies such as the FDA, though they do not ultimately stand before the judge in court, are often intimately involved in the development of public health laws and regulations. It is also important to build connections with them as early as possible in the policymaking process. These agency attorneys can help identify and avoid legal landmines, and they can subsequently play key roles in educating the attorney general's office or the Department of Justice about the underlying evidence supporting a given action.

Outside of government, various advocacy and academic groups support the defense of public health laws by providing *legal technical assistance.* These groups do not provide legal representation, but they can contribute subject-matter expertise, compile and share resources that have been developed and used in other communities, and offer connections to potential expert witnesses. Because the attorneys representing government entities may be generalists unfamiliar with the public health topic at issue, connections to such assistance can be extremely valuable. (One good example of such a resource is the Public Health Law Center at Mitchell Hamline School of Law, http://www.publichealthlawcenter.org.)

One important note of caution: When nongovernmental groups provide legal technical assistance to attorneys defending public health laws, those communications may not be covered by the attorney-client privilege. Under the attorney-client privilege, communications between an attorney and his or her client are considered confidential, and their disclosure cannot be compelled except in very rare instances. This protection is designed to foster free and forthright communication between an attorney and client, so that the attorney can provide effective representation. In most states, this privilege extends *only* from the attorney to his or her client—in this case, a legislature or other government entity. Communications with outside groups may not be covered by the privilege. Moreover, the presence of an outside advocate at, for example, a meeting between city council members and the city attorney, may prevent the attorney-client privilege from applying to those discussions.

Amicus Curiae Briefs

In addition to (or instead of) providing legal technical assistance, many public health organizations file *amicus curiae* briefs to advocate for public health causes in the courts. Literally, the phrase means "friend of the court," and these briefs (referred to as "amicus briefs" for short) are filed by entities that are not parties to a lawsuit but that have an interest in the case and want to advocate for a particular outcome. Amicus briefs can be filed by anyone—advocacy groups, professional organizations, governmental entities, academics, and others. Amicus briefs can be extremely influential, but it is important to be strategic about when to file them and what to address. Failure to do so can lead to a lot of wasted time, effort, and money. There are three main issues to consider: *whether* to file an amicus brief; *who* should file an amicus brief, and *what* the brief should address.

Amicus briefs are most useful when there is an important, unsettled *legal* issue at stake. By contrast, amicus brief are unlikely to be useful or influential if the case focuses on a specific *factual* dispute. For example, a case about whether or not state laws regulating lead paint are preempted by federal law may present an unresolved legal question, with implications for preemption jurisprudence that go beyond the context of lead paint. In such a case, as in many public health law cases, filing an amicus brief may be appropriate, particularly when other courts have issued conflicting opinions about the same question and the U.S. Supreme Court has not yet resolved the split. By contrast, a case about whether or not a landlord acted negligently in failing to remediate lead paint in a particular apartment building, without broader legal issues at stake, is a far less appropriate case for filing an amicus brief.

Amicus briefs are typically filed in appellate courts and at the U.S. Supreme Court. At the Supreme Court, briefs can be filed both at the *certiorari* stage (when the Court is being asked to consider taking a case) and also at the merits stage (once it has decided to hear a case). While amicus briefs are very common at the Supreme Court, they are less common in state courts and in federal appellate courts. For that reason, they can sometimes be highly effective in these other settings. In particular, since state supreme courts are the final authority on questions of state law, public health groups—particularly state-based ones—may have a strong interest in filing amicus briefs in important state supreme court cases.

When considering what people or entities should sign on to an amicus brief, the important point to remember is that you want the court to read the brief carefully and take its arguments seriously. Thus what is important is not the number of organizations that sign the brief but the expertise of those who do and the substance of the argument. Briefs from well-known and well-respected national organizations like the American Medical

Association or the American Cancer Society can be particularly impactful. Other types of expertise that can contribute new and valuable perspectives for the court to consider include

- Academics and practitioners with clear subject-matter expertise. This may include doctors, statisticians, economists, psychologists, public health experts, and others.
- "Neutral" parties that might not be expected to have a particular position. Courts will not find it surprising that public health groups support public health policies, but an amicus brief from the state chamber of commerce emphasizing the importance of a healthy workforce to the state's economy may intrigue the court and get its attention.
- Whistleblowers or people who have "switched" sides (e.g., a former tobacco industry executive or a politician who argued against a policy but now recognizes its merits).
- People who have key insights into the law at issue in the case, such as members of the legislature who can discuss the law's background and intent or public health officials who can discuss the law's implementation and effects.

The most important consideration for the content of the brief is to offer something *new* that will aid the court, and not just repeat what the parties have already said. After briefly describing the organization's qualifications and expertise, the amicus brief should lay out why the new perspective or information is being offered. There are several different ways that an amicus brief may be helpful to the court. First, it could go into much more depth on one of the key issues or sub-issues in the case. The parties' briefs are usually limited to a set number of pages, so they may not be able to fully explore each legal issue, especially when there are many different legal questions involved. The amicus brief may best go into depth on one issue (e.g., the First Amendment claim) or even one particular aspect of that issue that could have broad public health importance (e.g., which level of First Amendment scrutiny is appropriate).

Second, a brief may present a new and alternative argument that the parties have not raised, although it should be careful not to undermine the arguments of the party it is supporting. For example, if a state is arguing that a state law is not preempted by federal law, the amicus brief might present an alternative argument that the federal law in question is unconstitutional or otherwise invalid.

Finally, the brief can present nonlegal expertise that is relevant to the case. In public health cases, this type of amicus brief is probably the most common. Many public health cases turn on questions of epidemiology or other scientific issues—like whether or not cigarette warning labels reduce tobacco use—and amicus briefs are used to help educate the court on those issues. Communicating science to courts, however, can be a complicated endeavor. Some scholars have observed that judges, on the whole, are "not well trained in, or favorably inclined to learn, the nuts and bolts of scientific inquiry" (Faigman, 2006). (Indeed, an aversion to math and science may be part of the reason they went to law school.) Accordingly, they may be resistant to briefs that are too technically complex or that go against their intuitive assumptions. But translating the science into plain language and tying it to the doctrinal analysis can lend a crucial angle to a legal case.

In the *R.J. Reynolds* case, groups including the American Academy of Pediatrics and the American Lung Association filed a science-focused amicus brief demonstrating that graphic warnings labels help to accurately educate consumers about the dangers of smoking. As any good amicus brief does, this brief sought to connect the scientific research to a key legal issue in the case: whether the warnings were "factual," which was one part of the relevant First Amendment test. Though the court ruled against the FDA in this case, such amicus briefs can help educate the courts about important aspects of public health cases.

Conclusion

When public health laws and regulations are challenged, it is typically government attorneys who defend those laws in court. Ideally, these attorneys have been working with public health experts (practitioners, advocates, scholars, public health attorneys, and others) since the outset of the policymaking process. Largely behind the scenes, public health groups can play critical roles in supporting the legal defense of public health laws by working closely with government attorneys and by organizing amicus briefs. The importance of this phase in the policymaking process cannot be overstated. If a jurisdiction is deterred by the possibility of litigation, it will not pursue legal innovations for health. If a law cannot survive legal review, then the law cannot take effect, and the entire effort will need to start over from the beginning.

Further Reading

Kearney, J. D., & Merrill, T. W. (2000). The Influence of Amicus Curiae Briefs on the Supreme Court. *University of Pennsylvania Law Review*, *148*(3), 743–855.

Public Health Law Center. (2014). What Is Legal Technical Assistance? Retrieved April 3, 2018 from http://www.publichealthlawcenter.org/resources/what-legal-technical-assistance-

VI | Diffusing Effective Legal Solutions

POLICY SURVEILLANCE

AND EVALUATION

21 | Scientific Evaluation in Transdisciplinary Public Health Research and Practice

Learning Objectives

- Understand the importance of evaluation to public health law.
- Know how to use evaluation techniques to define important legal processes and outcomes.
- Understand basic evaluation designs and their advantages and limitations.
- Grasp the basic methods of scientific legal mapping and policy surveillance.
- Describe the five essential public health law services.

Introduction

By now, you have seen most of what we do in the practice of transdisciplinary public health law. The work begins with identifying problems through community engagement, professional experience, epidemiology and behavioral science, and then developing policy interventions that stakeholders think might help. Lawyers and others then work to turn those policy ideas into laws, regulations, or other formal legal instruments, which then go through the political process of enactment into law. You have learned that the work does not end once the laws are on the books: to be effective, laws have to be implemented, enforced, and sometimes defended against legal challenges. There is one more chapter in this story: learning whether all this work has paid off and acting accordingly.

Whether it is a new legal intervention or an old law that might be doing more harm than good, the only way to be certain of the impact a law is through testing its effects as rigorously as possible through evaluation research. Research evidence tells us whether more jurisdictions should adopt a new law or repeal a useless or harmful one. *Policy surveillance*, the scientific mapping of laws of public health importance, provides the legal data for this kind of evaluation and keeps track of the laws across jurisdictions. In this chapter, we cover the most important things you need to understand about mapping and evaluating laws to determine what impact they are having on the public's health.

Evaluation in Legal Epidemiology

Recall that we described three basic elements of legal epidemiology in Chapter 3: legal prevention and control, legal etiology, and policy surveillance. (See Figure 3.1.) All three depend upon scientific methods to measure the nature and distribution of law (which jurisdictions have what laws and with what characteristics), the implementation and impact of legal interventions on health, the implementation and impact of laws defining health agency powers and duties, and the health effects of non-health laws. *Evaluation research* uses scientific methods to measure things like how a law is implemented, how people enforcing the law or subject to its rules feel about it, whether it accomplishes its stated or immediate purposes, and whether it is having a long-term effect on health or other outcomes we care about. By using evaluation to show the impact of public health laws, we can build an evidence base upon which laws and policies can be better designed and more efficiently passed. As we will see, there are many approaches to evaluation, depending upon available resources and data, but it is always possible to learn something from approaching public health law from an evaluation point of view, and lawyers can play a key role in evaluation by helping scientists understand legal processes and identify processes and outcomes to measure.

Thinking Like an Evaluator

No matter what else you do, thinking like an evaluator can help you get the most out of public health law work. Evaluators have to think first about the resources needed for a study, including time and money. Studies to measure the law's effects take planning: evaluators carefully select the right time period to study, collect relevant data, and then analyze the results. People devising policy options, and lawyers drafting bills, should already be thinking about how an evaluation can be designed and funded. Legislators sometimes include a requirement (and funding) for an evaluation and report in a new law and should be urged in the lobbying process to do that. When the legislature does not require it, health agencies sometimes will commission or conduct one anyway. If there is limited funding, academics may be willing to do the work, or they may assign it as a student project in a graduate program or research class. Even if no formal evaluation is conducted, thinking through the design of an evaluation can put you in a better position to learn from the experience ahead.

Thinking like an evaluator helps you identify what effects you can expect the law to have, how you think they will happen, and where you should be looking for evidence of impact. In Chapter 7, we talked about causal models as a tool for developing good policy. Causal models work the same way in planning an evaluation. Your causal model is your theory of change: it requires you to specify who will be implementing the law, how you expect its targets to respond, and what effects you expect to see in the short, medium, and long terms. That in turn tells you what to measure—the data you need to collect—to see if the theory is correct. That is the core of an evaluation plan.

Let us take an example from the fight against HIV. Injecting drug users are at risk when they cannot get new, sterile syringes, but many states in the past had laws that made it hard for them to obtain new syringes (many still do). In 2000, the New York state legislature enacted a two-year Expanded Syringe Access Demonstration Program (ESAP; 2000) allowing pharmacies to sell 10 or fewer syringes to drug users without a prescription. Figure 21.1 is a simple causal model of the possible effects. As part of the law, the legislature ordered the Department of Health to submit an evaluation after two years that would assess ESAP's impact, both positive and negative.

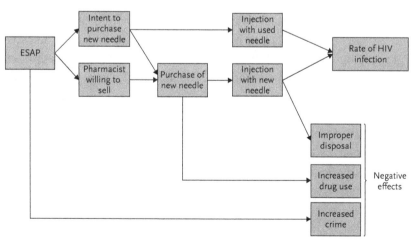

FIGURE 21.1. Causal model of implementation and effects of New York Expanded Syringe Access Program.

The Department of Health funded researchers at the New York Academy of Medicine, who were already conducting studies on syringe access, drug use, and HIV, to design and conduct the two-year evaluation. The evaluators had to define the impacts they needed to measure: what would existing theory and evidence predict as possible outcomes of pharmacy access, *and* what could be observed to measure those effects? The legislature also wanted the evaluation to look at specific negative side effects, like more crime, substance abuse, and improperly discarded needles in the community. Finding implementation indicators and outcomes that can be affordably measured are crucial in evaluation. Although everyone hoped that making syringes more available would cut the number of new HIV cases, the evaluators could not feasibly use this outcome in their evaluation. There is often a long lag between the time when people are infected and the time when their infection is diagnosed and reported to the health department, so accurate data on new infections after ESAP would not be available within the study period.

Fortunately, researchers could follow the causal chain back a step or two to identify things they *could* measure and that would be reasonably attributable to the law. They interviewed drug users about whether they shared used needles, where they got new needles, and whether, in their experience, pharmacists were willing to sell needles to drug users. The evaluators obtained syringe sales data and interviewed pharmacists about their willingness to sell to suspected drug users. To investigate negative side effects, the evaluators conducted neighborhood inspections to see if more needles were being improperly discarded and looked at data on crime rates and substance abuse to see if there were increases in either after the law.

The evaluation report found modest early improvements in access to and use of new syringes and no negative side effects (Center for Urban Epidemiologic Studies, 2003). Based on these findings, the legislature continued the program, and more sophisticated studies later confirmed that the intervention was increasing safe behavior without creating new harm (Cleland et al., 2007; Cooper et al., 2012). Over time, a substantial decline in new HIV cases among drug users—a decline that could not readily be explained in any other way—supported the conclusion that the expansion of syringe access through ESAP, syringe exchange programs, and other legal interventions had been a public health success.

Evaluation Designs

Legal evaluation has a life cycle. When a public health law is first enacted in one or more jurisdictions, research focuses on observing implementation

and getting early indications of possible impact. As in the ESAP evaluation, researchers look into whether people responsible for enforcing the
law are actually doing so, whether the people covered by the law know
about it, and whether the behaviors specified in the law are beginning to be
adopted. In a year or two, it becomes possible to compare health outcomes
before and after the law came into effect or to compare jurisdictions with
different laws at the same point in time.

As more time passes, and especially as more jurisdicions adopt their
own, differing versions of the law, there are more differences in law, behavior, and outcomes to observe and compare. More ambitious designs
become possible, testing the effect of the law and different, specific
provisions over time (*longitudinally*) and across many jurisdictions. This
helps us get to the ultimate question of whether the new law is causing the
effects and which parts of the law are important. The confidence we can
place in a causal inference from a study is directly related to the design of
the study.

Ideally, an evaluation would compare people who had been "treated"
by the law with those who had not, and exposure to the treatment would
be random, so there could be no systematic difference between those who
were treated and those who were not (and, indeed, neither the subjects nor
the researchers would be aware of who is in what group). If that sounds
familiar, that is because this is the double-blind randomized controlled
trial (RCT), often referred to as the gold standard of evaluation research.
True RCTs are scarce in legal epidemiology, because it is rarely possible
to randomize the application of the law or blind any of the participants
from the legal intervention. That said, it is not uncommon for RCTs to
test a practice or intervention required by law: RCTs have tested the impact of using rental housing vouchers to help people move from poorer
to less poor neighborhoods (Ludwig et al., 2012), whether Medicaid
insurance expansion improves recipient health (Baicker et al., 2013),
and whether treating water supplies prevents disease (Gerber, Green, &
Carnegie, 2013). If research can show that the underlying intervention
works—for example, that treating water supplies prevents disease—then
the only remaining research question is whether law is an effective way
to get more jurisdictions to treat their water. It is notable that both the
housing voucher and the Medicaid experiments were only possible because the practices tested were not funded at a level sufficient to make it
available to every eligible individual. Because the government resorted to
a lottery to fairly allocate the housing vouchers and Medicaid cards, the
researchers were able to build the study upon the randomized selection.

Experiments can also be used to test methods of enforcement. For example, a British study experimented with different forms of tax payment reminder letters to improve compliance with British tax laws (Hallsworth, List, Metcalfe, & Vlaev, 2014).

Given the difficulties of legal experiments, the practical gold standard for public health law evaluation is the well-designed *quasi-experiment*, a study that takes advantage of the variations in law between jurisdictions and over time. A quasi-experiment is a form of *natural experiment*, in which forces outside the researcher's control, in this case, lawmakers in different states or cities, create exposure and control groups that mimic a planned experiment in a way that resembles randomization. Randomization, however, is only one of many design elements that can be used to strengthen a study's ability to support inferences of causation. In a study of the impact of increasing the drinking age from 18 to 21 years old on car crashes, for example, researchers used a combination of tools to properly test the causal link:

- Making many repeated measures of outcomes over an extended period of time to distinguish real changes from seasonal or other unrelated variations in road safety;
- Using a time resolution that can detect a pattern of change predicted by theory; for example, if deterrence theory predicts that bar owners will immediately enforce the new age limits because of strong initial enforcement, one would expect an immediate reduction in alcohol-related crashes among the newly prohibited age groups; if enforcement is only being rolled out gradually, and widespread noncompliance is expected, the reduction in crashes may be more gradual, and researchers will need to wait longer to see an effect;
- Using comparison jurisdictions that are similar in demographics, drinking, and driving patterns to the jurisdictions that are raising the age;
- Using comparison groups of people who are similar to the target group but not themselves affected by the legal change; for example, if the drinking age is raised from 18 to 21, crashes among 18- to 20-year-olds, who can no longer buy alcohol legally, can be compared to 17- and 21-year-olds, who are not affected by the law change and among whom crashes should not decline; and
- Using comparison outcomes that are related to the primary outcome but are not affected by the law or policy under study; for example, a comparison of single-driver nighttime crashes (strongly associated

with alcohol consumption) and daytime crashes (generally unassociated with alcohol consumption) (Wagenaar & Komro, 2013).

These design elements are augmented by nuanced statistical techniques of analysis like *difference-in-difference analysis* (which compares the change over time in the outcomes observed in the people exposed to the law compared to the change in those not exposed to the law), *synthetic controls* (which uses statistical methods with longitudinal data to create a "control" group as similar to the group exposed to the law as possible), and *regression analysis* (processes for investigating the relationship among variables).

Research on implementation, typically using qualitative methods, is also important to causal inference, because it can reveal whether the theorized mechanisms of effect are working. Qualitative researchers use texts (like operational memos or social media posts) and interviews, surveys, and observation to study how people understand the law and integrate its requirements into their behavior (or refuse to). By looking at how police enforce a law or targets evade it, qualitative researchers can confirm that the law on the streets actually conforms to some degree with the law on the books or explain why a clearly written law may not actually be enforceable. For example, raising the drinking age will not have an effect if newly prohibited age groups find other ways to get alcohol. Ethnographic research can document how various segments of the underage population obtain alcohol and how drinking culture adapts to the new rules. Qualitative research finding that 18- to 20-year-olds are finding social substitutes for meeting up in bars would support the inference that bars are enforcing the age limit and therefore that a reduction in alcohol-related crashes in the age group could be caused by the law.

Criteria-based analysis of evidence can also be useful in assessing the impact of the law. In this approach, a checklist is used to assess the available evidence showing an association between a law and changes in behavior or health: the more the evidence satisfies the criteria, the stronger the inference of causation. The Bradford Hill criteria (Hill, 1965), shown in Figure 21.2, are the best known. In the case of raising the drinking age, which most states did in the mid-1980s, direct evidence showed that raising the drinking age was associated temporally with crash reductions, that the effect size (strength) was substantial, that the association was consistent across jurisdictions adopting the law, and that there was nothing else happening at the time that might have caused the effect (specificity). Mechanistic evidence included findings that bars and liquor stores were

CRITERION	EXAMPLE	IS CRITERION APPLICABLE TO LEGAL EPIDEMIOLOGY?
Strength of the association (i.e., effect size)	Raising the drinking age was associated with a 50% decrease in alcohol-involved traffic deaths in the target groups	Often. Note, a small effect may also be causally related to law, and important.
Consistency	The effect on deaths was observed everywhere the law was enacted.	Often.
Specificity	The decrease was seen primarily in drivers who were targeted by the new drinking age.	Often. Requires specification of the target population and the expected behavior change.
Temporality	The change occurred after the law was passed and at the time predicted by theory or seen in implementation research.	Often. Requires a theory or measurement of implementation.
Exposure gradient	The change in drinking was greater where fines were higher and/or enforcement more intense.	Often. Requires specification of measures of exposures, such as number of bars inspected or fined for serving underage drinkers.
Plausibility: there is a plausible mechanism that would explain the causal link	The law imposed sanctions on businesses furnishing alcohol to underage drinkers, enforced by inspectors. This led to rapid change in business practices, significantly reducing youth access.	Often. Requires specification of the theoretical mechanism(s) of legal effect.
Coherence: how well does all the evidence "hang together?"	The association is seen in all the criteria listed here, and there are no indications of other causes or contrary findings, such as a rise in self-reported drinking among the targeted age groups.	Often.
Experimental evidence	No experiments were available, but quasi-experiments relying on differences in law between states provided much of the evidence of the association.	True experiments are rare in law. Quasi-experiments are common and the "gold standard."
Analogy	The proven deterrent effect of drunk-driving laws generally provided support for causal inference by analogy.	Often.

FIGURE 21.2. Bradford Hill Criteria as a Tool for Assessing Causation in Legal Epidemiology.

McCartt AT, Hellinga LA, Kirley BB. The effects of minimum legal drinking age 21 laws on alcohol-related driving in the United States. *J Safety Res.* Apr 2010;41(2):173–181.

enforcing the law and that young people were less able to get alcohol. Finally, the similarity between the 21-year-old drinking age and a previous 18-year-old one that had been shown to be effective provided evidence of impact by analogy.

In the end, deciding whether a law works can be difficult. Experts can look at the accumulation of consistent evidence in single studies or at the strength of quasi-experiments, and they can use tools like the Bradford Hill criteria. Rigor and humility must be combined with practicality: we never have perfect data and cannot be expected to produce a gold standard study before acting. At the same time, there is no excuse for "treating" millions of people with a new law and then failing to do the best we can to assess its impact and side effects.

Legal Mapping and Policy Surveillance

Scientific policy surveillance is integral both to figuring out what laws work and to spreading good laws across the country. Mapping of public health laws has a long history in modern American public health law. As early as 1941, *Public Health Reports* featured a study of state vaccination laws (Fowler, 1941), and similar mapping studies frequently appear today.

More recently there has been a turn to conducting such legal research in a scientific way, using defined methods, coding, and quality control to objectively observe (rather than interpret) the text of the law and convert that text into quantitative data (Anderson, Tremper, Thomas, & Wagenaar, 2013; see Figure 21.3). This approach to legal mapping research, called *policy surveillance*, is defined as "the ongoing systematic, scientific collection and analysis of laws of public health significance" (Burris, Hitchcock, Ibrahim, Penn, & Ramanathan, 2016). The data these mapping studies produce are accompanied by a detailed protocol that defines the scope of the research, provides inclusion and exclusion criteria, and explains coding decisions—all of which combines to satisfy the basic scientific criterion of reproducibility. Translating complex legal text into digestible data also facilitates publication of legal information to the Internet for use by other stakeholders. Today, there are several websites that offer interactive access to legal mapping data, including downloadable files for research use. These include LawAtlas (www.LawAtlas.org), the Alcohol Policy Information System (https://alcoholpolicy.niaaa.nih.gov/), and the Centers for Disease Control and Prevention State Tobacco Activities Tracking and Evaluation System (https://www.cdc.gov/statesystem/).

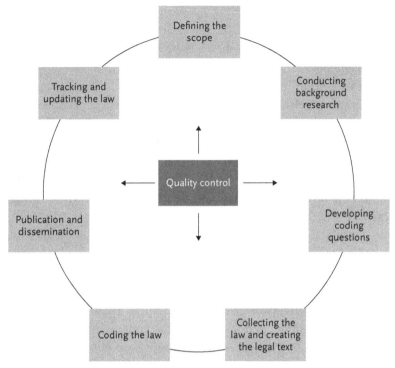

FIGURE 21.3. The policy surveillance process.

Policy surveillance meets at least three needs in public health research, practice, and policymaking. First, scientific collection and coding of important laws and policies creates data suitable for use in rigorous evaluation studies. Since its launch, more than 140 peer-reviewed papers have drawn on APIS for reliable legal data (Alcohol Policy Information System, 2015). The use of written research and coding protocols enhances the accuracy and efficiency of updating datasets to reflect changes in laws over time. Propagating public-domain legal datasets will lower the cost of and potentially speed the evaluation of important policies.

Second, policy surveillance addresses the chronic lack of readily accessible, nonpartisan information about status and trends in health legislation and policy. Accessible legal trend data is important to the accountability of the public health system, because laws and policies are frequently used as measures of progress or defined as goals in themselves in health policy guidance like Healthy People 2020. All participants in the process of translating knowledge and evidence into laws and regulations—researchers, health professionals, community members, policymakers—benefit from knowing where the need and onus for acting lies, what the trends are, how jurisdictions compare in individual policies and their overall policy portfolios, and what forms current policies are taking. When a government agency recommends the adoption of a law, or even just endorses it as evidence-based, those who make the recommendation, policymakers, and the public should be able to see where such legislation already exists, where it is still needed, and whether the recommendation is actually followed. Accessibility is an important issue for local health departments: local policy information is particularly difficult to collect, both because there are so many localities and local bodies with policymaking authority and because many forms of local policy are not available in general legal databases. Policy surveillance that includes state, tribal, local, and territorial policies, highlights important issues or categories, breaks legal texts into its component parts, takes advantage of data visualization tools, and provides full text or links to text can make it much faster and simpler for public health stakeholders to find and understand existing laws and policies and monitor trends across jurisdictions and over time.

A third important benefit of policy surveillance is the opportunity to build legal capacity in the public health workforce. Public Health Accreditation Board (PHAB) standards for health department accreditation recognize that "public health laws are key tools for health departments as they work to promote and protect the health of the population" and should be evidence-based and current with knowledge, practices, and emerging issues in public health (Public Health Accreditation Board 2013, 156). In order to meet PHAB standards, health departments must have the capacity to review laws, assess them for recommended changes, and collaborate with appropriate entities to effect needed reforms (Public Health Accreditation Board 2013). Local policy surveillance studies (Seattle-King County Public Health Department; 2015), if published, can make policy language and comparative analysis more accessible for day-to-day use by governments and communities, a powerful and needed form of data democratization. Some local and regional health departments may not have direct authority to effect change across their geographic coverage area because they overlap with multiple governmental subdivisions and institutions, including cities, school districts, and other special purpose districts. Policy surveillance capacity and cross-sector collaboration will support a policy assurance role not formerly possible.

Summing Up: The Five Essential Public Health Law Services

This book has taught you how legal skills can be used to support the design, implementation, monitoring, evaluation, and scale-up of legal measures that improve public health and health systems. Transdisciplinary public health law depends on traditional legal functions, such as advising health officers on legal options, drafting legislation, and litigating in court, but you have also seen that it also includes policy development, advocacy, enforcement, monitoring, evaluation, and other law-related activities that are most often performed by people without formal legal training. Figure 21.4 encapsulates these many functions in a framework of five essential public health law services.

As we discussed in Chapters 5 to 8, the first step is to identify a policy that has a reasonable chance of making a difference politically, legally, and epidemiologically. Devising a viable policy approach requires that the policymakers, practitioners, and advocates who are involved have access to relevant evidence and expertise. It requires collaboration with communities struggling with the problem and a recognition that the particular health issue you care about may be part of a web of health inequity. Developing policy strategically requires more than hoping that policy developers will find the research and experts they need. It involves creating relationship networks that span science, public health and legal practice, and communities.

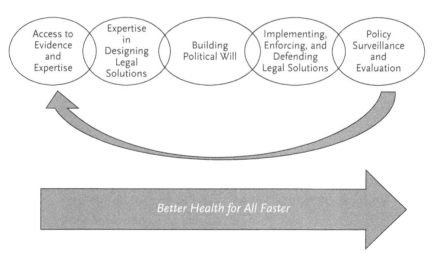

FIGURE 21.4. The five essential public health law services.

Burris S, Ashe M, Blanke D, et al. Better Health Faster: The 5 Essential Public Health Law Services. Public Health Reports. 2016;131(6):747-753.

Chapters 15 and 16 explained that a key public health law service is translating a policy idea into a legal form that is technically sound and politically acceptable, designed to gain maximum compliance with minimum enforcement, and calculated to avoid or overcome legal challenges. At the outset, lawyers must assess the authority of a policymaker to pass or promulgate new provisions. For example, a local alcohol tax may be preempted by state law and a tobacco labeling requirement would have to be considered in light of the Supreme Court's expansion of protection for commercial speech. Once authority is certain, lawyers can devise options that take full advantage of the legal instruments (e.g., statutes, regulations, executive orders, enforcement guidance, case law) and the many ways laws can be designed to influence behavior or environments. Lawyers can work with researchers to ensure the development of scientific evidence necessary for justifying a law and contribute political acumen to advocacy or litigation on an issue.

Proponents of healthy laws, even if armed with solid legal strategy and text, face the challenge of getting the legal intervention onto the books. We looked at public health law advocacy in Chapter 17. Just as lawyers are indispensable in designing legal solutions, partners' experiences in community engagement and advocacy are indispensable in getting healthy policies enacted. Building understanding and support is often the most difficult phase of the policy process, which is a very practical reason for working with community stakeholders from the very start of the policy development process. Mobilizing support at the advocacy stage can require educating the public about the problem and the solution, organizing the citizenry and building coalitions to mobilize active support, getting the public to participate in rulemaking and other policymaking processes, conducting research on opposition, and lobbying policymakers. All of these activities require resources, skills, and experience, and the literature explaining how to conduct these activities is vast.

Chapters 18 and 19 covered enforcement and compliance, which are critically important to the success of legal interventions. The effort to design, draft, and win enactment of a law can come to nothing if the ways of getting its targets to obey have not been carefully thought out, provided for in the law, and sufficiently resourced. Some interventions, such as smoke-free laws, rely heavily on information and social norms and may require little direct enforcement. Others, such as lead abatement regulations in housing, require consistent inspection and enforcement to reduce child exposure. Enforcement is difficult, and its importance has been chronically underestimated in public health law practice and research.

Chapter 20 talked about the important function of defending laws against legal challenge. Most public health legal interventions are never challenged. Those that are challenged often have an outsized role in shaping the perceptions of public health's mission and authority. Effective participation of external legal and health experts, for example by preparing legal briefs as *amici curiae* ("friends of the court") or advising the jurisdiction affected, can contribute greatly to the likelihood of success.

Finally, if law matters to health, then public health officers, policymakers, and researchers need to know what the law requires, where it applies, and whether or not it works. This is where policy surveillance and evaluation come in, as we discussed in this chapter. The five services framework can be used to "audit" health law capacity in agencies, communities, and specific advocacy movements. It can also be used for evaluating the quality and effectiveness of the services provided. In both ways, the public health approach of defining and evaluating health services can help public health law deliver better health faster.

Conclusion

Law plays a vital role throughout public health practice and advocacy. That means that lawyers are important in public health work but also that public health law is not just for lawyers. No matter what your discipline or official job description in public health, you are likely to be doing legal work some of the time. This book has introduced you to public health law as a transdisciplinary, collaborative practice in which many different kinds of professionals, policymakers, and citizens play important roles. Building on this introduction, you are ready to learn more about legal doctrine, legal epidemiology, policymaking, and advocacy.

We have taught you public health law as a rigorous professional discipline. We have emphasized the importance of scientific habits and data and a critical, rational approach to analysis. That is necessary for a useful career in public health law, but it is not everything you need. We close with these words from the Rev. Gary Gunderson, a minister and public health leader:

My counsel to our beloved field of public health is to *not* stop talking about facts, analytics, determinants, vectors, patterns and predictors. But we must *also* talk about our crazy love for the people—the public. And we talk about why we continue to hope for better, hope for more and simply won't quit hoping no matter what. You can take our money, put us in the dumpiest offices and cut our staff. You can relocate our building to a place so far down the road you can't find it in broad daylight. You can treat us as pitiful, hardly even as honorable as a primary care doctor, which in hospital world is hardly on the map. We won't quit. Why? Because we are in a lovers quarrel with the public we love.

If you are a public health professional and cannot profess love for the public, I'd recommend that you take your high end analytical tools and move on down the street to do hedge fund manipulation, which is not played for life and death stakes. If you don't love, you're a danger to the public and the rest of us in the field of public health. Don't even tweet.

This is the time for those who just can't stop loving the messy, disappointing, ever-muddling gaggle of humans called "the public." We are in *just* the right work at just the right time. While others rant, we must speak out of that love. Bring our facts and laptops, as we know that science is a friend of humans and what we are possible of. But we must speak out of love first, especially in public, especially with the public, especially about the public.

Further Reading

Burris, S., Ashe, M., Blanke, D., Ibrahim, J., Levin, D. E., Matthews, . . . Katz, M. (2016). Better Health Faster: The 5 Essential Public Health Law Services. *Public Health Reports*, *131*(6), 747–753.

Burris, S., Mays, G. P., Scutchfield, D. F., & Ibrahim, J. K. (2012). Moving from Intersection to Integration: Public Health Law Research and Public Health Systems and Services Research. *The Milbank Quarterly*, *90*(2), 375–408.

Wagenaar, A., & Burris, S. (Eds.). (2013). *Public Health Law Research: Theory and Methods*. San Francisco: John Wiley.

REFERENCES

Legal Materials

44 Liquormart, Inc. v. Rhode Island, 517 U.S. 484 (1996).

Administrative Procedure Act, 5 U.S.C. § 500 et seq., Pub. L. No. 79-404 (1946).

Ariz. Rev. Stat. Ann. § 41-194.01 (2016).

Bigelow v. Commonwealth of Virginia, 421 U.S. 809 (1975).

Brown v. Board of Education of Topeka, 347 U.S. 483 (1954).

Buck v. Bell, 200 U.S. 207 (1927).

Burwell v. Hobby Lobby, 573 U.S. __ ,134 S.Ct. 2751 (2014).

Camara v. Municipal Court of City and County of San Francisco, 387 U.S. 523 (1965).

Central Hudson Gas & Electric Corp v. Public Service Commission, 447 U.S. 557 (1980).

Chevron U.S.A., Inc. v. Natural Resources Defense Council, Inc., 467 U.S. 837 (1984).

Cipollone v. Liggett Group, Inc., 505 U.S. 504 (1992).

Citizens United v. Federal Election Commission, 558 U.S. 310 (2010).

City of Boerne v. Flores, 521 U.S. 507 (1997).

City of Cleburne, Tex. v. Cleburne Living Center, 473 U.S. 432 (1985).

City of New York v. New St. Mark's Baths, 497 N.Y.S.2d 979 (Sup. Ct. 1986).

Cleveland v. State, 989 N.E.2d 1072 (Oh. Ct. App. 2013).

Colonnade Catering Corp. v. United States, 397 U.S. 72 (1970).

Congressional Review Act, 5 U.S.C. 1801, Pub. L. No. 104-121 (1996).

Craig v. Boren, 429 U.S. 190 (1976).

DeShaney v. Winnebago County Dept. of Social Services, 489 U.S. 189 (1989).

Dimare Fresh, Inc. v. United States, 808 F.3d 1301 (Fed. Cir. 2015). *cert. denied*, 136 S. Ct. 2461 (2016).

Discount Tobacco City and Lottery, Inc. v. United States, 674 F. 3d 509 (6th Cir. 2012).

District of Columbia v. Heller, 554 U.S. 270 (2008).

Dred Scott v. Sandford, 60 U.S. 393 (1857).

Eisenstadt v. Baird, 405 U.S. 438 (1972).

Employment Division v. Smith, 494 U.S. 872 (1990).

Exemption from Tax on Corporations, Certain Trusts, Etc., 26 U.S.C. § 501 (2015).

Expanded Syringe Access Demonstration Program, Pub. L. No. 2000 Sess. Law News of N.Y. Ch. 56 (S. 6293–A, A. 9293–A) (2000).

Ferguson v. Skrupa, 372 U.S. 726 (1963).

First National Bank of Boston v. Bellotti, 435 U.S. 765 (1978).

Fl. Stat. Ann. § 790.33 (2017).

Floyd v. City of New York, 959 F. Supp. 2d 540 (S.D.N.Y. 2013).

Food and Drug Admin. v. Brown & Williamson Tobacco Corp., 529 U.S. 120 (2000).

Fountas v. Com'r of the Massachusetts Dept. of Revenue, 2009 WL 3792468 (Mass. Super. 2009). *aff'd* 76 Mass.App.Ct. 1116 (Mass.App.Ct. 2010), *review denied* 456 Mass. 1107 (2010).

Goldberg v. Kelly, 397 U.S. 254 (1970).

Gonzales v. Raich, 545 U.S. 1 (2005).

Graham v. R.J. Reynolds Tobacco Co., 782 F.3d 1261 (11th Cir. 2015).

Graham v. R.J. Reynolds Tobacco Co., 857 F.3d 1169 (11th Cir. en banc 2017).

Greene v. Edwards, 263 S.E.2d 661 (W.Va. 1980).

Grimes v. Kennedy Krieger Institute, 782 A.2d 807 (Md. 2001).

Griswold v. Connecticut, 381 U.S. 479 (1965).

Heart of Atlanta Motel, Inc. v. United States, 379 U.S. 241 (1964).

Hickox v. Christie, 205 F. Supp. 3rd 579 (D.N.J. 2016).

Hollis v. Lynch, 827 F.3d 436 (5th Cir. 2016).

Hunter v. City of Pittsburgh, 207 U.S. 161 (1907).

In re Civil Rights Cases, 109 U.S. 3 (1883).

Jacobson v. Massachusetts, 197 U.S. 11 (1905).

Jew Ho v. Williamson, 103 F. 10 (1900).

Johnson v. Robison, 415 U.S. 361 (1974).

Lindsley v. Natural Carbonic Gas Co., 220 U.S. 61 (1911).

Lobbying Disclosure Act of 1995, 2 U.S.C. § 1601 et seq. (2017).

Lochner v. New York, 198 U.S. 45 (1905).

Lorillard v. Reilly, 533 U.S. 525 (2001).

Lujan v. Defenders of Wildlife, 504 U.S. 555 (1992).

Mackey v. Montrym, 443 U.S. 1 (1979).

Marbury v. Madison, 5 U.S. 137 (1803).

Mathews v. Eldridge, 424 U.S. 319 (1976).

Matter of N.Y. Statewide Coal. of Hispanic Chambers of Commerce v. N.Y.C. Dept. of Health & Mental Hygiene, 970 N.Y.S.2d 200 (App. Div. 2013).

McCulloch v. Maryland, 17 U.S. 316 (1819).

McDonald v. Chicago, 561 U.S. 742 (2010).

Medtronic, Inc. v. Lohr, 518 U.S. 470 (1996).

Michigan v. EPA, 135 S. Ct. 2699 (2015).

Mississipi University for Women v. Hogan, 458 U.S. 718 (1982).

National Federation of Independent Business (NFIB) v. Sebelius, 567 U.S. 519 (2012).

North Carolina Board of Dental Examiners v. Federal Trade Commission, 574 U.S. __, 135 S. Ct. 1101 (2015).

Obergefell v. Hodges, 576 U.S. __, 135 S.Ct. 2584 (U.S. 2015).

Ohio Bureau of Employment Servs. v. Hodory, 431 U.S. 471 (1977).

Patient Protection and Affordable Care Act, Pub. L. No. 111-148, 124 Stat. 119 (2010).

Perez v. United States, 402 U.S. 146 (1971).

Phillips v. City of New York, 775 F.3d 538 (2d. Cir. 2015).

Planned Parenthood of Southeastern Pennsylvania v. Casey, 505 U.S. 833 (1992).

Powers and duties of the department, Wisc. Stat. Ann. § 250.04 (2017).

"Provider," Indiana Code § 25-1-9.5-4 (2016).

Public Health Service Act, 42 U.S.C. § 1 et seq. (1944).

R.J. Reynolds Tobacco Co. v. U.S. Food and Drug Administration, 823 F. Supp. 2d 36 (D.D.C. 2011).

R.J. Reynolds Tobacco Co. v. U.S. Food and Drug Administration, 845 F. Supp. 2d 266 (D.D.C. 2012). *aff'd by* 696 F.3d 1205 (D.D. Cir. 2012), *overruled by American Meat Institute v. U.S. Dept. of Agriculture*, 760 F.3d 18 (D.C.Cir. 2014).

R.J. Reynolds Tobacco Company et al. v. Food and Drug Administration et al., Brief of Defendants-Appellants, 2011 WL 6179451 (C.A.D.C. 2011).

R.J. Reynolds Tobacco Company et al. v. Food and Drug Administration et al., Brief of Plaintiffs-Appellees, 2012 WL 204198 (C.A.D.C. 2012).

Regulation of Firearms, Knives, and Explosives, Tex. Loc. Gov't Code Ann. § 229.001 (2017).

Reimbursement for Telehealth Services and Telemedicine Services for Certain Providers, Indiana Code § 12-15-5-11(b) (2013).

Religious Freedom Restoration Act, 42 U.S.C. § § 2000bb et seq. (1993).

Robert T. Stafford Disaster Relief and Emergency Assistance Act, 42 U.S.C. § 5121 et seq. (1988).

Roe v. Wade, 410 U.S. 13 (1973).

Senate of the United States. (1965). S. Rep. No. 195, 89th Cong., 1st Sess., 4.

Sorrell v. IMS Health, Inc., 564 U.S. 552 (2011).

South Dakota v. Dole, 483 U.S. 203 (1987).

Tarabochia v. Adkins, 766 F.3d 1115 (9th Cir. 2014).

Thompson v. Western States Medical Center, 535 U.S. 357 (2002).

Twining v. New Jersey, 211 U.S. 78 (1908).

U.S. v. Carolene Products Co., 304 U.S. 144 (1938).

U.S. v. Caronia, 703 F.3d 149 (2d Cir. 2012).

U.S. v. Darby Lumber Co., 213 U.S. 100 (1941).

U.S. v. Lopez, 514 U.S. 549 (1995).

United States Constitution § art. VI, cl. 2. (1787).

United States v. Hayes, 555 U.S. 415 (2009).

United States v. Philip Morris USA, Inc., 449 F. Supp. 2d 1 (D.C. Cir. 2006).

Unlawful Acts, 18 U.S.C. § 922(g)(2) (1994).

Virginia State Pharmacy Board v. Virginia Citizens Consumer Council, 425 U.S. 748 (1976).

Washington v. Davis, 426 U.S. 229 (1976).

Whole Women's Health v Hellerstedt, 136 S.Ct. 2292 (2016).

Wickard v. Filburn, 317 U.S. 111 (1942).

Williams v. City of Philadelphia, 164 A.3d 576 (Pa. Comm. Ct. 2016).

Williamson v. Lee Optical, 348 U.S. 483 (1955).

Winter v. Natural Resources Defense Council, Inc., 555 U.S. 7 (2008).

Wisconsin v. Yoder, 406 U.S. 205 (1972).

Young v. Cmty. Nutrition Inst., 476 U.S. 974 (1986).

Zauderer v. Office of Disc. Counsel, 471 U.S. 626 (1985).

Zinermon v. Burch, 494 U.S. 113 (1990).

Books, Articles, Reports, and Websites

Abouk, R., & Adams, S. (2013). Texting Bans and Fatal Accidents on Roadways: Do They Work? Or Do Drivers Just React to Announcements of Bans? *American Economic Journal: Applied Economics, 5*(2), 179–199.

Alcohol Policy Information System. (2015). Peer-Reviewed Publications Using APIS Data. Retrieved March 3, 2015, from https://alcoholpolicy.niaaa.nih.gov/peer-reviewed_publications_using_apis_data.html.

American Medical Association. (2016). *Principles of Medical Ethics*. Chicago, IL: American Medical Association.

Anderson, E., Tremper, C., Thomas, S., & Wagenaar, A. C. (2013). Measuring Statutory Law and Regulations for Empirical Research. In A. Wagenaar & S. Burris (Eds.), *Public Health Law Research: Theory and Methods* (pp. 237–260). San Francisco: Jossey-Bass.

Arkush, D. J. (2008). Situating Emotion: A Critical Realist View of Emotion and Nonconscious Cognitive Processes for Law and Legal Theory. *BYU Law Review, 2008*(5), 1275–1366.

Association of State and Territorial Health Officials. (2014). ASTHO Profile of State Public Health. *ASTHO Profile of State Public Health,* Vol. 3. Arlington, VA: ASTHO.

Badger, E. (2017, July 6). Blue Cities Want to Make Their Own Rules. Red States Won't Let Them. *New York Times*.

Baicker, K., Taubman, S. L., Allen, H. L., Bernstein, M., Gruber, J. H., Newhouse, J. P., . . . Finkelstein, A. N. (2013). The Oregon Experiment—Effects of Medicaid on Clinical Outcomes. *New England Journal of Medicine, 368*(18), 1713–1722.

Beecher, H. K. (1966). Ethics and Clinical Research. *New England Journal of Medicine, 274*(2), 1354–1360.

Berman, M. L. (2013). Defining the Field of Public Health Law. *DePaul Journal of Health Care Law, 15*(2), 45.

Blackmon, D. (2008). *Slavery by Another Name: The Re-Enslavement of Black Americans from the Civil War to World War II*. New York: Anchor Books.

Braithwaite, J., Walker, J., & Grabosky, P. (1987). An Enforcement Taxonomy of Regulatory Agencies. *Law & Policy, 9*(3), 323–351.

Brandt, A. M. (2007). *The Cigarette Century: The Rise, Fall, and Deadly Persistence of the Product That Defined America*. New York: Basic Books.

Briffault, R. (1990). Our Localism: Part I—The Structure of Local Government Law. *Columbia Law Review, 90*(1), 1–115.

Burris, S., Ashe, M., Levin, D., Penn, M., & Larkin, M. (2016). A Transdisciplinary Approach to Public Health Law: The Emerging Practice of Legal Epidemiology. *Annual Review of Public Health, 37*, 135–148.

Burris, S., Hitchcock, L., Ibrahim, J. K., Penn, M., & Ramanathan, T. (2016). Policy Surveillance: A Vital Public Health Practice Comes of Age. *Journal of Health Politics, Policy & Law, 41*(6), 1151–1167.

Burris, S., Wagenaar, A. C., Swanson, J., Ibrahim, J. K., Wood, J., & Mello, M. M. (2010). Making the Case for Laws That Improve Health: A Framework for Public Health Law Research. *Milbank Quarterly*, *88*(2), 169–210.

Center for Urban Epidemiologic Studies. (2003). New York State Expanded Syringe Access Demonstration Program (ESAP): Evaluation Report to the Governor and State Legislature. New York: New York Academy of Medicine.

Centers for Disease Control and Prevention. (2012). Anti-Lobbying Restrictions for CDC Grantees. Retrieved November 17, 2017, from https://www.cdc.gov/grants/documents/anti-lobbying_restrictions_for_cdc_grantees_july_2012.pdf.

Centers for Disease Control and Prevention. (2016a). Years of Potential Life Lost (YPLL). Retrieved December 9, 2017, from https://www.cdc.gov/injury/wisqars/years_potential.html.

Centers for Disease Control and Prevention. (2016b). Fact Sheets—Underage Drinking. Retrieved October 12, 2017, from https://www.cdc.gov/alcohol/fact-sheets/underage-drinking.htm.

Centers for Disease Control and Prevention. (2017a). National Diabetes Statistics Report, 2017. Atlanta, GA: Centers for Disease Control and Prevention, U.S. Department of Health and Human Services.

Centers for Disease Control and Prevention. (2017b). The Public Health System and the 10 Essential Public Health Services. Retrieved December 1, 2017, from https://www.cdc.gov/stltpublichealth/publichealthservices/essentialhealthservices.html.

Centers for Disease Control and Prevention. (2017c). Reproductive Health: Epidemiology Glossary. Retrieved December 9, 2017, from https://www.cdc.gov/reproductivehealth/data_stats/glossary.html.

Chemerinsky, E. (2015). *Constitutional Law: Principles and Policies* (4th ed.). New York: Wolters-Kluwer.

Cleland, C., Deren, S., Fuller, C., Blaney, S., McMahon, J., Tortu, S., . . . Vlahov, D. (2007). Syringe Disposal among Injection Drug Users in Harlem and the Bronx during the New York State Expanded Syringe Access Demonstration Program. *Health Education & Behavior*, *34*(2), 390–403.

Clinton, R. N. (1989). A Brief History of the Adoption of the United States Constitution. *Iowa Law Review*, *75*, 891–912.

Coan, A. B. (2012). Judicial Capacity and the Substance of Constitutional Law. *Yale Law Journal*, *122*, 422–458.

Cole, D., & Eskridge Jr, W. N. (1994). From Hand-holding to Sodomy: First Amendment Protection of Homosexual (Expressive) Conduct. *Harvard Civil Rights-Civil Liberties Law Review*, *29*, 319–351.

Cooper, H., Des Jarlais, D., Ross, Z., Tempalski, B., Bossak, B. H., & Friedman, S. R. (2012). Spatial Access to Sterile Syringes and the Odds of Injecting with an Unsterile Syringe among Injectors: A Longitudinal Multilevel Study. *Journal of Urban Health*, *89*(4), 678–696.

Deller, S., & Stallman, J. I. (2006). Tax and Expenditure Limitations and Economic Growth. *Marquette Law Review*, *90*, 497–554.

Faigman, D. L. (2006). Judges as Amateur Scientists. *Boston University Law Review*, *86*, 1207–1225.

Fowler, W. (1941). Principal Provisions of Smallpox Vaccination Laws and Regulations in the United States. *Public Health Reports, 56*(5), 167–189.

Franck, C., Grandi, S. M., & Eisenberg, M. J. (2013). Agricultural Subsidies and the American Obesity Epidemic. *American Journal of Preventive Medicine, 45*(3), 327–333.

Freidson, E. (2001). *Professionalism: The Third Logic*. Cambridge: Polity.

Frieden, T. R. (2010). A Framework for Public Health Action: The Health Impact Pyramid. *American Journal of Public Health, 100*(4), 590–595.

Gerber, A. S., Green, D. P., & Carnegie, A. J. (2013). Evaluating Public Health Law Using Randomized Experiments. In A. Wagenaar & S. Burris (Eds.), *Public Health Law Research: Theory and Methods* (pp. 283–306). San Francisco: Jossey-Bass.

Getz, W. M., Carlson, C., Dougherty, E., Porco Francis, T. C., & Salter, R. (2016). An Agent-Based Model of School Closing in Under-Vaccinated Communities During Measles Outbreaks. *Proceedings of the Agent-Directed Simulation Symposium, 2016*, 10.

Goldstone, L. (2011). *Inherently Unequal: The Betrayal of Equal Rights by the Supreme Court, 1865–1903*. New York: Walker & Company.

Gorovitz, E., Mosher, J., & Pertschuk, M. (1998). Preemption or Prevention? Lessons from Efforts to Control Firearms, Alcohol, and Tobacco. *Journal of Public Health Policy, 19*(1), 36–50.

Gostin, L. O., & Wiley, L. F. (2015). *Public Health Law: Power, Duty, Restraint*. Berkeley: University of California Press.

Gunningham, N. (2009). The New Collaborative Environmental Governance: The Localization of Regulation. *Journal of Law and Society, 36*(1), 145–166.

Haidt, J. (2012). *The Righteous Mind: Why Good People Are Divided by Politics and Religion* (1st ed.). New York: Pantheon Books.

Hallsworth, M., List, J., Metcalfe, R., & Vlaev, I. (2014). *The Behavioralist as Tax Collector: Using Natural Field Experiments to Enhance Tax Compliance* (NBER Working Papers). Cambridge, MA: National Bureau of Economic Research.

Hamilton, A. (1787). *The Federalist, 21*.

Hamlin, R. H. (1961). Public Health Law or the Interrelationship of Law and Public Health Administration. *American Journal of Public Health, 51*, 1733–1737.

Hays, S. P., Toth, J., Poes, M. J., Mulhall, P. F., Remmert, D. M., & O'Rourke, T. W. (2012). Public Health Governance and Population Health Outcomes. *Frontiers in Public Health Services and Systems Research, 1*(1). Retrieved from http://uknowledge.uky.edu/cgi/viewcontent.cgi?article=1004&context=frontiersinphssr.

Healthy Policy Institute of Ohio. (2013). What Is Advocacy? Retrieved November 17, 2017, from http://www.healthpolicyohio.org/wp-content/uploads/2014/02/whatisadvocacy_factsheet_final.pdf.

Hemenway, D. (2006). The Public Health Approach to Reducing Firearm Injury and Violence. *Stanford Law & Policy Review, 17*(3), 635–656.

Hill, A. B. (1965). The Environment and Disease: Association or Causation? *Proceedings of the Royal Society of Medicine, 58*, 295–300.

Himmelstein, D. U., & Woolhandler, S. (2016). Public Health's Falling Share of US Health Spending. *American Journal of Public Health, 106*(1), 56–57.

Holford, T. R., Meza, R., Warner, K. E., Meernik, C, Jeon, J, Moolgavkar, S. H., & Levy, D. T. (2014). Tobacco Control and the Reduction in Smoking-Related Premature Deaths in the United States, 1964–2012. *JAMA*, *311*(2), 164–171.

Huberfeld, N., Leonard, E. W., & Outterson, K. (2013). Plunging into Endless Difficulties: Medicaid and Coercion in National Federation of Independent Business v. Sebelius. *Boston University Law Review*, *93*, 1–88.

Institute of Medicine. (1988). *The Future of Public Health*. Washington, DC: National Academy Press.

Institute of Medicine. (2011). *For the Public's Health: Revitalizing Law and Policy to Meet New Challenges*. Washington, DC: National Academies Press.

Institute of Medicine. (2012). *Adverse Effects of Vaccines: Evidence and Causality*. Washington, DC: National Academies Press.

Internal Revenue Service. (2017a). Measuring Lobbying Activity: Expenditure Test. Retrieved November 17, 2017, from https://www.irs.gov/charities-non-profits/measuring-lobbying-activity-expenditure-test.

Internal Revenue Service. (2017b). Measuring Lobbying: Substantial Part Test. Retrieved October 13, 2017, from https://www.irs.gov/charities-non-profits/measuring-lobbying-substantial-part-test.

International Organization for Standardization. (2017). How We Develop Standards Retrieved November 16, 2017, from https://www.iso.org/developing-standards.html.

Israel, B. A., Coombe, C. M., Cheezum, R. R., Schulz, A. J., McGranaghan, R. J., Lichtenstein, R., . . . Burris, A. (2010). Community-Based Participatory Research: A Capacity-Building Approach for Policy Advocacy Aimed at Eliminating Health Disparities. *American Journal of Public Health*, *100*(11), 2094–2102.

Ivan Barkhorn, N. H., & Blau, J. (2013). Assessing Advocacy. *Stanford Social Innovation Review,* Spring, 58–64.

Jacob, J. T., Klein, E., Laxminarayan, R., Beldavs, Z., Lynfield, R., Kallen, A. J., . . . Cardo, D. (2013). Vital Signs: Carbapenem-Resistant Enterobacteriaceae. *Morbidity and Mortality Weekly Report*, *62*(9), 165–170.

Kania, J., & Kramer, M. (2011). Collective Impact. *Stanford Social Innovation Review,* Winter, 36–41.

Kersbergen, I., & Field, M. (2017). Alcohol Consumers' Attention to Warning Labels and Brand Information on Alcohol Packaging: Findings from Cross-Sectional and Experimental Studies. *BMC Public Health*, *17*, 123.

Kim, S., Russell, D., Mohamadnejad, M., Makker, J., Sedarat, A., Watson, R. R., . . . Muthusamy, V. R. (2010). Risk Factors Associated with the Transmission of Carbapenem-Resistant Enterobacteriaceae via Duodenoscopes. *Gastrointestinal Endoscopy*, *83*(6), 1121–1129.

Kirby, R. S. (2008). The Ghost Map: The Story of London's Most Terrifying Epidemic— And How It Changed Science, Cities, and the Modern World. *Geographical Review*, *98*(1), 139–140.

Koenig, T., & Rustad, M. (2001). *In Defense of Tort Law*. New York: New York University Press.

Komro, K. A., Livingston, M. D., Markowitz, S., & Wagenaar, A. C. (2016). The Effect of an Increased Minimum Wage on Infant Mortality and Birth Weight. *American Journal of Public Health*, *106*(8), 1514–1516.

Kronstadt, J., Meit, M., Siegfried, A., Nicolaus, T., Bender, K., & Corso, L. (2016). Evaluating the Impact of National Public Health Department Accreditation—United States, 2016. *Morbidity and Mortality Weekly Report*, *65*(31), 803–806.

Link, B. G., & Phelan, J. (1995). Social Conditions as Fundamental Causes of Disease. In Extra Issue: Forty Years of Medical Sociology: The State of the Art and Directions for the Future. *Journal of Health and Social Behavior*, *1995*, 80–94.

Longthorne, A., Subramanian, R., & Chen, C.-L. (2010). An Analysis of the Significant Decline in Motor Vehicle Traffic Crashes in 2008 (DOT HS 811 346). Washington, DC: National Highway Traffic Safety Administration, U.S. Department of Transportation. Retrieved March 25, 2018 from https://crashstats.nhtsa.dot.gov/Api/Public/ViewPublication/811346.

Ludwig, J., Duncan, G. J., Gennetian, L. A., Katz, L. F., Kessler, R. C., Kling, J. R., & Sanbonmatsu, L. (2012). Neighborhood Effects on the Long-Term Well-Being of Low-Income Adults. *Science*, *337*(6101), 1505–1510.

Madsen, K. M., Hviid, A., Vestergaard, M., Schendel, D., Wohlfahrt, J., Thorsen, P., . . . Melbye, M. (2002). A Population-Based Study of Measles, Mumps, and Rubella Vaccination and Autism. *New England Journal of Medicine*, *347*(19), 1477–1482.

Majone, G. (1994). The Rise of the Regulatory State in Europe. *West European Politics*, *17*(3), 77–101.

Mascini, P., & Wijk, E. V. (2009). Responsive Regulation at the Dutch Food and Consumer Product Safety Authority: An Empirical Assessment of Assumptions Underlying the Theory. *Regulation & Governance*, *3*(1), 27–47.

Massey, D. S., Albright, L., Casciano, R., Derickson, E., & Kinsey, D. N. (2013). *Climbing Mount Laurel: The Struggle for Affordable Housing and Social Mobility in an American Suburb*. Princeton, NJ: Princeton University Press.

Matthew, D. B., Rodrigue, E., & Reeves, R. V. (2016). Time for Justice: Tackling Race Inequalities in Health and Housing (Brookings Big Ideas for America). Retrieved December 19, 2016, from https://www.brookings.edu/research/time-for-justice-tackling-race-inequalities-in-health-and-housing/.

Matthews, G., Burris, S., Ledford, S. L., & Baker, E. L. (2016). Advocacy for Leaders: Crafting Richer Stories for Public Health. *Journal of Public Health Management and Practice*, *22*(3), 311–315.

Matthews, G., Burris, S., Ledford, S. L., Gunderson, G., & Baker, E. L. (2017). Crafting Richer Public Health Messages for a Turbulent Political Environment. *Journal of Public Health Management and Practice*, *23*(4), 420–423.

Mayo, M. L., Pitts, S. B., & Chriqui, J. F. (2013). Associations between County and Municipality Zoning Ordinances and Access to Fruit and Vegetable Outlets in Rural North Carolina, 2012. *Preventing Chronic Disease*, *10*, E203.

Mehta, N. (2009). Nonprofits and Lobbying. Retrieved November 17, 2017, from https://apps.americanbar.org/buslaw/blt/2009-03-04/mehta.shtml.

Mello, M. M., Pomeranz, J., & Moran, P. (2008). The Interplay of Public Health Law and Industry Self-Regulation: The Case of Sugar-Sweetened Beverage Sales in Schools. *American Journal of Public Health*, *98*(4), 595–604.

Metzger, G. E. (2012). To Tax, To Spend, To Regulate. *Harvard Law Review*, *126*, 83–116.

Mnookin, S. (2011). *The Panic Virus : A True Story of Medicine, Science, and Fear*. New York: Simon & Schuster.

Moher, D., Liberati, A., Tetzlaff, J., Altman, D. G., & Prisma Group. (2009). Preferred Reporting Items for Systematic Reviews and Meta-Analyses: The PRISMA Statement. *PLoS Medicine*, 6(7), e1000097.

Montoy, J. C. C., Dow, W. H., & Kaplan, B. C. (2016). Patient Choice in Opt-in, Active Choice, and Opt-out HIV Screening: Randomized Clinical Trial. *BMJ*, *352*, h6895.

National Association of County and City Health Officials. (2017). National Profile of Local Health Departments: Chapter 4, Leadership. Retrieved August 19, 2017, from http://nacchoprofilestudy.org/chapter-4/.

National Center for Health Statistics. (2015). Table 93. Gross Domestic Product, National Health Expenditures, per Capita Amounts, Percent Distribution, and Average Annual Percent Change: United States, Selected Years 1960–2014. Atlanta, GA: Centers for Disease Control and Prevention.

National Center for Health Statistics. (2016). Health, United States, 2016: With Chartbook on Long-Term Trends in Health. Hyattsville, MD: National Center for Health Statistics.

National Congress of American Indians. (2017). Tribal Public Health Law. Retrieved August 19, 2017, from http://www.ncai.org/policy-research-center/initiatives/projects/tribal-public-health-law.

National Highway Traffic Safety Administration. (2015). 2014 Crash Data Key Findings. Traffic Safety Facts. Washington, DC: U.S. Department of Transportation.

National Rifle Association Institute for Legislative Action. (2011). Three More Wins in Congress for Gun Owners. Retrieved November 17, 2017, from https://www.nraila.org/articles/20111222/three-more-wins-in-congress-for-gun-owners.

Ng, S. W., & Popkin, B. M. (2014). The Healthy Weight Commitment Foundation Pledge: Calories Purchased by U.S. Households with Children, 2000–2012. *American Journal of Preventive Medicine*, *47*(4), 520–530.

Ng, S. W., Slining, M. M., & Popkin, B. M. (2014). The Healthy Weight Commitment Foundation Pledge: Calories Sold from U.S. Consumer Packaged Goods, 2007–2012. *American Journal of Preventive Medicine*, *47*(4), 508–519.

Nguyen, H. B., Corbett, S. W., Steele, R., Banta, J., Clark, R. T., Hayes, S. R., . . . Wittlake, W. A. (2007). Implementation of a Bundle of Quality Indicators for the Early Management of Severe Sepsis and Septic Shock Is Associated with Decreased Mortality. *Critical Care Medicine*, *35*(4), 1105–1112.

Nichols, J. L., Tippetts, A. S., Fell, J. C., Eichelberger, A. H., & Haseltine, P. W. (2014). The Effects of Primary Enforcement Laws and Fine Levels on Seat Belt Usage in the United States. *Traffic Injury Prevention*, *15*(6), 640–644.

Nixon, S., & Lisa, F. (2008). Exploring Synergies between Human Rights and Public Health Ethics: A Whole Greater than the Sum of Its Parts. *BMC International Health and Human Rights,* 8(1), 1–9. doi:10.1186/1472-698x-8-2.

Noar, S. M., Hall, M. G., Francis, D. B., Ribisl, K. M., Pepper, J. K., & Brewer, N. T. (2016). Pictorial Cigarette Pack Warnings: A Meta-Analysis of Experimental Studies. *Tobacco Control*, *25*(3), 341–354.

Office of Management and Budget. (2011). Circular A—122; Cost Principles for Nonprofit Organizations—"Lobbying" Revision. Washington, DC: OMB.

Ogden, C., & Carroll, M. (2010). Prevalence of Obesity among Young Children and Adolescents: United States, Trends 1963–1965 through 2007–2008. Retrieved April

3, 2018 from http://www.cdc.gov/nchs/data/hestat/obesity_child_07_08/obesity_child_07_08.htm.

Ogolla, C. (2011). Non-Criminal Habeas Corpus for Quarantine and Isolation Detainees: Serving the Private Right or Violating Public Policy? *DePaul Journal of Health Care Law, 14*(135), 135–167.

Organisation for Economic Co-operation and Development. (2014). The Governance of Regulators (OECD Best Practice Principles for Regulatory Policy). Paris: OECD.

Pappworth, M. H. (1967). *Human Guinea Pigs; Experimentation on Man.* London: Routledge & Paul.

Parmet, W., & Smith, J. (2006). Free Speech and Public Health: A Population-Based Approach to the First Amendment. *Loyola of Los Angeles Law Review, 39*, 363–446.

Parmet, W. E. (1992). Health Care and the Constitution: Public Health and the Role of the State in the Framing Era. *Hastings Constitutional Law Quarterly, 20*, 267–335.

Parmet, W. E. (2016). Paternalism, Self-Governance, and Public Health: The Case of E-cigarettes. *University of Miami Law Review, 70*(3), 879–962.

Parmet, W. E., & Jacobson, P. D. (2014). The Courts and Public Health: Caught in a Pincer Movement. *American Journal of Public Health, 104*(3), 392–397.

Penman-Aguilar, A., Talih, M., Huang, D., Moonesinghe, R., Bouye, K., & Beckles, G. (2016). Measurement of Health Disparities, Health Inequities, and Social Determinants of Health to Support the Advancement of Health Equity. *Journal of Public Health Management and Practice, 22*, S33–S42.

Pertschuk, M., Pomeranz, J. L., Aoki, J. R., Larkin, M. A., & Paloma, M. (2013). Assessing the Impact of Federal and State Preemption in Public Health: A Framework for Decision Makers. *Journal of Public Health Management and Practice, 19*(3), 213–219.

Prescription Drug Monitoring Program Training and Technical Assistance Center. (2010). Prescription Monitoring Program Model Act 2010 Revision. Retrieved December 15, 2017, from http://www.pdmpassist.org/pdf/PMPModelActFinal20100628.pdf.

Reducing Regulation and Controlling Regulatory Costs, Executive Order 13771 (2017).

Public Health Accreditation Board. (2013). What Is Public Health Department Accreditation? Retrieved August 19, 2017, from http://www.phaboard.org/accreditation-overview/what-is-accreditation/.

Rogers, P. (2010, October 19). Prop. 26 Opponents: Measure Would Let Oil, Tobacco and Alcohol Companies Off the Hook. *The San Jose Mercury News.*

Ross, C. L., Leone de Nie, K., Dannenberg, A. L., Beck, L. F., Marcus, M. J., & Barringer, J. (2012). Health Impact Assessment of the Atlanta BeltLine. *American Journal of Preventive Medicine, 42*(3), 203–213.

Rothstein, R. (2017). *The Color of Law: A Forgotten History of How Our Government Segregated America.* New York: Liveright.

Safe Routes to School National Partnership. (2015). Fighting for Equitable Transportation: Why It Matters. Retrieved November 17, 2017, from https://www.apha.org/~/media/files/pdf/topics/environment/built_environment/srtsnp_equitytransp_factsheet2015.ashx.

Schadler, B. H. (2012). Introduction: Types of Exempt Organizations and What They May Do. Retrieved November 17, 2017, from https://www.bolderadvocacy.org/wp-content/uploads/2012/10/The_Connection_Intro_paywall.pdf.

Scott, C. (2001). Analysing Regulatory Space: Fragmented Resources and Institutional Design. *Public Law, 2001*, 329–353.

Scutchfield, F. D., & Keck, C. W. (2017). Deaths of Despair: Why? What to Do? *American Journal of Public Health, 107*(10), 1564–1565.

Seattle-King County Public Health Department. (2015). Local Medical Marijuana Laws in Washington State. Retrieved April 3, 2018, from http://www.lawatlas.org/datasets/local-recreational-marijuana-laws-in-washington-state-1417727078.

Shapiro, S. A. (2012). Blowout: Legal Legacy of the Deepwater Horizon Catastrophe: The Complexity of Regulatory Capture: Diagnosis, Causality, and Remediation. *Roger Williams University Law Review, 17*(1), 221–257.

Sonoma County Department of Health Services. (2012). A 2020 Vision for Sonoma County: Action Plan 2013–2016. Sonoma, CA: Sonoma County Department of Health Services.

Spanakis, E. K., & Golden, S. H. (2013). Race/Ethnic Difference in Diabetes and Diabetic Complications. *Current Diabetes Reports, 13*(6). doi:10.1007/s11892-11013-10421-11899.

Spitzer, H. (2015). "Home Rule" vs. "Dillon's r\Rule" for Washington Cities. *Seattle University Law Review, 38*(3), 809–860.

Stokols, D., Hall, K. L., Taylor, B. K., & Moser, R. P. (2008). The Science of Team Science: Overview of the Field and Introduction to the Supplement. *American Journal of Preventive Medicine, 35*(2, Suppl.), S77–S89.

Swanson, J., & Ibrahim, J. (2013). Picturing Public Health Law Research: Using Causal Diagrams to Model and Test Theory. In A. C. Wagenaar & S. Burris (Eds.), *Public Health Law Research: Theory and Methods* (pp. 217–236). San Francisco: Joseph Wiley and Sons.

Tang, K. C., Ståhl, T., Bettcher, D., & De Leeuw, E. (2014). The Eighth Global Conference on Health Promotion: Health in All Policies: From Rhetoric to Action. *Health Promotion International, 29*(Suppl. 1), i1–i8.

Terhune, C. (2015, February 18). Superbug Linked to 2 Deaths at UCLA Hospital. *Los Angeles Times*. Retrieved from http://www.latimes.com/business/la-fi-hospital-infections-20150218-story.html#page=1.

The Commonwealth Fund. (2017). U.S. Health Care from a Global Perspective: Spending, Use of Services, Prices, and Health in 13 Countries. Retrieved August 19, 2017, from http://www.commonwealthfund.org/publications/issue-briefs/2015/oct/us-health-care-from-a-global-perspective.

The Rockefeller Foundation. (2017). Social Impact Bonds. Retrieved August 19, 2017, from https://www.rockefellerfoundation.org/our-work/initiatives/social-impact-bonds/.

Thoma, M. E., Mathews, T. J., & MacDorman, M. F. (2015). Infant Mortality Statistics from the 2013 Period Linked Birth/Infant Death Data Set. *National Vital Statistics Reports, 64*(9), 1–30.

Thomas, J. C., Sage, M., Dillenberg, J., & Guillory, V. J. (2002). A Code of Ethics for Public Health. *American Journal of Public Health, 92*(7), 1057–1059.

Trust for America's Health. (2016). Investing in America's Health: A State-by-State Look at Public Health Funding and Key Health Facts. Washington, DC: Trust for America's Health.

Turnock, B. J., & Handler, A. S. (1997). From Measuring to Improving Public Health Practice. *Annual Review of Public Health*, *18*(1), 261–282.

Turnock, B. J., & Kelly, C. J. (1989). Mandatory Premarital Testing for Human Immunodeficiency Virus. The Illinois Experience. *JAMA*, *261*(23), 3415–3418.

Tyler, T. R. (1990). *Why People Obey the Law*. New Haven, CT: Yale University Press.

U.S. Food and Drug Administration. (2016). Executive Summary: Strategic Plan for Regulatory Science. Retrieved August 19, 2017, from https://www.fda.gov/ScienceResearch/SpecialTopics/RegulatoryScience/ucm268095.htm.

Vernick, J. S., Rutkow, L., & Salmon, D. A. (2007). Availability of Litigation as a Public Health Tool for Firearm Injury Prevention: Comparison of Guns, Vaccines, and Motor Vehicles. *American Journal of Public Health*, *97*(11), 1991–1997.

Wagenaar, A. C., & Komro, K. A. (2013). Natural Experiments: Research Design Elements for Optimal Causal Inference without Randomization. In A. Wagenaar & S. Burris (Eds.), *Public Health Law Research: Theory and Methods* (pp. 307–324). San Francisco: Jossey-Bass.

Wakefield, A. J., Murch, S. H., Anthony, A., Linnell, J., Casson, D. M., Malik, M., . . Walker-Smith, J. A. (1998). Ileal-Lymphoid-Nodular Hyperplasia, Non-Specific Colitis, and Pervasive Developmental Disorder in Children [Retracted]. *The Lancet*, *351*(9103), 637–641.

Wakefield, M. A., Loken, B., & Hornik, R. C. (2010). Use of Mass Media Campaigns to Change Health Behaviour. *The Lancet*, *376*(9748), 1261–1271.

Wernham, A., & Teutsch, S. M. (2015). Health in All Policies for Big Cities. *Journal of Public Health Management and Practice*, *21*, S56–S65.

West, W. F., & Raso, C. (2012). Who Shapes the Rulemaking Agenda? Implications for Bureaucratic Responsiveness and Bureaucratic Control. *Journal of Public Administration Research and Theory*, *23*(3), 495–519.

Wolff, T., Minkler, M., Wolfe, S. M., Berkowitz, B., Bowen, L., Butterfoss, F. D., . . . Lee, K. S. (2017). Collaborating for Equity and Justice: Moving Beyond Collective Impact. *Nonprofit Quarterly*, Winter.

World Health Organization. (2017a). Health Topics: Public Health Surveillance. Retrieved December 9, 2017, from http://www.who.int/topics/public_health_surveillance/en/.

World Health Organization. (2017b). Metrics: Disability-Adjusted Life Year (DALY). Retrieved July 30, 2017, from http://www.who.int/healthinfo/global_burden_disease/metrics_daly/en/.

INDEX

Tables, figures, and boxes are indicated by an italic *t, f,* and *b* following the page number.